The critics are raving over LOONEYSPOONS

"The zaniest, most reader-friendly cookbook you're likely to encounter. It's humorous, informative, motivational, and full of energy—just like its authors . . . Their lighthearted approach takes all the intimidation out of cooking . . . and the hands-down favorite? Rude Barb's Strawbapple Crisp, a delightfully easy blend of strawberries, apples, and rhubarb topped with crispy whole grain crumbs."
—*Prevention Magazine*

"A delight to the eye and can bring out the gourmet in all of us . . . *Looneyspoons* could very well set the tone for the next generation of cookbooks . . . Useful, common-sense strategies to help you adopt and maintain a healthy lifestyle."
—*Sun City News* (Sun City, CA)

"The perfect upbeat book for people who really have to change their eating habits and for people who just want to change their eating habits."
—*Rocky Mountain News* (Denver, CO)

"This unusual and inspirational cookbook offers not only low-fat recipes but also a heaping cup of humor along with dashes of helpful information . . . Quick and nutritious solutions to that age-old question, 'What's for dinner?'"
—*Times Leader*

"A very good low-fat recipe collection . . . Any cheesecake lover is bound to be delighted with the *Wake Up and Smell the Coffee Cheesecake* that is both easily prepared and vastly satisfying."
—*Post Crescent* (Appleton, WI)

"These recipes . . . will perk up appetites without adding much fat."
—*Tampa Tribune*

"Wonderfully hilarious . . . You don't have to be either a serious cook or a dieter to enjoy this book . . . A great holiday gift for anyone who likes to cook or who really enjoys eating."
—*San Ileandro Times*

"Uproariously entertaining . . . Great recipes."
—*Desert Sun*

"A fresh approach to low-fat cooking . . . Useful lifestyle information, cooking tips and food trivia."
—*Gazette* (Cedar Rapids, IA)

"Tasty, family-friendly recipes."
—*Sea Coast Echo* (Bay St. Louis, MS)

LOW-FAT FOOD MADE FUN!

Janet & Greta Podleski

Cartoons by Ted Martin

A Perigee Book

The recipes contained in this book are to be followed exactly as written. Neither the publisher nor the author is responsible for your specific health or allergy needs that may require medical supervision, or for any adverse reactions to the recipes contained in this book.

The following product and company names appearing in the book are trademarks or trade names of their respective companies: Barbie, Beano, Burger King, Campbell's, Chee•tos, Coke, Dole, Egg McMuffin, Flintstones, Fudgsicle, Grape-Nuts, Hamburger Helper, (Hershey's) Kisses, Jell-O, Jolly Time, Kellogg's, Kit Kat, Oil of Olay, Personal Pan Pizza (Pizza Hut), Reese, Rice Krispies, 7-Up, Snickers, Uncle Ben's, V8, Whopper, WonderBra.

Recipe analysis calculated using Nutribase Personal Nutrition Manager software (Cybersoft, Inc.).

A Perigee Book
Published by The Berkley Publishing Group
A division of Penguin Putnam Inc.
375 Hudson Street
New York, New York 10014

Copyright © 1997 by Granet Publishing Inc.
Cartoons by Ted Martin
Edited by Mary Goodbody
Food photography by Robert Wigington
Food styling by Ruth Gangbar
Cover photograph copyright © Susan Ashukian
Cover design by Jill Boltin
Page layout and design created exclusively with Corel DRAW!™, the world's leading graphics software.

Looneyspoons is a trademark of Granet Publishing Inc.

Granet Publishing Inc. edition: March 1998

First Perigee edition: September 2000

Perigee ISBN: 0-399-52563-7

All inquiries should be addressed to:
Granet Publishing Inc.
99 Northfield Dr. East, Suite 206
Waterloo, ONT.
N2K 3P9
1-800-470-0738
E-mail: spoons@magi.com
www.looneyspoons.com

The Penguin Putnam Inc. World Wide Web site address is
http://www.penguinputnam.com

The Library of Congress has catalogued the Granet Publishing Inc. edition as follows:

Podleski, Janet, 1965–
    Looneyspoons : low-fat food made fun / Janet Podleski and Greta Podleski.
        p.   cm.
    Includes bibliographical references and index.
    ISBN 0-9680631-1-X
    1. Cookery. 2. Low-fat diet—Recipes. 3. Food—Humor.
I. Podleski, Greta, 1966– . II. Title.
TX714.P637 1997   97-13876
641.5'638—dc21   CIP

Printed in the United States of America

10 9 8 7 6 5 4 3 2 1

To our mother,
who still, to this day,
insists that Polish sausage
is a health food

Contents

Introduction
by Dave Chilton, host of PBS' *The Wealthy Barber*

"**W**hat would possess a financial planning author to finance the publishing of a cookbook?" This is a question I've heard many times lately—from friends, family members, my stockbroker ("Remember your racehorse investment?" he reminds me), and even from the left side of my own brain.

"The last thing the world needs is another cookbook," my sister concluded in her standard open-minded fashion. This remark drew a knowing nod of support from my dad—the same man who had told me just prior to my writing *The Wealthy Barber*, "The last thing the world needs is another financial planning book." (It has since sold over 1.5 million copies.)

Finally, my cautious mother, who until that point had been silently reviewing the *Looneyspoons* manuscript, offered a response to my sister's comment that says it all: "This book is fantastic!" And it is.

Looneyspoons is full of unbelievably delicious low-fat recipes, interesting and useful lifestyle information, and lots of laughs. It makes healthy eating fun and, more important, it makes fun eating healthy. These meals taste great *and* they're good for you! The recipe ingredients are readily available and the serving sizes are generous. Plus, anybody, including me, can easily follow the recipe instructions.

I found myself fascinated by all the juicy tidbits of information alongside the recipes. They were fun to read and very informative. For instance, did you know you'd have to eat 200 pretzel twists to consume the 20 grams of fat found in just one hot dog? Even if that bit of knowledge doesn't change your eating habits (though it should!), it's fun to annoy your friends with.

Yes, I do love this book—in fact, everyone I've shown it to loves it. However, it wasn't just the unique manuscript that drew my interest—it was also the authors.

Janet and Greta Podleski are two of a kind. They're compelling, articulate women who believe passionately in this project. Last year, during the writing process, they both quit their jobs in order to work full time on *Looneyspoons*. Running short on funds, they were then forced to sell their car. When even that wasn't enough, Janet sold her wedding dress at a lawn sale. (Her husband, taking it in stride, noted, "I was hopeful she wasn't going to need it again anyway.")

Reluctant to give up control of their project to a conventional publishing house, they eventually decided to self-publish. Being *Wealthy Barber* fans and knowing self-publishing would be impossible on $317, they took a train (remember, the car was gone) to seek my advice over lunch, and to subtly coerce me into getting involved. They were armed with a complete business plan, some sample pages, and most important, a piece of Greta's low-fat cheesecake. Frankly, it's impossible not to give in to these two.

It quickly became clear to me that all the "ingredients" for success were in place: a fantastic book, together with authors whose energy and commitment are limitless.

I'd have been looney *not* to get involved.

The three of us wish you good reading and healthy eating!

DIPSY DOODLES

Slender snacks & appetizers

Don't Worry. Be Crabby.

If you're feeling down and out
There's no need to mope and pout
Don't worry. Be crabby.

This recipe is really hip
Pep up your mood with hot crab dip
Don't worry. Be crabby.

I'M REALLY HIP!

1-1/4 cups low-fat (1%) cottage cheese
3 ounces "light" cream cheese,
   softened
1/2 cup shredded reduced-fat
   sharp cheddar cheese (2 ounces)
2 tablespoons minced onions
1 tablespoon lemon juice
1 teaspoon *each* "lite" Worcestershire sauce
   and dry mustard
1 clove garlic, minced
3-4 dashes hot pepper sauce
1 pound lump crabmeat, chopped or broken up
   (imitation crabmeat works well)

Preheat oven to 350°.

In a food processor or blender, whirl cottage cheese and cream cheese until smooth. Transfer to a large bowl and stir in remaining ingredients.

Spray a medium casserole dish with non-stick spray. Spoon crabmeat mixture into casserole dish. Cover and bake for 25 minutes.

Remove from oven. Stir. Let cool, uncovered, for 5 minutes before serving. Serve as a spread for crackers or as a dip for baked tortilla chips.

Makes about 3-1/2 cups.

WHAT'S IN IT FOR ME?

PER SERVING (1/4 cup):
74 calories, 2.5 g fat,
4.9 g carbohydrate, 8.5 g protein,
425 mg sodium, 12 mg cholesterol
CALORIES FROM FAT: 29.8%

Show & Tell

Did you know that a crab has the ability to regenerate a claw? In fact, a mini-industry in Florida that was once threatened by depletion has revived thanks to the crab's special regenerative skill. Early crab hunters were accustomed to killing the crustacean for its two claws, its only marketable body parts. But as the crab population dwindled, so did crab hunting as a livelihood. In order to save the crabs (and their own jobs), crab hunters adopted the practice of breaking off only one of the crab's two claws and tossing the creature back into the sea. Incredibly, the handicapped crab manages to fend for itself, is still able to scrounge for food, grows a new appendage, and—if really unlucky—suffers through the whole ordeal again. (No wonder we describe someone who is grouchy or ill-tempered as "crabby"!)

Bad luck and grouchiness aside, crabmeat is a great low-fat food choice. One cup of canned crabmeat averages about 2 grams of fat and derives only 12% of calories from fat.

SAY IT AIN'T SO!

Health nuts, beware! Granola, granola bars, and trail mixes, even though they're often called "health foods" or "all natural," are full of calories, fat, and sugar. The average granola bar (hold the chocolate chips) derives 52% of its calories from fat. Groan-ola!

Many a person who goes on a diet finds that he is a poor loser.

Nacho Nacho Man

This recipe for a layered dip with nacho chips is a favorite of all the village people. And because it's made with low-fat ingredients, those health-conscious folks over at the YMCA give it the thumbs up, too.

The Bottom Layer (Creamy Bean Stuff)
1 cup canned low-fat refried beans
1/3 cup low-fat sour cream
2 tablespoons salsa
1 tablespoon lime juice

The Second Layer (Guiltless Guacamole)
1/2 cup peeled and chopped avocado
1/2 cup frozen green peas, cooked
1/4 cup low-fat sour cream
2 tablespoons chopped red onions
2 teaspoons lime juice
1 tablespoon chopped fresh cilantro
1 clove garlic, minced

The Third Layer (Sour Creamy Stuff)
1 cup low-fat sour cream (a thick brand)
1 teaspoon taco seasoning

The Fourth Layer (Simple and Spicy)
1 cup salsa (preferably chunky style)

The Top Layer (Cheesy Decorations)
1/2 cup shredded reduced-fat cheddar cheese (2 ounces)
1/4 cup chopped green onions

1 bag (7 ounces) *baked* tortilla chips

Combine all ingredients for bottom layer in a medium bowl. Spread evenly over the bottom of a 9-inch pie plate.

Combine all guacamole ingredients in a blender or food processor. Pulse on and off until mixture is well blended, but still slightly lumpy. Spread over bean mixture.

Combine sour cream and taco seasoning. Spoon over guacamole and spread evenly.

Pour salsa evenly over sour cream. Spread to sides of pie plate.

Sprinkle cheese over salsa and top with green onions. Cover and refrigerate for 1 hour before serving. Serve with baked tortilla chips.

Makes 8 servings.

PER SERVING: 212 calories, 4.6 g fat, 34.6 g carbohydrate, 11.3 g protein, 744 mg sodium, 7 mg cholesterol
CALORIES FROM FAT: 18.6%

WHAT'S IN IT FOR ME?

COOKING 101

When exposed to air, the flesh of an avocado discolors quickly. Mixing chopped or mashed avocado with lemon or lime juice is a simple way to keep the avocado from turning brown.

Chicken Case-a-dee-ahhhs

You'll be "ahhh-struck" by the "ahhh-some" flavor of these low-fat chicken quesadillas.

1 cup canned chickpeas, drained, rinsed, and mashed
1/2 cup low-fat sour cream
1/2 cup salsa (mild, medium, or hot)
1 large clove garlic, minced
8 7-inch flour tortillas
2 teaspoons vegetable oil
1 chicken breast half, cooked and shredded
1/4 cup *each* finely chopped red bell pepper and chopped green onions
1 tablespoon chopped fresh cilantro
1 cup shredded reduced-fat Monterey Jack cheese (4 ounces)

Preheat oven to 400°.

Combine mashed chickpeas, 2 tablespoons sour cream, 2 tablespoons salsa, and garlic in a small bowl. Mix well. Set aside.

Brush one side of each tortilla with oil. Arrange 4 tortillas, oil-side down, on a baking sheet. Spread 1/4 chickpea mixture over each tortilla, leaving a 1/2-inch border.

Combine shredded chicken, red pepper, green onions, and cilantro in a small bowl. Spread 1/4 chicken mixture over chickpeas, followed by 1/4 cheese. Cover with remaining tortillas, oil-side up.

Bake for 8-10 minutes, until tortillas are a light golden brown. Remove from oven. Let cool 5 minutes before cutting (this is important, otherwise tortillas will slide apart). Cut each quesadilla into 6 wedges. Serve with remaining sour cream and salsa.

Makes 24 wedges.

WHAT'S IN IT FOR ME?

PER WEDGE: 65 calories, 2.2 g fat, 8.4 g carbohydrate, 4.4 g protein, 90 mg sodium, 7 mg cholesterol
CALORIES FROM FAT: 27.5%

 COOKING 101

The easiest way to cut quesadillas is with a sharp pair of kitchen scissors, which are also handy for cutting open pita bread and snipping fresh herbs. If using a pizza cutter or knife, make sure it's super sharp, otherwise your quesadillas will pull apart.

Show me the WEIGH

When in doubt, laugh. Scientific studies have shown that humor and positive thinking have tremendous health benefits, guarding against illness and possibly even increasing longevity. Laughter actually helps people breathe easier, massages the heart and other vital organs, and increases the release of disease-fighting cells in the immune system. Having a few good laughs produces some of the same effects as exercise, quickening the pulse and stimulating the cardiovascular system. (Note: Flaking out on the couch with a bowl of pistachios on your chest watching the *Three's Company* re-run festival is no substitute for real exercise!) What's more, it seems that people who are able to find something funny in their dilemmas feel better sooner than those who have a good cry. So go ahead and laugh your headache off.

C'MON FIDO — ONLY 125 MORE CHRISTMAS CARDS TO GO!

Trivial Tidbit

Caution: Mass mailouts could be hazardous to your waistline! Licking a postage stamp will set you back anywhere from 2 to 8 calories, depending on how well you lick it.

Show & Tell

Looks like hot is now haute! Spicy salsa (the Spanish word for "sauce") is gaining in popularity over the traditional ketchup, with annual sales skyrocketing. A piquant blend of tomatoes, onions, cilantro, and chilies, salsa adds spark to potatoes, eggs, hamburgers, fish, chicken, meatloaf, rice, beans, Mexican dishes, sandwiches, pasta... and the list goes on. Various fruit salsas (pineapple, mango, and peach) are surfacing all over the place as condiments for fish, chicken, and meats. With hundreds of different brands to choose from (not to mention a darn good recipe over yonder), we shouldn't have any trouble getting our fill of this wonderful, low-fat sauce.

SAY IT AIN'T SO!

Roll out the barrel. We'll have a barrel of... fat? Yup, that finger-lickin' chicken is one of the worst fat culprits around. A typical meal from this leading franchise, consisting of 1 breast piece, 1 drumstick, coleslaw, fries, and a biscuit will ruffle your feathers with its horrifying 1000 calories, 56 grams of fat, and 50% calories from fat! Now there's no need to give up fried chicken cold turkey— just treat yourself to it *once* in a while!

You can have the most beautiful racecar in the world, but if you try to run it on beer, it's not going to work.

Anthony Robbins

Cindy Brady's Thizzlin' Thaltha

Oopth! That's *Sizzlin' Salsa!*
Cindy picked up this recipe while she and her family were visiting the Grand Canyon and generously decided to donate it for use in our cookbook. Thankth, Thindy!

THITH THALTHA REALLY THIZZLES

6 cups seeded and diced tomatoes (fresh, not canned)
2 cups diced onions
6 cloves garlic, minced
5 jalapeño peppers, seeded and minced
1 cup tomato sauce
1 tablespoon ground cumin
1/2 teaspoon *each* paprika and salt
2 tablespoons red wine vinegar or cider vinegar
1/8 teaspoon cayenne pepper (or to taste)
1/2 cup chopped fresh cilantro
3 tablespoons lime juice (preferably fresh)

Combine tomatoes, onions, garlic, and jalapeños in a large saucepan. Cook over medium-high heat for about 10 minutes, stirring often.

Stir in tomato sauce, cumin, paprika, vinegar, salt, and cayenne pepper. Continue to cook for another 10 minutes.

Remove from heat. Add cilantro and lime juice. Mix well. Serve when cool.

Makes about 8 cups.

Hint: Store salsa in the fridge in a sealed jar. It will keep for about 1 week (but it will never last that long). The fresh cilantro is what makes this salsa taste like the kind at Tex-Mex restaurants—don't leave it out. If you want a less-chunky-kinda salsa, transfer it to a blender and pulse on and off for a second or two. (Don't go crazy or you'll end up with soup!)

PER SERVING (1/4 cup):
18 calories, 0.2 g fat,
4 g carbohydrate, 0.7 g protein,
79 mg sodium, 0 mg cholesterol
CALORIES FROM FAT: 9.8%

WHAT'S IN IT FOR ME?

Plum Dandy Chicken Digits

Whodunnit? Any clue who's responsible for the abrupt disappearance of these ever-so-tasty chicken fingers? Could it be Professor Plum in the kitchen with a spoon? Or is it Colonel Mustard in the dining room with a fork? We suspect they're both mixed up in this mystery.

2/3 cup unseasoned dry bread crumbs
3 tablespoons *each* cornmeal and grated
** Parmesan cheese**
1 teaspoon *each* dried basil and dried oregano
3/4 teaspoon garlic powder
1/2 teaspoon *each* ground thyme and
** onion powder**
1/4 teaspoon cayenne pepper
4 large boneless, skinless chicken breast halves
** (about 1-1/4 pounds)**
1 egg white

Tangy Dipping Sauce
3/4 cup yellow plum jam (apricot and peach are tasty, too)
2 tablespoons white vinegar
1-1/2 teaspoons prepared mustard

In a medium bowl, combine bread crumbs, cornmeal, cheese, basil, oregano, garlic powder, thyme, onion powder, and cayenne pepper. Mix well and set aside.

Cut chicken breasts into 3/4 x 3-inch strips. Place strips in a medium bowl. Beat egg white lightly with a fork and pour over chicken. Toss to coat chicken with egg white.

Roll chicken strips, one at a time, in crumb mixture. Make sure chicken is well coated with crumbs. Place on a non-stick baking sheet. Bake for 15-20 minutes at 450°, until chicken is golden brown and no longer pink inside. Check for "doneness" after 15 minutes. If overcooked, the chicken will be dry.

While chicken is baking, prepare dipping sauce. Combine jam, vinegar, and mustard in a small saucepan. Cook over medium-high heat until jam is melted and bubbly, about 2 minutes. Serve chicken fingers with warm dipping sauce.

Makes 4 servings.

PER SERVING: 425 calories, 5.9 g fat, 54.6 g carbohydrate, 33 g protein, 329 mg sodium, 77 mg cholesterol
CALORIES FROM FAT: 13.1%

WHAT'S IN IT FOR ME?

Gotta MOVE It!

A minimum of 30 minutes of moderate, continuous exercise, four or five times a week, is the *weigh* to go if your goals are to burn fat, lose weight, and increase your cardio-endurance. And what better way to begin working towards those goals than walking? Walking is inexpensive, it's easy, it's versatile, it's enjoyable, and it works! Since exercise doesn't have to be intense to be beneficial, brisk walking is often the ideal choice to begin with. Go as far and as fast as you comfortably can. Swing your arms to increase the aerobic benefit. You'll know that you're going much too fast if you can't "whistle while you walk."

Slim Pickin's

You'd have to oink out on
23 WHOLE PITAS
to consume the
16 GRAMS OF FAT
found in
1/2 CUP FRENCH ONION CHIP DIP.
Which would fill you up more?

Go for quality *and* quantity!

Trivial Tidbit

An old wives' tale suggests sprinkling a little cayenne pepper in your socks to keep your feet super toasty warm during cold weather.

COOKING 101

What's the difference between crostini and bruschetta? Crostini is grilled or toasted bread with a savory topping (crostini means "toast" in Italian). On the other hand, bruschetta is grilled or toasted bread that's rubbed with raw garlic and drizzled with olive oil. Both are generally served as appetizers, but a few pieces of our Toast with the Most and a tossed salad can easily make a light lunch or dinner.

D. I. E. T.

is a four-letter word that really means...

DISALLOWING **I**MPERFECTIONS **E**QUALS **T**ROUBLE

For decades, men and women have been bombarded with contemporary ideals of beauty, from paper-thin supermodels to hard-bodied action heroes. As each new generation of body-image icons mount their pedestals, there is increased social pressure to live up to often impossible standards. These overblown body-image pressures have resulted in a widespread belief that there is an inverse relationship between worth and weight: you should feel bigger when you're smaller, and smaller when you're bigger. No wonder we're always dieting!

But you're only human, remember? If your body doesn't quite measure up to those celebrated in magazines, join the crowd! You're just like the vast majority of the population—and what's so bad about that? Although it's difficult to completely ignore the unattainable shapes of a Stallone or a Schiffer, it makes more sense to set your sights on a goal that's right for YOU. Ultimately, you are your own harshest judge—and the only one who can grant yourself a reprieve.

He's been eating frozen foods for so long, his stomach sends out blizzard warnings.

Toast with the Most

It's savory. It's crunchy. It's crostini—a tasty, toasty treat. Betcha can't eat just one!

2 medium red onions, cut into 1/2-inch thick rings
10 plum tomatoes (Roma), cut into 1/4-inch thick slices
3 tablespoons red wine vinegar
1 medium eggplant, unpeeled and cut crosswise into 1/2-inch thick slices
1/2 teaspoon salt
1/4 teaspoon black pepper
1 clove garlic, minced
2 tablespoons chopped fresh parsley
1 loaf Italian or French bread, cut into 3/4-inch thick slices (about 16 slices)
1 tablespoon grated Parmesan cheese

Preheat oven to 450°.

Spray two 13 x 9-inch baking pans or cookie sheets with non-stick spray.

Toss onion rings and tomatoes with vinegar and spread evenly over bottom of one pan.

In a separate pan, arrange eggplant slices in a single layer. Bake vegetables until eggplant is browned (about 30 minutes) and edges of tomatoes are browned (about 45 minutes).

Transfer eggplant, tomatoes, and onions to a food processor or blender. Add salt, pepper, garlic, and parsley. Pulse on and off to coarsely purée vegetables.

Arrange bread slices on a cookie sheet in a single layer and place under broiler for 1 or 2 minutes on each side (or until golden brown).

Spread each bread slice with 2 tablespoons tomato/eggplant mixture. Sprinkle Parmesan lightly over top. Serve warm.

Makes 8 servings.

PER SERVING: 179 calories, 2.2 g fat, 37.1 g carbohydrate, 6.5 g protein, 379 mg sodium, 1 mg cholesterol
CALORIES FROM FAT: 10.2%

WHAT'S IN IT FOR ME?

Bean There. Dunked That.

This creamy, garlicky dip made of lean, mean beans is sorta like hummus, only better (and lower in fat). It really gets around—make it once, and everyone will be begging you to make it again and again and again...

1 can (15 ounces) white kidney
    beans (cannellini), drained
    and rinsed
1/4 cup low-fat sour cream
3 tablespoons lemon juice
1 or 2 cloves garlic, minced
1 tablespoon tahini
1/2 teaspoon honey
1/4 teaspoon *each* ground
    coriander, salt, and
    black pepper

Combine all ingredients in a blender or food processor and process until smooth. Chill for at least 1 hour before serving. Serve with fresh wedges of pita bread for dunking.

Makes 1-1/2 cups.

WHAT'S IN IT FOR ME?

PER SERVING (1/4 cup):
73 calories, 1.9 g fat,
14.3 g carbohydrate, 5.8 g protein,
228 mg sodium, 0 mg cholesterol
CALORIES FROM FAT: 17.8%

What the heck is "tahini" and where can I buy it?

Despite what you may be thinking, tahini is not a tropical vacation destination. It's a rich and creamy paste made from hulled toasted sesame seeds that adds a mild, nutty flavor to sauces, dips, and dressings. It can be found in well-stocked supermarkets and natural or specialty food stores, and is best stored in the refrigerator.

SAY IT AIN'T SO!

A popular burger from a certain fast food chain—no McNames McMentioned—combined with a large order of fries totals 890 gut-bulging calories, with 50% of them coming from fat! Yikes! Opt instead for the lower-fat choices that this leading franchise does have to offer: leaner burgers, salads, low-fat muffins, and low-fat frozen yogurt. Definitely steer clear of the "special" sauce. You won't think it's so "special" when it ends up around your waistline later.

Tug or Slug?

Show & Tell

Yams and sweet potatoes are often considered to be one and the same. Although similar in size and shape, these nutritious vegetables come from different plant species, each with its own color, flavor, and texture characteristics. To add to the confusion, supermarkets often label both fresh and canned sweet potatoes as "yams." However, true yams are seldom grown and are not widely marketed in North America. They're popular in Latin American countries, the West Indies, as well as parts of Asia and Africa. When buying sweet potatoes or "yams," choose blemish-free specimens with unwrinkled skin. Because their flesh discolors rapidly after peeling, it's best to immerse them in cold water until you're ready to cook them. Since the differences between yams and sweet potatoes are only subtle, you can use both vegetables interchangeably in recipes.

Trivial Tidbit

Even though 64% of our taste buds are lost between the ages of 30 and 80, taste outlasts all the other senses over a lifetime. Our taste buds are so finely tuned, they can detect sweetness in a substance even if only 1 part in 200 is sweet. Sourness is detected in 1 part in 130,000, a sensitivity that developed for protective purposes since poisonous foods are more often bitter or sour than sweet.

Did you hear about the employee who fell into a huge vat of gum? His boss chewed him out.

I Yam What I Yam

Luscious yam medallions baked in a cheesy-herb coating. Yammit, these are yummy (and low-fat, too!).

4 medium yams or sweet potatoes, unpeeled, scrubbed
2 egg whites
1 clove garlic, minced
1/3 cup unseasoned dry bread crumbs
1/3 cup grated Parmesan cheese
1 teaspoon dried basil
3/4 teaspoon dried rosemary

Preheat oven to 425°.

Slice yams into 1/4-inch thick rounds or "medallions." Since peeled yams turn brown quickly when exposed to air, transfer them to a bowl of cold water until you're ready to proceed to the next step.

Pat yams dry using paper towels. Combine egg whites and garlic in a large bowl. Add yams and toss to coat.

In a small bowl, mix together bread crumbs, cheese, basil, and rosemary. Transfer crumbs to a dinner plate and spread evenly.

Coat yams on both sides with crumb mixture. Place in a single layer on a cookie sheet that has been sprayed with non-stick spray. Bake for 15 minutes. Remove from oven and flip yams over. Bake another 15 minutes until tender.

Makes 4 servings.

Hint: Try dunking these in your favorite low-fat ranch-flavored dip!

PER SERVING: 218 calories, 3.4 g fat, 39 g carbohydrate, 8.8 g protein, 268 mg sodium, 6 mg cholesterol CALORIES FROM FAT: 13.9%

Bermuda Triangles

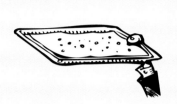

BERMUDA   BERMUDA SHORTS   BERMUDA TRIANGLES

These pizza-style appetizers are guaranteed to disappear without a trace. They're fun to make, and kids just seem to love them. Hey adults! You'll love them, too! These delectable triangles make a fine and fancy finger food that's sure to please those pernickety guests.

Crust
1 large baking potato
1/3 cup skim milk
1 tablespoon butter or margarine, melted
1 cup all-purpose flour
1-1/2 teaspoons baking powder
1 teaspoon sugar
1/4 teaspoon salt

Topping
1 clove garlic, minced
1 cup sliced mushrooms
1/2 cup *each* chopped red bell pepper, sliced red onion rings, and thinly sliced zucchini
1 teaspoon dried oregano
1 cup seeded and diced tomato
1/2 cup pizza sauce (or spaghetti sauce)
1/4 cup grated Parmesan cheese

Pierce baking potato all over with a fork. Microwave on high power for 10-12 minutes, until tender. Cut in half and let potato cool. When cool, peel off and discard skin. Place potato in a medium bowl. Add skim milk and butter. Beat with an electric mixer on medium speed until smooth, about 1 minute.

In a separate bowl, combine flour, baking powder, sugar, and salt. Add to potato mixture. Mix well using a wooden spoon. Form dough into a ball. Cut into quarters. Roll out each quarter on a lightly floured surface to a diameter of 7 inches.

Spray a large skillet with non-stick spray. Heat over medium-high heat. Working one at a time, cook pizza crusts for 2-3 minutes on each side, until golden brown and puffed slightly. Transfer crusts to a baking sheet.

Preheat oven to 400°.

Re-coat skillet with non-stick spray. Add garlic, mushrooms, red pepper, onions, zucchini, and oregano. Cook over medium-high heat until vegetables are tender-crisp, about 6 minutes. Remove from heat and stir in tomatoes.

Spread 2 tablespoons pizza sauce over each crust. Top each with 1/4 vegetable mixture, followed by 1 tablespoon Parmesan cheese. Bake for 8-10 minutes, until cheese is melted. Using a pizza cutter or sharp knife, slice each pizza into 6 triangles. Serve immediately.

Makes 24 triangles.

WHAT'S IN IT FOR ME?

PER TRIANGLE: 42 calories, 1 g fat, 7 g carbohydrate, 1.5 g protein, 94 mg sodium, 2 mg cholesterol
CALORIES FROM FAT: 20.7%

A garlic press is a useful tool. It produces a quicker and more intensely flavored result than garlic minced with a knife, as the pressing releases more of the garlic's essential oils.

COOKING 101

Show me the WEIGH

You may ask yourself, "Why should I bother with low-fat food? Nothing comes close to the taste of a nice, juicy cheeseburger and french fries anyway." Actually, you've got it all wrong. *Nothing tastes as good as being fit feels!* Making smarter food choices will help change your body for the better. If you change the way you look and feel, chances are the overall quality of your life will improve as a result. Think about it. If you don't feel good about yourself, it's hard to feel good about the world around you. Poor nutrition can contribute to a poor self-image, which affects your mood, and this may in turn affect your personal relationships, your job, and your health. So think twice about the greasy burger—your family, friends, and co-workers may end up thanking you!

Mixed-Up Meatballs

Some are sweet, some are sour. But personal differences aside, they do make an unforgettable pair. Mmmm! Delicious!

**1-1/2 pounds lean ground turkey
  or chicken (skinless)**
1/2 cup unseasoned dry bread crumbs
1/3 cup minced onions
1/4 cup chopped fresh parsley
1 egg white
**1/2 teaspoon *each* garlic
  powder and ground sage**
**1/4 teaspoon *each* salt and
  black pepper**
**1 cup seedless raspberry
  jam**
1/4 cup prepared mustard
**1-1/2 tablespoons prepared
  horseradish**

Combine ground turkey or chicken, bread crumbs, onions, parsley, egg white, garlic powder, sage, salt, and pepper in a medium bowl. Mix well (using your hands works best). Form mixture into bite-size meatballs, about 1-inch diameter. You should end up with 65-70 meatballs.

Place meatballs on a large baking sheet that has been sprayed with non-stick spray. Bake at 400° for 12-15 minutes, until cooked through (test for "doneness" after 12 minutes). Remove from oven and transfer to a large saucepan.

In a small saucepan, stir together jam, mustard, and horseradish. Cook over medium-high heat for 2-3 minutes, stirring often. Sauce will be thick and bubbly. Pour sauce over meatballs. Stir well. Cover and simmer over medium-low heat for 10 minutes. Transfer to a serving dish and serve hot.

Makes 8 servings.

PER SERVING: 233 calories, 1.8 g fat, 33.2 g carbohydrate, 22.2 g protein, 307 mg sodium, 41 mg cholesterol CALORIES FROM FAT: 6.9%

WHAT'S IN IT FOR ME?

The only exercise he gets is when his flesh crawls during a horror movie.

Slim Dunk

When it comes to dips, especially the ones served at parties, most people end up letting their defenses down, indulging and bulging from fat-crammed treats. Now, there's no need to foul-out of your healthy eating plan. This dip's so light, it won't interfere with your hang time.

**2 cups low-fat sour cream
(see hint below)**
**1/4 cup non-fat or low-fat
mayonnaise**
**1 10-ounce package frozen
spinach, thawed, squeezed
dry, and chopped**
**1 envelope (1.8 ounces)
Knorr brand leek soup
mix**
**1/4 cup minced red bell
pepper**

Combine all ingredients in a medium bowl. Stir well. Cover and refrigerate for 3 hours before serving.

Makes about 3 cups.

Hint: This recipe works best when the low-fat sour cream is very thick. Select a brand that lists "gelatin" in the ingredients, otherwise your dip may be runny.

WHAT'S IN IT FOR ME? ➔ PER SERVING (1/4 cup):
45 calories, 1.1 g fat,
7.4 g carbohydrate, 2.6 g protein,
250 mg sodium, 1 mg cholesterol
CALORIES FROM FAT: 19.8%

COOKING 101

This dip tastes great served with your favorite fresh vegetables for dunking. You could also spoon the dip into a hollowed-out round pumpernickel loaf, chop the scooped-out bread into large chunks, and use these for dunking. Serious yum factor!

Gotta MOVE It!

Most athletes know that they should "eat to win." Funny thing is, many of them decide not to eat real food, opting instead to waste their money on every new dietary supplement they read about in fitness magazines—from energy pills and protein supplements to seaweed and bee pollen. Forget the Do-It-Yourself Instant Super Hero Protein Pak. The truth is, you don't need a special diet or a particular vitamin supplement to keep your body in peak condition. A sensible, well-balanced diet is all you need to get a head start on the competition. And guess what kind of fuel is the most efficient for feeding muscles during vigorous activity? No, not a chocolate bar! You got it—good ol' complex carbohydrates—bread, cereal, pasta, potatoes, rice, beans, veggies, and fruit. These carbohydrates are stored in your muscle tissue as glycogen, which is readily broken down into glucose, the ultimate "high performance" muscle fuel. Remember, Snickers bars may be the official chocolate bars of the Olympics, but that doesn't mean they'll give you the strength or stamina to win the gold.

Flintstone vitamins are so potent, every time I take one I get the urge to stop the car with my feet.

What the heck is "mixed herb seasoning" and where can I buy it?

You'll find several varieties of pre-mixed herb seasonings in the spice section of your grocery store, all designed to enhance the flavor of food without adding a lot of salt. Most brands include a combination of dehydrated garlic, onion, parsley, paprika, oregano, and/or basil. Some are hot 'n spicy. Others are mild. You can sprinkle these seasonings directly on vegetables, chicken, potatoes, fish, pasta, or in this case, pita chips. They're a smart way to boost flavor without boosting your fat, sodium, and calorie intake.

Oil Beauty Pageant: The Good, the Bad, and the Really Ugly

Vying for the title of "Healthiest Oil," contestants were judged on their fat compositions. Higher scores were given to oils that exhibited a combination of low saturated fat content (really ugly fat) and high monounsaturated fat content (better fat). In plain English, saturated fat isn't good for you, so the less saturated fat, the healthier the oil. In the event of a tie, contestants then went on to compete in the swimsuit and evening gown competitions.

And the winner of the "Healthiest Oil" competition is...(where is Bob Barker when we really need him?)

1. **Canola Oil!**
   followed by, from most healthy to least healthy:

2. **Olive Oil**
3. **Safflower Oil**
4. **Sunflower Oil**
5. **Sesame Oil**
6. **Peanut Oil**
7. **Corn Oil**
8. **Soybean Oil**
9. **Cottonseed Oil**

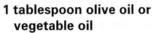
Chip Chip Hooray!

If you love chips, but not the fat
Our slimmed-down version
   is where it's at
Great for snacking, dunking too
These guiltless chips are good
   for you!

**1 tablespoon olive oil or
   vegetable oil**
1 egg white
4 6-inch whole wheat pitas
Mixed herb seasoning

Preheat oven to 350°.

Whisk together olive oil and egg white in a small bowl. Set aside.

Using scissors, cut the pitas in half. Open up the pockets, and cut each half into 2 half circles. Stack half circles 2 at a time, then cut into 3 wedges. You should end up with 12 "chips" from each whole pita.

Using a pastry brush, lightly brush the inside of each pita chip with olive oil mixture. Place chips on a baking sheet, oil-side up, in a single layer. Sprinkle herb seasoning over each chip.

Bake for 15 minutes, or until golden brown and crispy. (If you bite into a chip and it's chewy, that means they're not done yet!)

Store chips in an airtight container or plastic bag.

Makes 4 servings.

PER SERVING: 188 calories, 5.7 g fat, 28.4 g carbohydrate, 7 g protein, 431 mg sodium, 0 mg cholesterol
CALORIES FROM FAT: 26.6%

WHAT'S IN IT FOR ME?

Note: **Coconut Oil** and **Palm Oil** were both disqualified from the competition for being much too high in saturated fat content. Boo! Hiss!

GREEN ACRES

Salads for hungry people,
not rabbits!

Cool Chick Salad

What's so cool about this chicken salad? Well, it's really hoppin' with black beans, not to mention a zesty, rockin' and rollin' combination of lime and cilantro that'll knock your socks off.

2 cups chopped cooked chicken breast
1 cup canned black beans, drained
   and rinsed
1-1/2 cups diced tomato
1 cup whole kernel corn
1/2 cup diced red onions
1/4 cup chopped fresh cilantro

Dressing
2 tablespoons lime juice
1 tablespoon olive oil
1/2 teaspoon *each* ground cumin
   and sugar
1/4 teaspoon *each* salt and black pepper

Combine first 6 ingredients in a large bowl and mix well.

In a small bowl, whisk together dressing ingredients. Pour over bean mixture and stir until dressing is evenly distributed.

Cover and refrigerate until ready to serve.

Makes 6 servings.

WHAT'S IN IT FOR ME?

PER SERVING: 273 calories, 7.7 g fat, 26.8 g carbohydrate, 26.6 g protein, 427 mg sodium, 60 mg cholesterol
CALORIES FROM FAT: 24.6%

Show me the WEIGH

Fat is undoubtedly a dietary scoundrel when over-consumed. But believe it or not, fat's not so bad once you get to know it. It does have redeeming qualities, too! In fact, we need a certain amount of fat to survive. Dietary fat supplies us with lineolic acid, an essential fatty acid which is important for proper growth, especially in children.

Fat is also the vehicle that transports fat-soluble vitamins (A, D, E, and K) through the body, and is required for the maintenance of healthy skin and for the metabolization of cholesterol.

So eating a low-fat diet doesn't mean eating *no* fat, and it doesn't have to mean *never* eating a high-fat food. Expect that you'll have cravings for chocolate or a T-bone steak every now and then, treat yourself, and then get back on track with low-fat choices for the rest of the week.

Slim Pickin's

If you choose to eat a scrawny
1 TABLESPOON OF MARGARINE,
you'll be choosing a surprising
11 GRAMS OF FAT,
the equivalent of eating
12 CUPS OF BOILED LOBSTER.
Which would fill you up more?

Go for quality *and* quantity!

A hungry bear was prowling the forest looking for something to eat when he came upon two men sitting under a tree. One was reading a novel and the other was writing in a journal. The bear immediately pounced upon the man reading the novel and gobbled him up. Apparently, the bear knew that readers digest and writers cramp.

Show & Tell

Water chestnuts really aren't nuts at all! They're tubers (underground stem parts) of an aquatic plant originating in Southeast Asia. Water chestnuts are commonly used in Chinese and Vietnamese cooking for their delicate flavor and crunchy texture. Best of all, they're virtually fat-free!

Gotta MOVE It!

Uggghhh! Cellulite! Those unsightly dimples! If you're thinking of using creams, pills, or injections to "spot-reduce" in areas where Plenty O'Cellulite lives, you should hold on to your wallet —its contents are all you'll be losing. You can't spot-reduce fat, no matter where it is. Getting rid of the cellulite look involves the same process as reducing fat anywhere else on the body: cutting back on the fat you eat and getting some regular exercise. A healthy, varied diet along with exercise minimizes overall body fat, allowing the underlying muscle to show through. Throw in some weight or resistance training and the appearance of your muscles will improve further. But you can't eliminate fat from a certain part of your body by exercising that part alone. Your body doesn't selectively draw energy from fat stores in the parts being exercised. It draws on fat from all areas. So don't waste your time and money on miracle pills, potions, creams, or schemes to fight cellulite. Just move it!

Acme
MIRACLE
FLAB B GONE
CREAM
New York • Paris • Ottawa

Melrose Plates

Why not invite everyone in your trendy apartment building over for a taste of this tangy, zesty, California-style salad? Invite the fashion designer who lives upstairs, invite her nasty sister, invite the advertising executives, call over the owner of the local bar and his photographer friend, invite the doctors...

6 ounces uncooked rotini or other
shaped pasta (about 2 cups dry)
2 cups chopped cooked chicken breast
1 cup diced celery
1 cup mandarin orange sections
(try apples if you hate
mandarins)
1/2 cup water chestnuts,
cut into slivers
2 tablespoons chopped fresh parsley
3/4 cup non-fat plain yogurt
2 tablespoons honey
1 tablespoon frozen orange juice
concentrate
1 teaspoon poppy seeds
1/2 teaspoon dry mustard
1/4 teaspoon black pepper
Lettuce (any kind you like)

Cook pasta according to package directions. Drain and rinse with cold water. Transfer pasta to a large bowl. Add the chicken, celery, orange sections, water chestnuts, and parsley. Mix well.

In a separate bowl, stir together yogurt, honey, orange juice concentrate, poppy seeds, mustard, and pepper. Pour yogurt mixture over chicken/pasta mixture and toss. Serve on a bed of lettuce.

Makes 4 servings.

Hint: If you don't have any chicken on hand (or on foot or on head or on...), try tuna, turkey, crabmeat, or shrimp in its place.

PER SERVING: 418 calories, 5 g fat, 63 g carbohydrate, 31 g protein, 128 mg sodium, 60 mg cholesterol CALORIES FROM FAT: 10.6%

WHAT'S IN IT FOR ME?

Nature gave us two ends—one to sit on and the other to think with. Our success depends on which end we use the most.

Rootie Toot Fruit Salad

A creamy, orangy sauce (low in fat, of course) makes this a refreshing, light dessert for that weekend barbeque party. Toss in the fruits that you like best and put your taste buds to the test!

2 cups low-fat sour cream
   (look for a thick brand)
2 tablespoons honey
1 tablespoon frozen orange juice
   concentrate
1 teaspoon grated orange zest
6 cups chopped fresh fruit
   (try a combination of bananas, oranges,
   kiwi fruit, strawberries, and apples,
   or choose your favorites)

Mix first four ingredients together in a small bowl. Cover and refrigerate for 1 hour.

Stir sauce and fruit together in a large bowl. Serve immediately.

Makes 6 servings.

Hint: To prevent the flesh of apples from turning brown after cutting or peeling them, dip them in lemon juice. Make sure you mix the sauce and fruit together just before serving, otherwise the salad will be runny.

WHAT'S IN IT FOR ME? ➡ PER SERVING: 168 calories, 1.6 g fat, 35.3 g carbohydrate, 6.1 g protein, 3 mg sodium, 3 mg cholesterol CALORIES FROM FAT: 7.9%

COOKING 101

When a recipe calls for the "zest" of a citrus fruit, it's referring to the colorful outer part of the skin, not the inner white part, which is known as the pith. The zest contains all of the aromatic citrus oils and provides a hint of citrus tang to the recipe. A simple method of obtaining a fine zest is by rubbing the fruit against the smallest holes of a cheese grater.

SAY IT AIN'T SO!

What popular food is concocted with bits of animal hooves, teeth, bone fragments, and other unmentionable parts? Sound like the contents of a witch's brew? Actually, this describes something that a lot of people wash down *with* a brew at a ball game. That's right, it's a hot dog, one of the *wurst* food choices you can make if you care about your health. Hot dogs, sausages, and luncheon meats sometimes contain substandard animal parts, and even though they might not make you ill, they certainly don't sound appealing, do they? Questionable ingredients should be enough to repulse most people, but fat content also should. The average 2-ounce hot dog (wiener only) has 16 grams of fat. To be frank, that's just too much fat to eat on a regular basis.

I do whatever my Rice Krispies tell me to do.

HOWS ABOUT A LITTLE SUGAR, SUGAR?

What the heck is "radicchio" and where can I get some?

Radicchio is a relative of the endive and looks like a small, reddish-purple cabbage. Its wonderful color and mildly bitter taste give ordinary green salads a boost. It's a bit expensive compared to other lettuces, but luckily you don't need to use much here. Almost all grocery stores now carry radicchio in their produce sections.

The Naked Truth About Dressing

Keeping fat content to a minimum while maximizing flavor is the goal here with our Tangy Vinaigretta salad dressing. This is accomplished by using only 2 teaspoons of olive oil, which is then distributed among 4 servings. Fat-laden dressings are what choke otherwise healthy salads to death, and most people don't even realize it, piling on the dressing with reckless abandon. Blue cheese dressing, oil and vinegar, and ranch dressing all have *8 grams of fat per tablespoon*, and who uses just one tablespoon? Let's assume that on average we use 2 tablespoons of dressing. That's a total of 16 grams of fat—about the same as an order of greasy fries! Oily, creamy, and cheesy dressings are best avoided. Make your own low-fat dressings, go wild with herbs and spices, or look for low-fat or even fat-free versions in your grocery store.

Russian Dressing

Beyond Be-Leaf Garden Salad

Be-leaf it or not, this mouthwatering, colorful salad boasts a unique dressing that's not crammed with fat like most other salad dressings.

AHM A BE-LEAFER

5 cups shredded/torn romaine or green leaf lettuce, or mixed greens
1 cup chopped radicchio
1 cup alfalfa sprouts
1 cup grated carrot
1 small red onion, thinly sliced into rings
8 cherry tomatoes, halved
24 thin slices unpeeled English cucumber
1 cup Seasoned Croutovs (page 36)
Tangy Vinaigretta Dressing (recipe follows)

To assemble salad, divide lettuce among 4 serving plates. Sprinkle each with 1/4 cup radicchio and 1/4 cup alfalfa sprouts, followed by 1/4 cup grated carrot and 1/4 of the red onion. Arrange 4 cherry tomato halves, 6 cucumber slices, and 1/4 cup Croutovs on top.

Drizzle dressing over individual salads and serve immediately.

Makes 4 servings.

Tangy Vinaigretta Dressing
3 tablespoons *each* red wine vinegar and apple juice
2 teaspoons olive oil
1 clove garlic, minced
1 teaspoon sugar
1/2 teaspoon *each* Dijon mustard and dried oregano
1/8 teaspoon black pepper

Whisk all ingredients together in a small bowl. Serve at room temperature.

PER SERVING: 114 calories, 3.7 g fat, 17.7 g carbohydrate, 3.4 g protein, 142 mg sodium, 0 mg cholesterol
CALORIES FROM FAT: 28.5%

WHAT'S IN IT FOR ME?

Trivial Tidbit

Romaine lettuce derives its name from the Romans who admired its healthful properties. In fact, the Emperor Augustus put up a statue praising the lettuce for curing him of an illness.

Of Rice and Men

Sure, this unique rice salad with a tangy-sweet lime dressing and chunks of cantaloupe is a real hit with men, but women love it too, and can't seem to resist a second or even a third helping. You know what they say: "Once, rice, three times a lady."

1 cup uncooked long grain brown rice (see hint below)
1 cup orange juice
1-1/3 cups low-sodium, reduced-fat chicken broth
1-1/2 cups diced cantaloupe
1 cup peeled and diced English cucumber
1/2 cup *each* diced red bell pepper and chopped green onions
2 tablespoons chopped fresh cilantro

Dressing
3 tablespoons lime juice
2 tablespoons honey
1 tablespoon olive oil
1 teaspoon prepared mustard
1 clove garlic, minced
1/2 teaspoon ground cumin
3-4 dashes hot pepper sauce
1/4 teaspoon salt

Combine rice, orange juice, and chicken broth in a medium saucepan. Bring to a boil. Reduce heat to medium-low. Cover and simmer until rice is tender and all liquid has been absorbed, about 25 minutes. Let rice cool completely.

In a large bowl, stir together rice, cantaloupe, cucumber, red pepper, green onions, and cilantro. In a small bowl, whisk together all dressing ingredients. Pour over rice mixture and stir well. Cover and refrigerate for 1 hour before serving.

Makes 8 servings.

Hint: Make sure the brown rice you're using is the quicker-cooking variety (cooks in 25 minutes), but not instant rice.

WHAT'S IN IT FOR ME? → PER SERVING: 151 calories, 2.6 g fat, 30.2 g carbohydrate, 3.1 g protein, 162 mg sodium, 0 mg cholesterol CALORIES FROM FAT: 15.1%

Show & Tell

A variety of muskmelon, the cantaloupe's name is derived from the town of Cantalupo, Italy, where the melon was first grown after being brought into the country from Armenia in the first century A.D. Rich in beta-carotene and fiber, half a 5-inch cantaloupe also packs in 100 percent of the recommended daily allowance of vitamins A and C, with less than 1 gram of fat! Given these health-promoting qualities, maybe we should forget the name cantaloupe and start thinking *CAN*aloupe!

Gotta MOVE It!

Round and round you go. It's a vivacious circle! Physical activity sets off a chain of events that keeps you coming back for more. The more active you are, the more energy you have. The more energy you have, the better you feel. The better you feel, the more you want to do... Getting on the right track is as easy as walking to the grocery store instead of driving.

Low-fat eating is for those who are thick and tired of dieting.

Slim Pickin's

You'd have to oink out on
37 KIWI FRUIT
to consume the
13 GRAMS OF FAT
found in
1 PACKAGE OF REESE'S PEANUT BUTTER CUPS.
Which would fill you up more?

Go for quality *and* quantity!

D. I. E. T.

is a four-letter word that really means...
DANGEROUSLY INADVISABLE EATING TACTICS

Reducing caloric intake to unrealistically low daily targets means you're not getting the nutrients that your body needs to function properly and to be healthy. What's more, if you don't eat, your body goes into "starvation mode," it slows your metabolism and tries to hoard any fuel that comes along, with fat being the prime candidate because it lasts the longest in famine. As far as liquid diets go, it's absurd to think your body can survive this way. What happens when you start eating regular food again? The answer: weight gain. It seems the only thing you *do* lose on dangerously restrictive diets is your health and self-esteem.

Rotini Riot

Expect a really rollickin' shindig when word gets out that you've created a super-savory pasta salad that's not drowning in oil. Sure to cause a stir!

12 ounces uncooked tri-color rotini (about 4 cups dry)
1 cup broccoli florets
1/2 cup carrots, cut into matchsticks
1/2 cup *each* chopped red and green bell pepper
1/2 cup thinly sliced mushrooms

Dressing
1/4 cup plus 1 tablespoon red wine vinegar
1/4 cup apple juice
3 tablespoons olive oil
1 tablespoon *each* lemon juice and sugar
2 teaspoons Dijon mustard
1 large clove garlic, minced
1 teaspoon *each* dried basil and dried oregano
1/4 teaspoon *each* crushed red pepper flakes, salt, and black pepper
2 teaspoons grated Parmesan cheese

Cook pasta according to package directions. Drain. Rinse well with cold water and drain again. Transfer pasta to a large bowl.

Place broccoli and carrots in a small microwave-safe dish with 1/4 cup water. Microwave on high power for 1-1/2 minutes. Drain. Add to pasta along with red and green peppers and mushrooms.

Combine all dressing ingredients in a small bowl. Stir well using a whisk. Pour dressing over pasta and vegetables. Stir well to coat pasta with dressing. Cover and refrigerate for 4 hours before serving. Tastes even better the next day!

Makes 8 servings.

PER SERVING: 238 calories, 6.6 g fat, 38 g carbohydrate, 6.3 g protein, 117 mg sodium, 0 mg cholesterol
CALORIES FROM FAT: 25.2%

WHAT'S IN IT FOR ME?

Impastable Slim Chick Salad

You'll be a slim chick if this low-fat chicken salad is one of your lunchin' mainstays (unless you're a guy, and then you'd be a slim Chuck). Sesame oil gives it a distinct flavor that'll have you drooling for a second helping.

4 cups cooked shaped pasta such as rotini, radiatore, or wagon wheels (about 2 cups dry)
2 cups chopped cooked chicken breast
1 cup *each* thinly sliced red bell pepper and broccoli florets
1 cup snow peas, trimmed and halved
1/4 cup chopped green onions
3 tablespoons red wine vinegar
1 tablespoon reduced-sodium soy sauce
1 tablespoon tomato-based chili sauce
2 teaspoons sesame oil
1 teaspoon *each* grated ginger root and honey
1 clove garlic, minced
1/4 teaspoon black pepper

In a large bowl, toss cooked pasta with chicken, red pepper, broccoli, snow peas, and green onions. Set aside.

In a small bowl, whisk together vinegar, soy sauce, chili sauce, sesame oil, ginger root, honey, garlic, and pepper.

Pour dressing over pasta mixture and stir to coat evenly. Refrigerate until ready to serve.

Makes 6 servings.

Hint: This salad tastes best when eaten within a day.

Slim Chick Slim Chuck

WHAT'S IN IT FOR ME?

PER SERVING: 251 calories, 4.4 g fat, 32.2 g carbohydrate, 20.2 g protein, 394 mg sodium, 40 mg cholesterol
CALORIES FROM FAT: 15.8%

SAY IT AIN'T SO!

Think you're a dietary saint because you ordered salad for lunch? Well say goodbye to your halo and harp if you've ordered a fast food taco salad! With ranch dressing, this healthy-sounding selection has 87 grams of fat, 1167 calories, and 67% of calories from fat. You don't necessarily have to wait until hell freezes over to indulge in a taco salad, but at least wait for a frost warning.

Show me the WEIGH

Feel like you've been running on empty? It just may be that you're not eating enough (imagine!) or that you're not eating enough high-quality foods. Think of food as your gas-o-lean, your fuel, your energy. A car doesn't run without fuel, a furnace doesn't run without fuel, and neither does your body. So don't be fuelish! Fill 'er up with smart choices like grains, veggies, pasta, fruit, and beans—all loaded with nutrients, low in fat, and satisfying, too. Perfect food to rev up your engine!

Diet: A short period of starvation preceding a gain of five pounds.

There's no need to crack up over cracked boiled eggs. There's a simple scientific explanation behind this occurrence, as well as a foolproof method to prevent simmering eggs from cracking and oozing out some of their egg white in the process.

Every egg contains an air pocket at the larger, rounded end. When placed in simmering water, the heat of the water expands the air in the pocket, creating a higher atmospheric pressure within the egg than in the water. The fragile egg shell is easily cracked by the built-up pressure.

The solution? From now on, remove your eggs from the refrigerator and pierce the larger, rounded end with a pushpin. This will make a convenient hole for the air to escape through as it expands. Ease the cold eggs into a pot of boiling water. Reduce heat and simmer eggs for 5 minutes for soft-cooked eggs and 12 minutes for hard-cooked eggs. Cool the eggs in cold water, then peel them. The result: perfectly cooked, uncracked eggs.

Trivial Tidbit In 1924, an Italian-American chef named Caesar Cardini, who opened a string of restaurants in Tijuana between the wars, created the salad that bears his name. He didn't, however, include the anchovies that appear in modern Caesar salads—he considered it a perversion.

He's been on a garlic diet. He hasn't lost any weight, but he's lost quite a few friends.

Seize Her Salad

Why? Because *her* salad is undoubtedly the best Caesar since the days of Julius (and we don't mean Dr. J, either!) Apparently, the ancient Romans were quite concerned about the fat content in their meals. When you're erecting coliseums, fighting lions, and overthrowing empires, who can afford to carry those extra pounds? So *she* created this delicious, low-fat Caesar salad for *her* subjects to enjoy. It's a taste worth capturing. (Who *she* is remains a mystery to this day.)

1/2 cup low-fat mayonnaise
1/4 cup low-sodium, reduced-fat chicken broth
2 tablespoons grated Parmesan cheese
1-1/2 tablespoons lemon juice
1 tablespoon red wine vinegar
1 hard-cooked egg
2 cloves garlic, minced
1/2 teaspoon *each* Dijon mustard and "lite" Worcestershire sauce
1/8 teaspoon black pepper
1 large head of romaine lettuce, torn
1-1/2 cups Seasoned Croutovs (page 36)

Combine first 10 ingredients in a blender or food processor and blend until smooth. Cover and refrigerate for at least 1 hour.

Toss romaine and dressing in a large bowl until lettuce is evenly coated with dressing. Add Croutovs just before serving. Sprinkle lightly with additional Parmesan cheese and pepper, if desired. Serve immediately.

Makes 6 servings.

Hint: Since the Seasoned Croutovs are not coated in oil like most commercially made croutons, they easily absorb moisture. You'll want to add them just before serving the salad to prevent them from becoming soggy.

PER SERVING: 93 calories, 2.6 g fat, 14.2 g carbohydrate, 4.3 g protein, 374 mg sodium, 37 mg cholesterol
CALORIES FROM FAT: 23.9%

WHAT'S IN IT FOR ME?

We're Talkin' Small Potatoes

It may be small red potatoes we're cookin' for this zesty, filling salad, but we don't want you to think that this is just another "mash in the pan." No siree! Not this one. This spud's for you!

10 small red potatoes, unpeeled,
   cut into 1/4-inch thick slices
   (about 2-1/2 pounds)
1/2 cup diced carrots
3/4 cup diced celery
1/4 cup *each* diced red onions and
   chopped green onions
2 tablespoons chopped fresh parsley
1/4 cup red wine vinegar
1 tablespoon olive oil
1 teaspoon sugar
1/2 teaspoon *each* Dijon mustard and celery seeds
1 large clove garlic, minced
1/4 teaspoon black pepper

Steam potato slices until tender, about 10 minutes. Add carrots and continue to steam for another 5-7 minutes. Drain off water.

In a large bowl, toss potatoes, carrots, celery, red onions, green onions, and parsley until well mixed. In a small bowl, whisk together vinegar, oil, sugar, Dijon mustard, celery seeds, garlic, and pepper. Pour over potato mixture and stir gently until evenly coated with dressing. Serve warm or cold.

Makes 6 servings.

WHAT'S IN IT FOR ME?

PER SERVING: 262 calories, 3 g fat, 54.7 g carbohydrate, 5.4 g protein, 48 mg sodium, 0 mg cholesterol
CALORIES FROM FAT: 10%

Show & Tell

Green onions are also referred to as scallions, spring onions, and salad onions. Although there are subtle differences between these members of the onion family, all may be used interchangeably in recipes. These long, slender onions have a white base that has not fully developed into a bulb and long, straight green leaves. When a recipe calls for chopped green onions, include both the white base and the green tops, since both parts are edible.

SAY IT AIN'T SO!

Was the sandwich invented because someone realized that man cannot live on bread alone? What a shame, because bread is much healthier *without* some of the things we put on it. Take a grilled cheese sandwich, for instance. Start out with two pieces of perfectly healthy bread, clothe them in butter, cloak them with cheese, and you've got 22 grams of fat! Don't be shy about having naked bread once in a while. It'll rise to the occasion.

Fat makes you fat
There's no denying that
But mind over platter
Makes a body to be flattered

WHY HARRIET! YOU LOOK ABSOLUTELY INEDIBLE

THANKS ELSIE. I'VE SWITCHED TO SKIM MILK

Slim Pickin's

If you choose to eat
1 MEASLY APPLE TURNOVER,
you'll be choosing
17 GRAMS OF FAT,
the equivalent of eating
17 CUPS OF SPAGHETTI.
Which would fill you up more?

Go for quality *and* quantity!

Show me the WEIGH

What would Chief Executive Officers of corporate North America possibly have to gain by taking an interest in low-fat, healthy eating? The answer is simple: $$$! Numerous studies suggest that at least 60-70% of illnesses have a dietary link, with fat being the worst dietary villain. Cutting back on fat yields tremendous health benefits, and for employers, this could mean reduced employee absenteeism, enhanced employee energy, and improved creativity, focus, and overall work capacity. So if employees in general were to increase their consumption of nutritious, low-fat foods, this could translate into significantly increased productivity for their employers. And that's the bottom line that would probably interest the big boss.

L.A. Slaw

Objection, your Honor! Isn't coleslaw a notorious fat offender because it's dripping with mayo? Objection overruled. This particular coleslaw is a slaw with a "**L**ean **A**ttitude." The verdict is in: Not guilty!

5 cups coarsely shredded green cabbage
2 cups coarsely shredded red cabbage
1 cup grated carrot
3/4 cup thinly sliced celery
1/4 cup *each* white vinegar and sugar
1 tablespoon vegetable oil
1 teaspoon Dijon mustard
1/2 teaspoon celery seeds
1/4 teaspoon *each* salt and black pepper

Place first four ingredients in a very large bowl and toss until well mixed.

To prepare dressing, combine vinegar, sugar, vegetable oil, Dijon mustard, celery seeds, salt, and pepper in a small saucepan. Heat over medium-high heat until mixture comes to a boil and sugar dissolves. Add to cabbage mixture and stir until well blended.

Cover and chill at least 2 hours before serving.

Makes 8 servings.

PER SERVING: 66 calories, 2.1 g fat, 11.5 g carbohydrate, 1.1 g protein, 107 mg sodium, 0 mg cholesterol
CALORIES FROM FAT: 26.9%

Wife: "There's a burglar in the kitchen. He's eating the casserole we had for dinner."
Husband: "Go back to sleep. I'll bury him in the morning."

Seasoned Croutovs

Special thanks to our Russian cousins, Olga and Vladislav Croutov, who six years ago risked their lives in order to send us this secret, KGB-protected recipe for low-fat croutons. The recipe cleared Customs just in time for the printing of this book.

1 teaspoon garlic powder
1 teaspoon dried oregano
1 teaspoon dried basil
1 teaspoon grated Parmesan cheese
3 cups cubed fresh bread
Olive-oil-flavored cooking spray

Preheat oven to 350°.

Mix garlic, oregano, basil, and cheese in a small bowl until well blended. Pour mixture into a large plastic freezer bag or plastic grocery bag. Dust bread cubes lightly with a shot of olive-oil-flavored cooking spray. Add bread cubes to bag and shake until coated with spices. Not all spices will stick to bread, but that's O.K.

Place bread cubes in a single layer on baking sheet. Bake until Croutovs are crisp and golden brown, about 10-15 minutes (it depends on the kind of bread you use, so keep your eye on them). Let cool.

Store in an airtight container or plastic bag for up to 1 week.

Makes 3 cups.

Some cooks recommend that you use slightly stale bread when making home-made croutons. That works great when you're coating them with butter or olive oil. Our low-fat Croutovs aren't soaking in fat, so they require that the bread be fresh, otherwise the seasonings won't stick. Just about any type of bread will do: French, Italian, sourdough, whole wheat, and pumpernickel all work well.

Gotta MOVE It!

Keeping the fun and enjoyment in exercise is sometimes challenging, especially on those occasions when your body may be willing but your brain is saying "I absolutely cannot run another step! Jogging is soooo boring!" To stay motivated and to distract yourself from your physical efforts, try listening to music. Evidence suggests that listening to music helps people to exercise longer and stronger because they tend to think their workouts are easier. One side of a ninety-minute tape is perfect for a workout and it'll give you a target to shoot for. Tuning in to some lively music is a doggone good way to keep your mind interested in continuing, and who knows—you may find yourself breaking into a little jig along the way! So just put your favorite tape into your Walkman and go ahead—walk, man!

WHAT'S IN IT FOR ME?

PER SERVING (1/4 cup):
32 calories, 0.5 g fat,
5.7 g carbohydrate, 1 g protein,
70 mg sodium, 0 mg cholesterol
CALORIES FROM FAT: 14%

Husband: "Dear, what will I get if I cook another meal like tonight's?"
Wife: "My life insurance!"

No Peeking! We're Dressing!

Just because you're cutting back on fat doesn't mean your salads have to go naked! Dress them up with one of these ultra-flavorful low-fat dressings instead of the traditional oil-packed varieties for substantial fat savings. Remember, most traditional salad dressings are over 90% fat! Eeek!

Creamy Dill and Cucumber

1/2 cup non-fat or low-fat mayonnaise
1/2 cup peeled and diced English cucumber
2 tablespoons skim milk
1 tablespoon white vinegar
1 tablespoon chopped fresh dill *or* 1 teaspoon dried dillweed
1 clove garlic, minced
1/4 teaspoon salt

Combine all ingredients in a food processor and whirl until smooth. Store in a jar in the refrigerator.

Makes about 1 cup.

Sun-dried Tomato

6 sun-dried tomatoes
1/2 cup non-fat or low-fat mayonnaise
1/4 cup buttermilk
2 tablespoons white vinegar
1 clove garlic, minced
1 teaspoon sugar
1/2 teaspoon dried oregano

Place sun-dried tomatoes in a small bowl. Pour 1/4 cup boiling water over tomatoes and let soak for 10 minutes. Remove tomatoes and reserve the soaking liquid. Finely dice tomatoes. Combine tomatoes, soaking liquid, mayonnaise, buttermilk, vinegar, garlic, sugar, and oregano in a food processor. Whirl until smooth. Store in a jar in the refrigerator.

Makes about 1-1/4 cups.

Zesty Orange Poppy Seed

You can serve this dressing warm or cold. It tastes especially good on spinach salad.

1 tablespoon all-purpose flour
1/4 cup sugar
1/2 teapoon salt
3/4 cup skim milk
1/4 cup white vinegar
1 tablespoon frozen orange juice concentrate
1-1/2 teaspoons prepared mustard
1 clove garlic, minced
3/4 teaspoon poppy seeds
1/8 teaspoon black pepper

Combine flour, sugar, and salt in a small saucepan. Whisk in milk until mixture is smooth. Add remaining ingredients. Cook and stir over medium-high heat until mixture comes to a boil and thickens. Remove from heat. Let cool slightly if serving warm. Otherwise, store in a jar in the refrigerator until ready to serve.

Makes about 1-1/4 cups.

Creamy Dill and Cucumber
PER SERVING (1/4 cup):
26 calories, 0.1 g fat,
7 g carbohydrate, 0.4 g protein,
408 mg sodium, 0 mg cholesterol
CALORIES FROM FAT: 1.5%

Sun-dried Tomato
PER SERVING (2 tablespoons):
9 calories, 0.1 g fat,
1.7 g carbohydrate, 0.4 g protein,
39 mg sodium, 0 mg cholesterol
CALORIES FROM FAT: 11.6%

Zesty Orange Poppy Seed
PER SERVING (2 tablespoons):
33 calories, 0.2 g fat,
7.2 g carbohydrate, 0.8 g protein,
124 mg sodium, 1 mg cholesterol
CALORIES FROM FAT: 5.3%

WHAT'S IN IT FOR ME?

Spinnochio Salad

We're extremely confident that the following statement will *not* make our noses grow: This remarkable spinach salad drizzled with a delectable warm bacon dressing is THE BEST SPINACH SALAD YOU'LL EVER TASTE! C'mon—would we we string you along?

6 cups packed fresh spinach leaves, stems removed
1-1/2 cups thinly sliced mushrooms
1 cup thinly sliced red onion rings
1 can (11 ounces) mandarin oranges, drained
2 slices raw bacon
1 clove garlic, minced
1 tablespoon lemon juice
2-1/2 tablespoons honey
1 tablespoon white vinegar
1/8 teaspoon black pepper

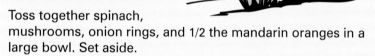

Toss together spinach, mushrooms, onion rings, and 1/2 the mandarin oranges in a large bowl. Set aside.

In a small skillet, cook bacon over medium-high heat until crisp. Shake off excess drippings and transfer bacon to a blender or food processor. *Don't discard the bacon drippings! Leave them in the skillet!*

Add remaining mandarin oranges and lemon juice to bacon in blender. Whirl briefly until oranges and bacon are puréed. Return orange/bacon mixture to skillet with bacon drippings. Add garlic, honey, vinegar, and pepper. Mix well. Mixture should still be quite warm, however, you may reheat it over medium heat, if desired.

Divide salad among 6 serving plates and drizzle warm dressing over top. Serve immediately.

Makes 6 servings.

WHAT'S IN IT FOR ME? ➜ PER SERVING: 106 calories, 3.4 g fat, 18.8 g carbohydrate, 3 g protein, 116 mg sodium, 5 mg cholesterol
CALORIES FROM FAT: 26.1%

When you eat raw spinach, some of the vitamins and minerals pass unused through the body because the human digestive system can't break down the vegetable's tough cellular walls to extract the nutrients. Cooking solves this problem. The fact that Popeye ate his spinach directly from the can and in one big gulp tells us that his super strength included a super-charged stomach!

Slim Pickin's

If you choose to eat one meager **RESTAURANT-STYLE EGG ROLL**, you'll be choosing a total of **6 GRAMS OF FAT**, the equivalent of eating **60 FRESH PEACHES**. Which would fill you up more?

Go for quality *and* quantity!

SAY IT AIN'T SO!

It's a wonder that Gilligan managed to stay so slim with all that coconut cream pie Mary Ann made! Most people aren't aware that the coconut's most abundant nutrient is fat (80% of its calories are derived from fat). Unlike other vegetable fats, coconut oil has almost no polyunsaturated fatty acids. In fact, coconut oil has a higher concentration of saturated fatty acids than any other food. Half a cup has a mind-boggling 964 calories and 109 grams of fat! Vacationer's alert: You might want to go easy on the Piña Coladas—a few of these coconut-laced cocktails won't make slipping into a bathing suit any easier!

WANTED
COCONUT SAMMY
ADIPOSE OUTLAW
WANTED FOR AIDING AND ABETTING WEIGHT GAIN

THE BOWLED

and

THE BEAUTIFUL

Soup's on, fat's off

14 Carrot Gold Soup

What's for supp, Doc? This creamy carrot soup, that's what. And it's so delicious we've awarded it the 14 Carrot Gold Rating!

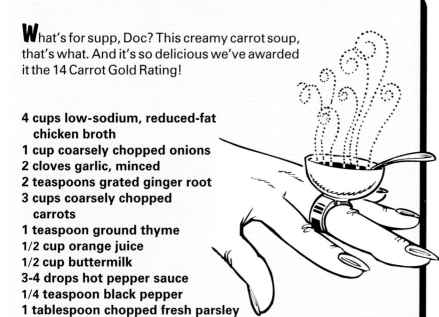

4 cups low-sodium, reduced-fat chicken broth
1 cup coarsely chopped onions
2 cloves garlic, minced
2 teaspoons grated ginger root
3 cups coarsely chopped carrots
1 teaspoon ground thyme
1/2 cup orange juice
1/2 cup buttermilk
3-4 drops hot pepper sauce
1/4 teaspoon black pepper
1 tablespoon chopped fresh parsley

Pour 1/2 cup of the chicken broth in a large saucepan. Add onions, garlic, and ginger root. Cook over medium-high heat for 3 minutes.

Stir in remaining broth, carrots, thyme, and orange juice. Bring to a boil. Reduce heat to medium-low. Cover and boil gently for 20 minutes, or until carrots are tender.

Working in batches, transfer soup to a blender and process until smooth. Return to saucepan. Reduce heat to low. Stir in buttermilk, hot pepper sauce, and pepper. Do not let soup boil. Stir until heated through, about 2 minutes.

Ladle into serving bowls and sprinkle with chopped fresh parsley.

Makes 6 servings.

WHAT'S IN IT FOR ME? ➡ PER SERVING: 99 calories, 2.1 g fat, 18 g carbohydrate, 4.1 g protein, 122 mg sodium, 1 mg cholesterol CALORIES FROM FAT: 17.6%

*T**he fat you eat is the fat you wear.**

SAY IT AIN'T SO!

Not a good way to start your day: Packed into an average chocolate chip breakfast bar are 11 grams of fat and 200 calories. This amounts to 49% calories from fat and that's reason enough to *bar* excess consumption.

The "Not-So-Square" Root

Carrots aren't just fare for waskly wabbits. Bet you didn't know that munching on a carrot a day is like signing a daily health insurance policy. That's because carrots are potent protectors against cancer and they also promote a healthy immune system, good vision (have you ever heard of a rabbit being called "four eyes"?), and healthy skin, hair, bones, and teeth.

At the root of the carrot's nutritional prowess is beta-carotene, a powerful antioxidant that is converted by the body to vitamin A. Beta-carotene protects the body's cells from harmful free radicals which are a result of cigarette smoke, alcohol, environmental pollutants, and daily wear and tear. Free radicals can damage cells and contribute to diseases such as cancer and cataracts.

Though most vegetables are more nutritious when eaten raw, carrots are an exception. Cooked carrots are actually better for you than raw ones. This is because cooking partially dissolves the tough, cellulose-stiffened cell walls of the carrot, making its nutrients more readily available for the body's use. The best news of all: Research has suggested that beta-carotene may even delay the aging process! Will "Carrots of Olay" soon be bottled to keep them guessing?

FOUR EYES! FOUR EYES!

COOKING 101

Low-fat sour cream is an excellent substitute for the fat-laden heavy cream or whipping cream traditionally used to flavor and thicken creamy soups. Just be careful when adding sour cream to a hot dish, because it sometimes curdles. One remedy is to bring the sour cream to room temperature beforehand. After adding the sour cream, stir often, and be sure to remove the pot from the stove before it reaches the boiling point.

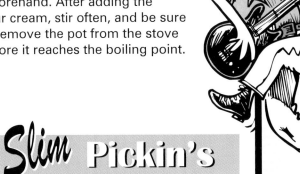

Slim Pickin's

If you choose to eat a measly
1/2 CUP OF REGULAR TRAIL MIX,
you'll be choosing an incredible
22 GRAMS OF FAT,
the equivalent of eating
56 BOWLS OF KELLOGG'S RICE KRISPIES
with skim milk.
Which would fill you up more?

Go for quality *and* quantity!

I'LL HAVE THE TURTLE SOUP AND MAKE IT SNAPPY!

It's Only Brocc 'n Bowl

But I like it. Like it. Yes I do!
Hard to believe that a broccoli and cheese soup so creamy and delicious isn't rollin' in fat.

1 cup chopped onions
1 clove garlic, minced
1/2 cup chopped celery
2-1/2 cups low-sodium, reduced-fat
    chicken broth
3 cups broccoli florets
1 cup peeled, cubed potatoes
1/2 cup low-fat sour cream
3/4 cup shredded reduced-fat sharp
    cheddar cheese (3 ounces)
1/2 teaspoon *each* ground thyme, black
    pepper, and "lite" Worcestershire
    sauce
1/4 teaspoon salt
4-5 dashes hot pepper sauce

Spray a large saucepan with non-stick spray. Add onions, garlic, and celery. Cook and stir over medium heat until celery begins to soften, about 5 minutes. Add broth, 2 cups broccoli, and all potatoes. Bring to a boil. Reduce heat to medium-low. Cover and simmer for 10-12 minutes, until broccoli and potatoes are tender.

While soup is simmering, steam the reserved 1 cup broccoli until tender, about 5 minutes. Set aside.

Transfer soup to a blender or food processor, working in batches if necessary. Pulse on and off until soup is coarsely puréed (still kind of chunky). Return puréed soup to pot over low heat. Add reserved steamed broccoli, sour cream, cheese, thyme, pepper, Worcestershire sauce, salt, and hot pepper sauce. Stir until smooth. Serve immediately.

Makes 4-6 servings.

Hint: If re-heating the soup, don't allow it to boil. The sour cream may cause the soup to curdle.

PER SERVING (based on 6 servings):
109 calories, 3.4 g fat,
13.1 g carbohydrate, 8.9 g protein,
252 mg sodium, 11 mg cholesterol
CALORIES FROM FAT: 25.7%

WHAT'S IN IT FOR ME?

Butternut Shout

You butternut cry. You butternut pout, we're telling you why: Fan applause is comin' to town! (Make that a standing ovation for this curried butternut squash soup that's good for goodness sake.)

1 tablespoon reduced-fat butter or margarine (not fat-free)
1/2 cup chopped onions
1 teaspoon curry powder
1-1/2 cups low-sodium, reduced-fat chicken broth
1/2 cup apple juice
4 cups peeled, cubed butternut squash
1 cup peeled, chopped pears
1/4 teaspoon salt
1/3 cup low-fat sour cream
Fresh parsley for garnish (optional)

Melt butter in a medium saucepan. Add onions and cook over medium heat until tender, about 5 minutes. Sprinkle curry powder over onions and cook 1 more minute.

Add broth, apple juice, squash, and pears. Bring to a boil. Reduce heat to medium-low. Cover and simmer for 15-20 minutes, until squash is tender.

Transfer soup to a blender or food processor. Pulse on and off until mixture is puréed. Return to pot. Add salt.

To serve, ladle soup into individual bowls and spoon a generous tablespoonful of low-fat sour cream in the center. Garnish with fresh parsley, if desired.

Makes 4 servings.

WHAT'S IN IT FOR ME? ➡ PER SERVING: 147 calories, 2.4 g fat, 30.8 g carbohydrate, 4 g protein, 181 mg sodium, 4 mg cholesterol CALORIES FROM FAT: 13.6%

Show & Tell

Gourdness gracious! With so many varieties of squash out there, how will I ever know which one is butternut? It's simple. Butternut squash is easily distinguished by its elongated pear shape. Usually weighing between 1-1/2 and 5 pounds, it has a light-brown skin and orange flesh, with inedible seeds stored in the round "bulbous" area. The hard, thick skin of this winter squash protects the flesh and allows it to be stored a lot longer than summer squash (like zucchini). It doesn't require refrigeration and can be kept in a cool, dark place for about a month.

Show me the WEIGH

Limiting fat intake to 30% of total daily calories is ideal for maintaining a healthy weight and a healthy body in adulthood, but for children it's a different story. Experts agree that fat intake should not be reduced in children under the age of 2 because infants need higher levels of fat for growth and development. In fact, breast-fed children receive 50% of their calories from fat. That's why nutritionists don't recommend skim milk or 1% milk for small children. The progression to a lower-fat diet (30% of calories from fat) should be a gradual one for children.

Don't go out of your "weigh" to please anyone but yourself.

Women who have been coerced into that "Dieting Thing" again, read on.

It seems that striving for a size 8 figure just doesn't cut it anymore. You know, it's all fine and dandy that the typical female model happily subsists on the same daily caloric intake as that of the common canary, but that shouldn't mean that *we* have to. And just because the average female model weighs in at a walloping 123 pounds (while standing on a scale carrying 3 bags of groceries and an entire set of Encyclopedia Britannica), that shouldn't mean that *we* have to.

Apparently, the constant barrage of advertisements featuring perfect size 2, "20% thinner than the average female" bodies is supposed to inspire us. Yes, we mere mortals should be incited to shed those final unsightly, unwanted pounds, so that someday, we too may appear in underwear ads. (By the way, why is it that underwear models always seem to be gripped in the throes of some inexplicable passion? Obviously, it's considered bad form to simply stand around in a WonderBra, casually inspecting the dirt under your fingernails.)

The most intriguing advertisement of all is the familiar "before and after" approach, which usually features an unfortunate lass, her abdomen bulging alarmingly and her posterior shaped like a prize-winning jack-o-lantern. The second view features the same sorry lass after two easy weeks on the ACME "Fat B Gone" Instant Meal Plan (just add water to lose weight). She's now pictured wearing a microscopic, neon pink Spandex leotard which has not only rendered her midriff smooth and slender, but has miraculously removed the dark circles from under her eyes, straightened her front teeth, and eliminated the gray from her hair.

What kind of fools do they take us for, anyway?

♪ Mother Souperior's Best Barley

This un*convent*ional chunky, hearty soup is second to nun.

2 teaspoons canola or vegetable oil
1 pound boneless, skinless turkey or chicken breasts, cut into cubes
1-1/2 cups *each* chopped celery and chopped carrots
1 cup chopped onions
4 cups low-sodium, reduced-fat chicken broth
1 can (28 ounces) tomatoes, undrained, cut up
1/3 cup pearl barley
3/4 teaspoon dried marjoram
1/2 teaspoon *each* ground thyme, ground sage, salt, and black pepper
1/4 cup chopped fresh parsley

Heat oil in a large saucepan over medium-high heat. Add turkey cubes and cook until no longer pink.

Add all remaining ingredients. Mix well. Bring soup to a boil over high heat. Reduce heat to low. Cover and simmer for 30-35 minutes, until turkey and barley are tender.

Makes 6 servings.

PER SERVING: 257 calories, 5.4 g fat, 25 g carbohydrate, 26.5 g protein, 762 mg sodium, 59 mg cholesterol
CALORIES FROM FAT: 19%

She's been on several diets. The only thing that grew thin was her temper.

Chowdown Chickpea Chowda

Howdy, pardner! Howdya like some chowwwda? This here grub is so dang good, you'll wanna rustle up some o' yer kinfolk to mosey on over fer a brimmin' bowl of soup that would do Granny Clampett proud! Fill yer belly!

4 cups low-sodium, reduced-fat chicken broth
2 cans (15 ounces each) chickpeas, drained and rinsed
3 cups peeled, cubed potatoes
1-1/2 cups thinly sliced carrots
1/2 cup *each* chopped onions and chopped celery
1 tablespoon lemon juice
1 bay leaf
1 clove garlic, minced
1/2 teaspoon *each* ground sage and ground thyme
1/4 teaspoon *each* black pepper and salt
1/2 cup chopped fresh parsley

Combine all ingredients except parsley in a large saucepan. Bring to a boil. Reduce heat to medium-low. Cover and simmer for 20 minutes.

Using a potato masher, mash vegetables until soup resembles a coarsely puréed mixture. Stir in parsley and serve.

Makes 6 servings.

WHAT'S IN IT FOR ME? ➜ PER SERVING: 197 calories, 2 g fat, 38.5 g carbohydrate, 9 g protein, 415 mg sodium, 0 mg cholesterol CALORIES FROM FAT: 8.8%

A Healthy Serving

Show & Tell

Chickpeas, also known as garbanzos, aren't peas at all. They're beans! Chickpeas are rich in carbohydrates, protein, phosphorous, calcium, and iron. They have a very adaptable flavor and texture, and are available dried or canned. Canned chickpeas should be rinsed and drained before using to wash away the added salt.

Slim Pickin's

You'd have to oink out on
110 ORANGES
to consume the
22 GRAMS OF FAT
found in a mere
2 TABLESPOONS OF BUTTER.
Which would fill you up more?

Go for quality *and* quantity!

Gotta MOVE It!

When you feel the urge to exercise, do you lie down until the urge goes away? If so, read on for the kick in the butt that you desperately need! Most people are aware that exercise burns calories, raises metabolism, and develops lean muscle mass, which raises metabolism further. What most people don't realize is that the benefits of exercise are mental as well as physical. Exercise helps relieve tension and stress, which is why you feel less tired afterward than before. And when people exercise, they just generally feel better about themselves, especially when they're zipping the zipper that hasn't zipped in years! Think about it. You've probably never heard anyone leaving the gym, tennis court, or cross-country ski trail saying, "I wish I hadn't done that!"

The Stock Market

If the only capital gains you've made lately are around your midriff, you'll profit from trying these low-fat, flavorful stocks as bases for your soups and sauces. What's the difference between stocks and broths, you ask? Well, broths are made from both the meat and bones of the chicken or beef, while stocks are made from the bones only. Which tastes better? There's no stock answer—it's simply a matter of preference.

Vegetable Stock

8 cups water
4 celery stalks, including leaves, chopped
2 leeks, white parts only, cleaned and sliced
2 large carrots, peeled and chopped
1 large onion, quartered
1 large apple, cored and quartered
1 large potato, scrubbed and chopped
1 cup chopped parsley with stems
4 cloves garlic, minced
2 bay leaves
1/2 teaspoon *each* ground thyme and dried rosemary
Salt and pepper to taste

Combine all ingredients in a large pot. Bring to a boil over medium-high heat. Reduce heat to low. Cover and simmer for 1 hour.

Remove from heat and let cool. Cover and refrigerate overnight. The next day, pour stock through a fine strainer into a bowl. Discard residue. Pour into containers with tight-fitting lids. Stock will keep 1 week in refrigerator or indefinitely if frozen.

Makes about 8 cups.

Chicken Stock

8 cups water
1 chicken carcass or 1 large chicken back (ask your butcher)
2 carrots, peeled and chopped
2 celery stalks, including leaves, chopped
1 large onion, quartered
1 leek, white part only, cleaned and sliced
5 cloves garlic, minced
1/2 cup chopped parsley with stems
1 bay leaf
6 peppercorns
3/4 teaspoon ground thyme
Salt to taste

Combine all ingredients in a large pot. If using whole chicken carcass, crack into 2 or 3 pieces. Bring to a boil over medium-high heat. Skim off any foam that rises to surface. Reduce heat to low. Cover and simmer for 2 hours.

Pour stock through a fine strainer into a bowl. Discard bones and residue. Refrigerate stock overnight. Skim off any fat that has congealed on surface. Pour into containers with tight-fitting lids. Stock will keep 3-4 days if refrigerated, or several months if frozen.

Makes about 8 cups.

Beef Stock

2 pounds beef bones
8 cups water
3 celery stalks, including leaves, chopped
2 carrots, peeled and chopped
1 large onion, quartered
2 bay leaves
4 cloves garlic, minced
6 peppercorns
2 whole cloves
1/2 teaspoon *each* ground thyme and dried marjoram
Salt to taste

To develop a fuller flavor and deeper color in the final stock, first place the beef bones in a roasting pan and roast at 400° for 20 minutes.

Place roasted bones in a large pot and add all remaining ingredients. Bring to a boil. Reduce heat to low. Cover and simmer for 4 hours. Skim off any foam that rises to surface.

Pour stock through a fine strainer into a bowl. Discard bones and residue. Refrigerate stock overnight. Skim off any fat that has congealed on surface. Pour into containers with tight-fitting lids. Stock will keep 3-4 days if refrigerated, or several months if frozen.

Makes about 8 cups.

PER SERVING: Due to variations in ingredients and the fact that the vegetables are discarded after cooking, precise nutritional information is not available. The nutritional values of all three stocks would be similar to canned stocks, with the sodium content dependent upon how much or how little salt you choose to add.

WHAT'S IN IT FOR ME?

Crammed Chowder

Stuck for something to serve for supper? Suppose someone suggested serving soup that's simply swimming with seafood and savory stuff. Sounds so succulent!

1 cup *each* chopped onions and
   sliced mushrooms
1 clove garlic, minced
2 cans (6-1/2 ounces each) shucked clams
   and their juice
2 cups low-sodium, reduced-fat
   chicken broth
1/2 cup dry white wine
1-1/2 cups peeled, cubed potatoes
1/2 cup chopped celery
1/4 cup chopped green onions
1/2 pound fish fillets (try cod, haddock,
   or salmon), cut into chunks
3/4 teaspoon dried basil
1 teaspoon "lite" Worcestershire sauce
3-4 drops hot pepper sauce
1/2 teaspoon *each* salt and black pepper
2 tablespoons chopped fresh parsley
1/3 cup whipping cream
3/4 cup low-fat sour cream

Spray a large saucepan with non-stick spray. Add onions, mushrooms, and garlic. Cook over medium heat until vegetables are softened, about 5 minutes.

Meanwhile, drain and reserve juice of clams. Set clams aside. Add reserved clam juice to onions and mushrooms, along with chicken broth, wine, potatoes, celery, and green onions. Bring to a boil. Reduce heat to medium. Cover and cook for 15 minutes, until potatoes are tender.

Add clams, fish chunks, basil, Worcestershire sauce, hot pepper sauce, pepper, and salt. Simmer over medium heat for 5 minutes, until fish turns opaque.

Turn heat to low. Gradually stir in whipping cream, then sour cream. *Do not boil*. Add parsley and continue to stir until heated through.

Makes 6 servings.

WHAT'S IN IT FOR ME?

PER SERVING: 202 calories, 6.4 g fat,
17.1 g carbohydrate, 16.3 g protein,
546 mg sodium, 40 mg cholesterol
CALORIES FROM FAT: 28.2%

COOKING 101

While homemade chicken, beef, and vegetable stocks are far superior to and more flavorful than those from a can or made from bouillon powder, it's quite okay to use the latter as a base for soups and sauces when you're not able to make your own. The recipes in this book call for the lower-sodium, reduced-fat canned broth that's available at most supermarkets. Although it's time-consuming, making your own stocks and broths really is pretty simple—a good project for a lazy Sunday afternoon. Instructions for making homemade stocks can be found in The Stock Market on the previous page.

Slim Pickin's

You'd have to oink out on
200 PRETZEL TWISTS
to consume the
20 GRAMS OF FAT
found in
1 HOT DOG.
Which would fill you up more?

Go for quality *and* quantity!

Self-discipline is when your conscience tells you to do something and you don't talk back.

Show & Tell

When you "brown" onions, heat converts their sulfurous flavor and aroma compounds into sugars. This explains why cooked onions taste sweet. The sugars and amino acids on the onion's surface caramelize to a deep rich brown which intensifies the flavor (a process called the Maillard reaction, after the French chemist who first identified it). Since heat breaks down the offensive-smelling sulfur compounds, choosing cooked onions rather than fresh ones is probably the wisest and most socially-beneficial menu choice you can make when you're on a dinner date.

The Crying Game

When you slice an onion, you cut into its cell walls and a gas called propanethial-S-oxide is released that reacts with the water in your eyes to form sulphuric acid. Yikes! Your eyes respond by producing tears to wash away the agitation.

To help prevent the flow of tears, try one of the following tricks:

- Chill the onion before slicing to reduce the effect.

- Place the onion or onions in a bowl of cold water in the sink and peel them under the water—the eye-irritating compounds are less likely to escape.

- Wait as long as possible to trim the root end where the tear-producing fumes are concentrated.

- Wear a scuba diving mask (really!)

Soup to Cry For

Not crying, as in tears, silly! Crying, as in "crying out for more!" Tears of joy! So happy because you've never tasted a better French Onion Soup, and even happier because it's low in fat! Hollering for a second bowlful! Get it?

2 large yellow onions, sliced into rings
1 clove garlic, minced
2 cups low-sodium, reduced-fat chicken broth
2 cups low-sodium, reduced-fat beef broth
1/2 cup unsweetened apple juice
1 teaspoon *each* "lite" Worcestershire sauce and ground thyme
1/2 teaspoon ground rosemary
4 slices French stick bread
2 cloves garlic, peeled and halved
1/3 cup shredded reduced-fat mozzarella or Jarlsberg cheese (about 1-1/2 ounces)
Fresh parsley for garnish

Combine onions, garlic, and 1/4 cup of the chicken broth in a large saucepan. Cook over medium-low heat for 25 minutes. Onions should be tender and golden brown. Add remaining chicken broth, beef broth, apple juice, Worcestershire sauce, thyme, and rosemary. Bring to a boil. Reduce heat to low. Cover and simmer for 15 minutes.

Meanwhile, toast bread slices under the broiler for 1-2 minutes on each side. Be careful not to burn them. Remove from oven and rub each piece of toasted bread with the cut sides of the garlic halves (keep broiler on).

Ladle soup into 4 oven-proof bowls. Place toasted bread slice in each bowl and top with shredded cheese. Broil until cheese is melted. Garnish with fresh parsley. Serve immediately.

Makes 4 servings.

PER SERVING: 228 calories, 4 g fat, 37.2 g carbohydrate, 10.9 g protein, 276 mg sodium, 11 mg cholesterol
CALORIES FROM FAT: 15.6%

WHAT'S IN IT FOR ME?

Just Veggin' Out

Maximum taste with minimum fuss! That's what this chunky, hearty soup is all about. Easy to prepare and exploding with vegetable goodness. What more could you ask for?

2 teaspoons olive oil
1 cup *each* chopped celery and chopped onions
1 clove garlic, minced
4 cups low-sodium, reduced-fat beef broth
1 can (14-1/2 ounces) tomatoes, undrained, cut up
1-1/2 cups V8 juice
3 cups frozen "California-style" mixed vegetables (broccoli, cauliflower, and carrots)
2 cups peeled, cubed potatoes
2 cups shredded or chopped cabbage
1 teaspoon "lite" Worcestershire sauce
1 teaspoon dried marjoram
1 bay leaf
3/4 teaspoon salt
1/2 teaspoon *each* ground thyme and black pepper

Heat olive oil in a large saucepan over medium heat. Add celery, onions, and garlic. Cook until vegetables are softened, about 5 minutes.

Add remaining ingredients. Stir well. Bring to a boil. Reduce heat to medium-low. Cover and simmer for 25 minutes, until potatoes and cabbage are tender. Remove bay leaf before serving.

Makes 8 servings.

WHAT'S IN IT FOR ME?

PER SERVING: 120 calories, 2.4 g fat, 22.2 g carbohydrate, 4 g protein, 661 mg sodium, 0 mg cholesterol
CALORIES FROM FAT: 16.8%

Eating soup with a mustache can be quite a strain.

Just the Fats, Ma'am

We're faced with different types of fat in our diets, and each has a different effect on the body (mostly ill effects). Research suggests that two types of fat are good for us, although they are beneficial only when eaten in moderation. Our best bet is to find ways to eat less of all types of fat.

Saturated Fats are solid at room temperature and turn to oil when heated. Most saturated fats are animal in origin, derived from meat, poultry, and dairy products (butter, cheese, milk, cream, eggs). It's wise to limit intake of foods that contain saturated fat. They tend to raise cholesterol and triglyceride levels, and studies indicate that they seem to interfere with immune functioning. Coconut oil and palm kernel oil are high in saturated fat even though they're plant oils.

Polyunsaturated Fats originate from plant sources and are liquid at room temperature. They're considered to be a "healthier" fat because they help lower total cholesterol and triglyceride levels. Vegetable oils such as safflower, sunflower, sesame, cottonseed, and corn oil are polyunsaturated fats.

Monounsaturated Fats include olive oil, canola, and peanut oil. Oils that are high in monounsaturated fats are the "healthiest" choice of oil, as they help decrease the levels of LDL (the "bad" cholesterol).

Hydrogenated Fats start out as liquid fats but are solidified when hydrogen atoms are added. In essence, a healthy fat (unsaturated) is converted into an unhealthy fat (saturated), a nutritional trick that adds to the profit margins of food manufacturers. Why the magic show? Hydrogenated oils give products longer shelf lives since the oil is less likely to break down over time and become rancid. Most of the hydrogenated fats we eat come from partially hydrogenated vegetable oils which are commonly found in packaged foods such as cookies, crackers, snack foods, sauces, pastries, and muffins as well as margarines, shortenings, peanut butter, and deep-fried foods. Needless to say, hydrogenated fats shouldn't be taken "lightly." Read the label before you buy.

What the heck are "shallots" and where can I buy them?

Shallots are a member of the onion family with golden brown skin, white flesh, and just a tinge of purple. Their flavor is more subtle than onion and less harsh than garlic. They look like oversized cloves of garlic and can be found in mesh bags or bins where you find regular onions at the supermarket.

SAY IT AIN'T SO!

Heart attack on a plate! That's exactly what the following traditional restaurant meal describes: 12 ounces of prime rib, a baked potato slathered with sour cream, buttered veggies, and a salad with blue cheese dressing. Who needs dessert when the main course alone totals a whopping 1800 calories and over 70% fat? Finished eating? Feeling absolutely stuffed? Instead of calling the waiter for your check, why not buy yourself some time and call 911?

What did the leftovers say when they were put into the freezer? Foiled again!

Much Ado About Mushrooms

Why all the fuss about mushroom soup? Well, we've cut the fat dramatically without jeopardizing the flavor, and that's nothing to *shake a spear* at. (Um...Er... that's "shake a stick" at.)

1 clove garlic, minced
1/4 cup minced shallots
4 cups sliced mushrooms
2 cups low-sodium, reduced-fat chicken broth
1/4 cup all-purpose flour
1/4 cup white wine
1 teaspoon "lite" Worcestershire sauce
1/2 teaspoon dried basil
1/2 cup non-fat plain yogurt
1 teaspoon cornstarch
1 cup 1% milk
1/2 cup half and half cream
1/2 teaspoon black pepper
1/4 teaspoon salt

Spray a medium saucepan with non-stick spray. Add garlic and shallots. Cook and stir over medium heat for 1 minute. Add mushrooms and continue to cook for 3-4 minutes, until mushrooms are tender. Add 1-1/2 cups of the chicken broth. Mix remaining 1/2 cup chicken broth with the flour until smooth. Add to pot along with wine, Worcestershire sauce, and basil. Stir well. Reduce heat to medium-low. Cover and simmer for 10 minutes, stirring occasionally.

Transfer 1/2 of soup to a blender or food processor. Pulse on and off to coarsely purée mixture. Return mixture to saucepan and stir well.

Mix yogurt and cornstarch in a small bowl. Add to soup, along with milk and cream. Don't allow soup to boil. Stir until well blended and heated through, 2-3 minutes. Season with salt and pepper. Serve immediately.

Makes 4 servings.

PER SERVING: 164 calories, 4.6 g fat, 18.8 g carbohydrate, 8.5 g protein, 239 mg sodium, 18 mg cholesterol
CALORIES FROM FAT: 24.4%

Borscht Karloff Soup

We were thinkin' (that's a first!) that if good ol' growling and grumbling Frankenstein had cooked this scrumptious, hearty beet soup more often, perhaps he would have ended up with a sunnier disposition! You know, it's fitting that borscht originated in Russia—you'll definitely be *russian* home for a big, brimmin' bowl!

**5 cups low-sodium, reduced-fat
  beef broth
2 cups *each* coarsely grated beets,
  shredded cabbage, and peeled,
  cubed potatoes
1/2 cup coarsely chopped
  red onions
2 tablespoons *each* red wine
  vinegar and tomato-based
  chili sauce
1 tablespoon "lite"
  Worcestershire sauce
1 bay leaf
1 clove garlic, minced
1/2 teaspoon dried
  marjoram
1/4 teaspoon black pepper
1/2 cup low-fat sour cream
1/4 cup chopped fresh parsley**

> PLEASE DOC, MAY I HAVE SOME MORE?

Combine all ingredients except sour cream and parsley in a large saucepan. Bring to a boil. Reduce heat to medium, cover, and gently boil for 15-20 minutes, or until potatoes are tender. Stir occasionally.

Remove from heat. Measure the sour cream in a 2-cup measuring cup. Add 1 cup of soup to the same measuring cup. Blend until smooth. Return sour cream mixture to pot and stir well. Add parsley and stir again. Serve immediately.

Makes 4-6 servings.

> WHAT'S IN IT FOR ME?

PER SERVING (based on 6 servings):
115 calories, 0.5 g fat,
24.2 g carbohydrate, 4.7 g protein,
212 mg sodium, 1 mg cholesterol
CALORIES FROM FAT: 4%

Let's kick the habit! Nothing to fear, Sister Mary Theresa, we're talkin' *fat* habit here. Most of the fat we get in our diets is a result of habit. It's second nature to add butter or margarine to bread and vegetables, to put mayonnaise on sandwiches, to slather sour cream on baked potatoes, to drown otherwise healthy salads with fat-laden dressings, and to munch on potato chips and chocolate bars. So let's replace the old high-fat habits like these with new low-fat habits, like putting salsa on baked potatoes instead of sour cream, skipping the butter and adding jam, honey, or cinnamon-sugar to toast, and trying some of the new and widely available fat-free dressings, mayonnaises, cheeses, and low-fat potato chips. Once you become addicted to feeling better, there's no *weigh* you'll want to go back to your old habits.

Show & Tell

We've got the beet! The red beet, or beet-root, is not only eaten, but is also used as a food coloring. Beets are a good source of fiber and are high in folate, which is believed to help prevent fatigue and depression. When choosing fresh beets, select small, young beets for the nicest texture. Very large beets are often tough (and tough beets are tough eats!).

SAY IT AIN'T SO!

Frequent flyers take note! Airline food may be hazardous to your physique. A measly 1 ounce of peanuts (airline snack-size) is on a veritable crash course with your waistline! You'd be much better off asking for pretzels, because this puny serving of peanuts derives an astronomical 74% of calories from fat (14 grams fat, 170 calories)! Fuel... Check. Wheels...Check. Lights... Check. Fat...Roger! Roger! We've got 74% calories from fat! I can't get this plane off the ground!

> DUMP THE PEANUTS! I CAN'T GET THIS THING OFF THE RUNWAY...

IF YOU BAKE IT

THEY WILL COME

**Breads, muffins
& other stuffins**

Go Ahead. Bake My Bread.

Rumor has it, Dirty Harry can often be spotted happily chewing on a chunk of this luscious cheese bread. Best thing about it, besides its wonderful texture and taste, is ease of preparation— no need to knead!

2 cups all-purpose flour
2 teaspoons baking powder
1 teaspoon baking soda
1 tablespoon sugar
1/2 teaspoon *each* dry mustard
 and salt
1/4 teaspoon garlic powder
1 cup shredded reduced-fat
 sharp cheddar cheese (4 ounces)
1-1/4 cups buttermilk
2 egg whites
1 tablespoon butter or
 margarine, melted
2 tablespoons minced onions

Preheat oven to 325°.

Combine flour and next 7 ingredients in a large bowl. Set aside.

In a small bowl, beat together buttermilk, egg whites, butter, and onions using a whisk.

Add buttermilk mixture to flour mixture, stirring just until moistened.

Spray an 8 x 4-inch loaf pan with non-stick spray. Pour batter into pan. Bake for 45 minutes or until wooden pick inserted in center comes out clean. Let cool in pan for 10 minutes before serving. Serve warm.

Makes 1 loaf, 12 slices.

WHAT'S IN IT FOR ME? ➡ PER SLICE: 120 calories, 3 g fat, 17.1 g carbohydrate, 6.6 g protein, 361 mg sodium, 10 mg cholesterol CALORIES FROM FAT: 22.3%

 COOKING 101

Baking powder is a leavener that contains a combination of baking soda, an acid (such as cream of tartar), and a moisture absorber (such as cornstarch). Baking powder releases carbon dioxide gas bubbles when mixed with liquid, and this is what causes breads and cakes to rise. It loses its potency over time, so if you've had the same supply for eons, better perform this simple test before using it as a leavening agent: Pour 1/4 cup hot tap water over 1/2 teaspoon of the baking powder and observe—the fresher the powder, the more actively it will bubble. If a weak reaction occurs, or none at all, your baked goods will end up flat as a tortilla. Time to get a new supply!

Show me the WEIGH

Filling up on potatoes and bread will make you fat. This is a myth many of us grew up with, and it's not an easy one to shake. But get with the program! Get a grip! The truth is, carbohydrate-rich foods should be the focal point of all healthy eating plans. Carbohydrates like potatoes, bread, pasta, rice, beans, and vegetables are filling, satisfying, strengthening foods, and are low in fat. Be skeptical, however, of their high-fat pals like butter, sour cream, mayonnaise, and creamy, cheesy sauces.

In the 1800's, the first bakery was officially opened on the yeast coast.

Sure, supporting minor hockey is a worthwhile charitable activity, but next time leave the almonds behind with your donation. Chocolate covered almonds (a piddling 1-ounce serving—as if you can resist the temptation to hoover the entire box!) will cost you 161 calories and 12 grams of fat. With a mammoth 67% calories from fat, it would seem that your thighs stand to gain the most from this charitable donation.

Slim Pickin's

If you choose to eat a paltry
1/2 CUP OF SUNFLOWER SEEDS,
you'll be choosing a whopping
35 GRAMS OF FAT,
the equivalent of eating
**2 ENTIRE LOAVES OF
MULTIGRAIN BREAD.**
Which would fill you up more?

Go for quality *and* quantity!

NOTHIN'!

She went through that new 14-day diet, but all she lost was two weeks.

Oatstanding Choco-Chip Muffins

Muffins sent directly from chocolaty, chewy heaven! Oatbursts of flavor make these a sure-fire, oat-of-this-world hit!

**1-1/4 cups quick-cooking rolled oats
1-1/2 cups boiling water
1-1/2 cups all-purpose flour
3/4 cup unpacked brown sugar
1/4 cup granulated sugar
1-1/2 teaspoons baking powder
1 teaspoon baking soda
1/2 teaspoon salt
1 teaspoon ground cinnamon
2 egg whites
1/4 cup puréed canned peaches
  (purée canned peaches, without juice,
  in blender)
1/4 cup reduced-fat butter or
  margarine, melted (not fat-free)
1 teaspoon vanilla
1/2 cup mini chocolate chips**

Preheat oven to 325°.

Pour boiling water over oats in medium bowl. Stir and let stand for 20 minutes.

Combine flour and next 6 ingredients in a large bowl. Set aside.

In a small bowl, combine egg whites, puréed peaches, butter, and vanilla. Beat with a whisk until well mixed. Add peach mixture to oats and stir until smooth. Add oat mixture to flour mixture and stir until dry ingredients are moistened. Batter will be thick. Fold in chocolate chips.

Spray large muffin tin with non-stick spray (or use paper muffin cups). Divide batter among 12 muffin cups. Bake for 25 minutes, or until wooden pick inserted in center comes out clean. Remove muffins from pan and let cool.

Makes 12 muffins.

PER SERVING: 200 calories, 4.7 g fat, 35.9 g carbohydrate, 4.1 g protein, 272 mg sodium, 4 mg cholesterol
CALORIES FROM FAT: 20.9%

WHAT'S IN IT FOR ME?

Bisquito Bites

These scrumptious biscuits are definitely worth making from scratch, especially if you're itching for melt-in-your-mouth texture and a taste guaranteed to cause a real buzz at dinner parties. Perfect for dunking in stew, chili, and soup.

TRY ONE, I MADE THEM FROM SCRATCH

1-1/4 cups all-purpose flour
1/2 cup whole wheat flour
1 tablespoon sugar
1-1/2 teaspoons baking powder
1 teaspoon baking soda
1/4 teaspoon salt
1 cup mashed potatoes (unseasoned)
1 cup buttermilk
3 tablespoons butter or margarine, melted

Preheat to 425°.

Combine first 6 ingredients in a large bowl. Mix well and set aside.

In a medium bowl, whisk together potatoes, buttermilk, and melted butter. Add buttermilk mixture to flour mixture and stir until a soft ball forms. Knead for one minute on a lightly floured surface (add more flour to dough, if needed, to prevent dough from sticking). Roll out 3/4-inch thick. Cut into 2-1/2-inch rounds using a cookie cutter or the rim of a wine glass.

Transfer biscuits to a baking sheet that has been sprayed with non-stick spray. Bake for 13-15 minutes, until biscuits have puffed up and are golden brown.

Makes 14 biscuits.

WHAT'S IN IT FOR ME?

PER BISCUIT: 106 calories, 2.8 g fat, 17.7 g carbohydrate, 2.8 g protein, 148 mg sodium, 7 mg cholesterol
CALORIES FROM FAT: 23.4%

Let your food be your medicine and your medicine be your food.

Hippocrates

COOKING 101

The worst part about making your own dough is trying to clean up the little bits that stick to your countertop. If you don't have a slab of marble to work on (like the professionals use), here's a tip that will definitely help save on clean-up time: When rolling out dough for pizza crusts or biscuits, work on a large piece of wax paper that has been "anchored" to the countertop. Simply moisten the back of the paper with water before laying it down. This will hold it in place while you work. Just toss it out when you're done and voilà—no sticky mess!

Gotta MOVE It!

Killing two birds with one stone sounds kind of cruel, and it might not sit well with the animal rights groups, but what the heck, let's do it anyway! Doing two things at once may be just the way to fit exercise into an already busy daily schedule. When taking Fido for a walk, for instance, try keeping up with his pace for a change instead of choking him down to your turtle trot. Catch up on the latest gossip with your best friend while hiking, biking, or golfing. Wear your cross trainers when you take your kids to soccer practice, so you can walk or jog instead of just sitting there for an hour. Take up active hobbies. Be flexible and creative in combining every-day activities with exercise. Hey, if you can kill two birds with one stone, maybe you should take up baseball. The Yankees could use your arm!

HONEY HOW ARE YOU COMING ALONG WITH THE SCRAMBLED EGGS?

What the heck are "canned green chilies" and where can I get them?

Popular and widely available, the canned green chilies called for in this recipe are of the Anaheim variety. They range from mild to hot on the "heat-o-meter," and you can find them in small cans at the grocery store next to the salsa.

D. I. E. T.

is a four-letter word that really means...

DEPRIVATION INEVITABLE EVERYTHING TABOO

Because diets deprive you of the foods you like to eat, these "taboo" foods are the ones you will desperately crave. You end up throwing in the towel—you "cheat" on your diet. The "cheating" mentality associated with dieting is very damaging to self-esteem and self-motivation because you often begin questioning yourself. "Why can't I stick with this simple diet plan? I have no willpower whatsoever. I'm a miserable failure." Obviously, when everything you enjoy is taken away from you, the odds are that you'll rebel in order to get them back. If you want to avoid the cheating mentality, then strike the word "diet" from your vocabulary for good. Variety and moderation are certainly a lot easier to stomach than self-denial and deprivation. A lifetime eating plan includes all the foods you enjoy. No foods are bad or taboo.

AMAAAZING GRAZE

A-maize-ing Cornbread

This one's a corn of plenty, a regular corn-u-copia of good-for-you-stuff—all low in fat, of course. Perfect for snacking and for dunking in chili, soup, and stew.

1-1/4 cups all-purpose flour
1 cup cornmeal
2 teaspoons baking powder
1 teaspoon baking soda
1/4 teaspoon salt
3/4 cup buttermilk
1 egg, lightly beaten
1/2 cup low-fat (1%) cottage cheese
2 tablespoons honey
2 tablespoons butter or margarine, melted
1 can (4 ounces) diced green chilies, drained
1 cup whole kernel corn (thaw first if using frozen)

Preheat oven to 375°.

In a large bowl, combine flour, cornmeal, baking powder, baking soda, and salt. Mix well.

In a medium bowl, combine buttermilk, egg, cottage cheese, honey, butter, chilies, and corn. Beat with a whisk until well blended.

Add corn mixture to flour mixture and stir until dry ingredients are moistened. Pour batter into an 8 x 8-inch baking pan that has been sprayed with non-stick spray. Bake for 35 minutes or until a wooden pick inserted in center comes out clean. Cut into 9 squares and serve warm.

Makes 9 servings.

PER SERVING: 190 calories, 4.4 g fat, 32.7 g carbohydrate, 6.4 g protein, 395 mg sodium, 32 mg cholesterol
CALORIES FROM FAT: 20.2%

WHAT'S IN IT FOR ME?

Another One Bites the Crust

And another one. And another one. That's because this honey of a bread is moist on the inside and crusty on the outside. Great for sandwiches!

2 packages (1/4 ounce each)
   active dry yeast
1 teaspoon sugar
1/2 cup warm water
3/4 cup warm skim milk
1 cup warm water
1/3 cup honey
1/4 cup canola oil
2 teaspoons salt
3 cups whole wheat flour
3-4 cups all-purpose flour

Stir together yeast and sugar in a small bowl. Add 1/2 cup warm water. Let sit for 10 minutes, until frothy.

In a large bowl, combine skim milk, second amount of warm water, honey, oil, and salt. Mix well. Add yeast mixture and stir again.

Using an electric mixer on low speed, beat in all of the whole wheat flour. Beat until smooth, about 1 minute. Using a wooden spoon, stir in enough of the all-purpose flour to make a dough that's easy to handle. Knead dough on a lightly floured surface for 6-7 minutes, until smooth and elastic. Dust lightly with more flour if dough is too sticky to handle.

Spray a large bowl with non-stick spray. Place dough inside. Turn to coat. Cover and let rise in a warm place until double in size, about 45 minutes.

Punch down dough. Divide dough in half. Shape into 2 loaves. Place dough in 9 x 5-inch loaf pans. Cover and let rise in a warm place until double in size, about 35-40 minutes. Don't let dough rise over the edge of pan, as it will need room to grow while it's baking.

Bake at 375° for 35-40 minutes, until crust is a deep golden brown and bread sounds hollow when tapped. Remove from pans immediately and let cool on a wire rack.

Makes 2 loaves, 16 slices each.

WHAT'S IN IT FOR ME? ➡ PER SLICE: 111 calories, 2.1 g fat, 20.2 g carbohydrate, 3.2 g protein, 137 mg sodium, 0 mg cholesterol CALORIES FROM FAT: 16.7%

Show & Tell

When it comes to yeast, there's no business like dough business! Yeast is really a microscopic fungus that multiplies rapidly when given its favorite foods: starch or sugar. It's used as a leavening (raising) agent in various kinds of dough. When added to the dough, the yeast converts the sugar and starch into ethanol and carbon dioxide. The carbon dioxide gas is what causes the dough to rise.

Show me the WEIGH

The occasional pig-out is O.K. The habitual pig-out is NOT O.K. The truth is that if you want to lose weight, the worst thing you can do is stop eating. You're a lot more likely to lose weight and keep it off if you eat pleasurably—a balanced diet with healthy and nourishing low-fat foods and some occasional treats so that you won't feel deprived. A good guideline to follow is the "80/20" rule: Make healthy choices 80% of the time, and eat whatever you want 20% of the time. If you look at it this way, the occasional pig-out won't mean you'll pork out!

Wife: "What's wrong with this cake, dear? It tastes kind of gritty."
Husband: "Nothing, sweetheart. The recipe called for three whole eggs and I guess I just didn't get the shells beaten up fine enough."

COOKING 101

Wouldn't it be nice to have freshly baked muffins available first thing in the morning? Well, there's "muffin to it"! Separately mix the wet and dry ingredients the night before. Cover the dry ingredients and keep them at room temperature overnight. Cover the wet ingredients and refrigerate. Before hopping in the shower in the morning (don't slip and fall), simply preheat the oven, spray the muffin tin with non-stick spray, combine the wet and dry ingredients, fill the muffin cups, and pop them in the oven. The muffins can bake while you shower and get dressed!

SAY IT AIN'T SO!

One half cup of butter pecan ice cream— Wait! That's a completely unrealistic serving size! Make that 1 cup of butter pecan ice cream: 48 grams of fat, 620 calories, and 70% calories from fat! Hey! What's the story? Are we talking about 1 cup of butter pecan ice cream or 1 cup of *butter*?

A balanced meal is one from which the diner has a 50-50 chance of recovering.

Sinnamon Apple Muffins

Bless me Father, for I have sinn...amon apple muffins that are so mouthwatering and moist, they're certain to lead to temptation. The confession: They're sinfully delicious!

THEY'RE SIN FREE

1-1/2 cups quick-cooking rolled oats
1-1/2 cups boiling water
1 cup whole wheat flour
1/2 cup all-purpose flour
3/4 cup unpacked brown sugar
1-1/2 teaspoons baking powder
1 teaspoon baking soda
1/2 teaspoon salt
1 teaspoon ground cinnamon
1/4 cup *each* honey and unsweetened applesauce
2 egg whites
3 tablespoons butter or margarine, melted
1 teaspoon vanilla
1-1/2 cups peeled, cored, and finely chopped apples
Cinnamon-sugar to sprinkle on top (optional)

Preheat oven to 325°.

Pour boiling water over oats in a medium bowl. Stir and let stand for 20 minutes.

Combine flours and next 5 ingredients in a large bowl. Set aside.

In a small bowl, whisk together honey, applesauce, egg whites, butter, and vanilla. Add applesauce mixture to oats and stir until smooth. Add oat mixture to flour mixture and stir until dry ingredients are moistened. Fold in chopped apples.

Spray large muffin tin with non-stick spray (or use paper muffin cups). Divide batter among 12 muffin cups. Sprinkle each muffin lightly with cinnamon sugar, if desired. Bake for 25 minutes, or until wooden pick inserted in center comes out clean. Remove from pan and let cool.

Makes 12 muffins.

PER MUFFIN: 192 calories, 3.9 g fat, 36.4 g carbohydrate, 4.2 g protein, 252 mg sodium, 8 mg cholesterol
CALORIES FROM FAT: 17.7%

WHAT'S IN IT FOR ME?

Loaf of my Life

Spice up your loaf life by following the directions in this recipe! This one's a sweetheart of a zucchini loaf that's *not* bogged down with oil, so you and that special someone can enjoy it to your heart's content!

1-3/4 cups all-purpose flour
2 teaspoons baking powder
1 teaspoon *each* baking soda
   and ground cinnamon
1/4 teaspoon *each* salt and
   ground nutmeg
1 cup packed brown sugar
1/4 cup *each* canola oil and
   unsweetened applesauce
1 egg
1 egg white
1 teaspoon vanilla
1-1/2 cups finely shredded
   zucchini
2/3 cup Grape-Nuts cereal

Preheat oven to 350°.

Combine flour, baking powder, baking soda, cinnamon, salt, and nutmeg in a large bowl. Stir well and set aside.

In a small bowl, whisk together brown sugar, oil, applesauce, egg, egg white, and vanilla. Add to flour mixture. Mix until dry ingredients are moistened. Stir in zucchini and Grape-Nuts. Batter will be thick.

Spray an 8 x 4-inch loaf pan with non-stick spray. Spoon batter into pan. Bake for 45-50 minutes or until a wooden pick inserted in center comes out clean. Cool on a wire rack.

Makes 1 loaf, 12 slices.

Carrot-Pineapple Loaf: Omit zucchini and add 3/4 cup shredded carrots and 8 ounces canned, drained crushed pineapple. Reserve 1/4 cup juice from pineapple and add to the wet ingredients. Bake as directed for zucchini loaf.

Zucchini Loaf
PER SLICE:
202 calories, 5.3 g fat,
36.2 g carbohydrate, 3.5 g protein,
258 mg sodium, 18 mg cholesterol
CALORIES FROM FAT: 23.1%

Carrot-Pineapple Loaf
PER SLICE:
214 calories, 5.5 g fat,
39.2 g carbohydrate, 3.5 g protein,
261 mg sodium, 18 mg cholesterol
CALORIES FROM FAT: 22.3%

SHE LOAFS ME – SHE LOAFS ME NOT

WHAT'S IN IT FOR ME?

COOKING 101

The most common complaint people have about low-fat baked goods is that they taste dry. There are a few things you can do to help keep the moistness in your low-fat muffins, cakes, and breads, while still cutting back on fat. First of all, make sure you don't overbake your baked goods. Low-fat goodies cook quicker than their higher-fat versions, so check for doneness before the suggested cooking time has elapsed (keep in mind that oven temperatures vary). Secondly, store your low-fat baked goods in an airtight container or covered snugly with plastic wrap to retain moisture. And remember, when it comes to muffins, breads, and other baked goods, *reducing* fat, not eliminating it altogether, is the key. It's a matter of chemistry: Fat contributes to a moist and tender texture, so it can't be completely removed from these foods—unless you want your muffins to double as tennis balls!

Slim Pickin's

You'd have to oink out on
146 CUPS CREAM OF WHEAT
to consume the
44 GRAMS OF FAT
found in a mere
1/2 CUP OF WHIPPING CREAM.
Which would fill you up more?

Go for quality *and* quantity!

WAITER, THIS SAUSAGE HAS MEAT AT ONE END AND BREAD AT THE OTHER...

WELL SIR, YOU KNOW HOW HARD IT IS TO MAKE BOTH ENDS MEAT THESE DAYS

COOKING 101

If you're using fewer nuts in a recipe to cut back on fat, first toast and cool them to intensify their flavor. Spread them in a 9-inch microwave-safe pie plate. Microwave, uncovered, on high power for about 3 minutes, until lightly browned. Stir midway through. Let them cool for 3-4 minutes before adding to the other ingredients. You can also toast nuts in a skillet over medium heat. Just be sure to keep your eye on them and stir often, so they don't burn.

Gotta MOVE It!

If you love to dance, you're already one step ahead of the rest of us as far as fitness goes. That's because dancing is a fantastic fat burner and a marvelous muscle toner. Line dancing, disco, cha cha, meringue, jive, two-step, square-dancing, you name it—it's easy to tap into the enormous physical benefits derived from cutting a rug. And since many people embark on a night of dancing, you can bet that they'll end up having put in at least 30-45 minutes of sustained physical movement, which is ideal for fat burning. Now if you want to burn calories like you've never burned them before, try the Polka. It's exhausting, but if you do it regularly, there's no way that Bobby Vinton will be referring to you when he sings, "I don't want her. You can have her. She's too fat for me!"

Trivial Tidbit

Who'da thunk? Some people actually polish their leather shoes with banana peels! It's true! Apparently, the slippery skin conditions and shines shoes quite nicely. But what if shoes were actually *made* from banana peels? Would we call them slippers? Maybe someone should use banana skins to create a nifty briefcase for attorneys. It could be used exclusively by lawyers who want to appeel their cases!

Gone Bananas!

Are you climbing the walls trying to decide what to serve your guests along with coffee and tea? Well forget the fatty cakes and pastries and start monkeying around! Serve this delectable, low-fat banana bread to really get your party swinging!

2 cups all-purpose flour
3/4 cup whole wheat flour
1 cup unpacked brown sugar
1-1/2 teaspoons baking powder
1/2 teaspoon baking soda
1 teaspoon ground cinnamon
1/2 teaspoon salt
3 egg whites
2 tablespoons butter or margarine, melted
3/4 cup non-fat plain yogurt
1 teaspoon vanilla
2 cups mashed bananas (ripe!)
1/2 cup chopped walnuts

Preheat oven to 325°.

Combine flours and next 5 ingredients in a large bowl. Set aside.

In a medium bowl, beat egg whites, butter, yogurt, and vanilla with a whisk until smooth. Add bananas and whisk again.

Add banana mixture to flour mixture. Stir until dry ingredients are moistened. Stir in walnuts.

Spray a 9 x 5-inch loaf pan with non-stick spray. Pour batter into pan. Bake for 1 hour and 20 minutes, or until toothpick inserted in center comes out clean. Remove from pan and let cool.

Makes 1 large loaf, 16 slices.

Hint: Make sure you use a large loaf pan (9 x 5-inch, 2 qt.) to make this banana bread. If you use a smaller pan (8 x 4-inch, 1-1/2 qt.), the outside of the bread will burn before the inside is cooked.

PER SLICE: 176 calories, 4.1 g fat, 31.6 g carbohydrate, 4.4 g protein, 162 mg sodium, 4 mg cholesterol
CALORIES FROM FAT: 20.5%

WHAT'S IN IT FOR ME?

Bananaberry Bombs

You'll be blown away by the great taste and moist texture of these banana blueberry muffins! Flavor explosion! Ka-pow!

1 cup quick-cooking rolled oats
1/2 cup *each* all-purpose flour
   and whole wheat flour
1/4 cup wheat germ
1/2 cup sugar
1-1/2 teaspoons baking
   powder
1 teaspoon baking
   soda
1/2 teaspoon salt
1-1/2 cups mashed
   bananas (make sure
   they're ripe)
2 egg whites
1/4 cup reduced-fat butter or margarine,
   melted (not fat-free)
1 cup fresh or frozen blueberries

Preheat oven to 375°.

Combine oats, flours, wheat germ, sugar, baking powder, baking soda, and salt in a large bowl. Stir well and set aside.

In a small bowl, whisk together bananas, egg whites, and melted butter until smooth. Add banana mixture to dry ingredients and mix until just moistened. Gently fold in blueberries.

Spray large muffin tin with non-stick spray (or use paper muffin cups). Divide batter evenly between 12 muffin cups. Bake for 20 minutes, or until wooden pick inserted in center comes out clean.

Makes 12 muffins.

WHAT'S IN IT FOR ME? ➡ PER MUFFIN: 173 calories, 3.1 g fat, 33.5 g carbohydrate, 4.5 g protein, 269 mg sodium, 4 mg cholesterol CALORIES FROM FAT: 15.3%

In the Victorian era, muffins were bought in the street from sellers who balanced trays of them on their heads! They'd ring bells, like modern day "Dickee Dee" ice cream vendors, to announce their wares. In days gone by, muffins were considered breakfast or tea fare, but nowadays they're eaten any time of the day.

Making your own fresh muffins can be simple and fun—just be sure to follow these essential muffin-baking tips:
1) Pre-heat the oven, since muffins need a *hot* oven to rise properly; 2) Mix the wet and dry ingredients only until the dry ingredients are moistened, since over-mixing will make the muffins tough and rubbery; and 3) Fill empty muffin cups with water when you're not using all of the cups in a muffin pan. This trick helps prevent your pan from warping or burning. Carefully drain off the water when you're ready to remove the muffins.

What the heck is "wheat germ" and where can I buy it?

Every grain of wheat consists of a husk (bran) and a kernel. The kernel is made up of starch and a mixture of proteins called gluten. Inside the kernel is the seed or embryo, known as wheat germ. It contains important nutrients such as iron, vitamin E, riboflavin, and thiamin. Look for wheat germ in the grocery store near the cereals or rice.

Two groups of people are preoccupied with the last supper—clergymen and dieters.

MEATLESS IN SEATTLE

Viceless vegetarian vittles

Chili Chili Bang Bang

A magical blend of vegetables, beans, and spices, this fiery hot invention is guaranteed to rev up your engine! Tastes great served with A-maize-ing Cornbread (page 55).

- **1-1/4 cups coarsely chopped onions**
- **1 cup *each* chopped green and red bell pepper**
- **3/4 cup *each* chopped celery and chopped carrots**
- **3 cloves garlic, minced**
- **1 tablespoon chili powder**
- **1-1/2 cups quartered mushrooms**
- **1 cup cubed zucchini**
- **1 can (28 ounces) tomatoes, undrained, cut up**
- **1 can (15 ounces) black beans, drained and rinsed**
- **1 can (15 ounces) chickpeas, drained and rinsed**
- **1 can (11 ounces) kernel corn, undrained**
- **1 tablespoon ground cumin**
- **1-1/2 teaspoons *each* dried oregano and dried basil**
- **1/2 teaspoon cayenne pepper (adjust to taste)**

Spray a large saucepan with non-stick spray. Add onions, green and red peppers, celery, carrots, garlic, and chili powder. Cook over medium heat, stirring often, until vegetables are softened (about 6 minutes).

Add mushrooms and zucchini. Cook and stir for 4 more minutes. Add tomatoes, beans, chickpeas, corn (with liquid), cumin, oregano, basil, and cayenne pepper. Stir well. Bring to a boil. Reduce heat to medium-low. Cover and simmer for 20 minutes, stirring occasionally.

Makes 8 servings.

WHAT'S IN IT FOR ME? ➔ PER SERVING: 159 calories, 1.9 g fat, 31 g carbohydrate, 7.8 g protein, 548 mg sodium, 0 mg cholesterol
CALORIES FROM FAT: 9.8%

You'd have to oink out on
18 BAGELS
to consume the
27 GRAMS OF FAT
found in a measly
1 CUP OF SCRAMBLED EGGS.
Which would fill you up more?

Go for quality *and* quantity!

Show me the WEIGH

You can actually eat like a king on the budget of a pauper if you're eating high volume, low-fat foods. Filling, satisfying foods like grains, vegetables, beans, fruit, pasta, and potatoes are inexpensive, convenient, easy to prepare, and can be eaten in larger quantities than foods which are higher in fat, and you won't have to pay the same health penalties either. Many of the chronic diseases that afflict North Americans can be linked to diets that are high in fat and low in fiber. These diseases, sometimes referred to as "diseases of affluence," include heart disease, diabetes, some types of cancer, high blood pressure, and obesity. So it seems that the simple foods, or the foods of the peasant, give us a greater overall return on our investment than the feast fit for a king.

Sky High Vegetable Pie

Hi! Remember me? I passed you at the broccoli level

With a crust that tastes like Thanksgiving stuffing and a filling piled high with a delicious combination of veggies and cheese, this could easily be the tallest free-standing, man-made vegetable structure in the world!

Crust

1 tablespoon reduced-fat butter or margarine, melted (not fat-free)
1/2 cup *each* diced celery and diced onions
1 clove garlic, minced
6 cups slightly stale whole wheat bread cubes (about 8 slices)
1/2 teaspoon *each* dried oregano, dried basil, ground sage, ground thyme, and black pepper
1/4 teaspoon salt
1/3 cup low-sodium, reduced fat chicken broth

Filling

2 cups sliced mushrooms
1/2 cup chopped onions
1/2 10-ounce package frozen spinach, thawed, squeezed dry, and chopped (5 ounces total)
3/4 cup shredded reduced-fat sharp cheddar cheese (3 ounces)
1/2 cup thinly sliced red bell pepper
1 cup broccoli florets
1 medium tomato, thinly sliced
1-1/2 cups fat-free egg substitute

Preheat oven to 400°.

To prepare crust, melt butter or margarine in a medium skillet over medium-high heat. Add celery, onions, and garlic. Cook until vegetables are softened, about 4 minutes. Toss vegetables with bread cubes and remaining crust ingredients, except broth. Sprinkle the broth over bread mixture and toss again.

Line an 8-inch springform pan with aluminum foil. Press bread mixture into bottom of pan to form crust. Set aside.

To prepare filling, spray a medium skillet with non-stick spray. Add mushrooms and onions. Cook and stir over medium heat until vegetables are tender, about 5 minutes. Remove from heat and stir in spinach.

Layer 1/2 the cheese over crust. Top with 1/2 spinach/mushroom mixture, followed by the broccoli and red peppers. Sprinkle remaining cheese over red peppers, followed by remaining spinach/mushroom mixture. Top with tomato slices. Pour egg substitute over all.

Bake for 45 minutes, until vegetables are tender and egg is "set." Let cool 5 minutes. Run a sharp knife around edge of pan to loosen sides. Remove sides, slice, and serve.

Makes 6 servings.

PER SERVING: 201 calories, 5.3 g fat, 21.4 g carbohydrate, 17.2 g protein, 513 mg sodium, 12 mg cholesterol
CALORIES FROM FAT: 23.6%

What's in it for me?

COOKING 101

To remove excess water from frozen spinach that has been thawed, place the spinach in a wire strainer and press down on it with your hands or the back of a spoon. Then blot the spinach dry using paper towel.

Fajita Pita Without the Meata

You-a just-a gotta try-a this-a one-a. It's-a great-a!

1/2 cup low-fat sour cream
1/2 cup salsa (mild, medium, or hot)
2 tablespoons diced canned green chilies (mild)
1 teaspoon olive oil
2 cloves garlic, minced
1 large red bell pepper, seeded and
   cut into strips
1 large green bell pepper, seeded
   and cut into strips
1 large onion, cut into rings
2 medium carrots, cut into
   matchsticks
1 medium zucchini, cut into strips
1 tablespoon chopped fresh cilantro
2 teaspoons lime juice
4 10-inch whole wheat pitas (large size)
1 cup shredded lettuce
1 cup seeded and diced tomato
1/2 cup shredded reduced-fat cheddar cheese (2 ounces)

Combine sour cream, salsa, and chilies in a small bowl. Cover and refrigerate until serving time.

Heat olive oil over medium heat in a large non-stick skillet. Add garlic and sauté for 1 minute. Add red and green peppers, onions, carrots, and zucchini. Cook and stir for about 10-12 minutes, until vegetables are tender-crisp. Stir in cilantro and lime juice. Remove from heat.

While vegetables are cooking, stack pitas and wrap them in aluminum foil. Warm in a 350° oven for 10 minutes.

Spread 1/4 of the vegetable mixture down the center of each pita. Top with salsa/sour cream mixture, lettuce, diced tomato, and cheese. Roll up to enclose filling. Wrap bottom half of sandwich in aluminum foil for easier eating.

Makes 4 servings.

WHAT'S IN IT FOR ME? ➡ PER SERVING: 383 calories, 8.1 g fat, 64.3 g carbohydrate, 17.9 g protein, 770 mg sodium, 11 mg cholesterol CALORIES FROM FAT: 18.1%

COOKING 101

If your pita bread cracks in half when you roll it, chances are it's not fresh. Try to buy fresh pita bread from a Lebanese bakery or specialty store and use it the same day. There's really no comparison between freshly baked pitas and the dry, often stale pitas found on many supermarket shelves.

Gotta MOVE It!

Friend or foe? When it comes to maintaining a healthy lifestyle, the gang you hang with may not be helping your cause, especially if all of your social activities revolve around food. Instead of meeting for chicken wings and beer, plan gatherings around enjoyable activities that don't involve food but do involve movement. You can still gab *and* burn flab while playing tennis, golf, or baseball, or hiking, biking, or walking. Altering an unhealthy lifestyle begs for encourage-ment and support, and surrounding yourself with like-minded pals may end up saving you cals!

I always do my exercises regularly in the morning. Immediately after waking, I say sternly to myself, "Ready now. Up. Down. Up. Down." After two strenuous minutes, I tell myself, "Okay. Now try the other eyelid."

Bursting with a medley of colorful vegetables and a unique honey-mustard sauce, this family-sized veggie submarine is the perfect vehicle for exploring the unknown depths of your appetite.

A Mellow Submarine

Filling
2 cups sliced mushrooms
1 cup *each* **sliced red bell pepper, red onion rings, and sliced zucchini**
1 cup broccoli florets
2 tablespoons chopped fresh basil *or* **3/4 teaspoon dried basil**

Honey Mustard Sauce
1/4 cup low-sodium, reduced-fat chicken broth
1 clove garlic, minced
2 tablespoons honey
1 tablespoon *each* **Dijon mustard and tomato paste**
1/2 teaspoon dried oregano
1/4 teaspoon black pepper

1 fresh loaf Italian bread, unsliced (about 15 inches long)
2 teaspoons olive oil
1/8 teaspoon garlic powder
1/2 cup shredded reduced-fat Swiss cheese (2 ounces)

Spray a large skillet with non-stick spray. Add mushrooms, red pepper, onions, zucchini, broccoli, and basil. Cook over medium-high heat, stirring often, until vegetables are tender-crisp, about 6-7 minutes. Remove from heat and drain off any liquid. Set aside.

To prepare honey-mustard sauce, combine all sauce ingredients in a small saucepan. Cook over medium-high heat for 2-3 minutes, until mixture is thick and bubbly. Remove from heat and set aside.

Using a sharp bread knife, slice loaf lengthwise into 2 pieces, 1/3 of the way down (your top piece will be smaller than your bottom piece). Pick out some of the bread from the bottom piece to create a partially hollowed-out boat (about 1/2-inch deep).

Combine olive oil with garlic powder. Using a pastry brush, brush the cut sides of the top and bottom loaf pieces with the oil. Sprinkle bottom piece with 1/2 the cheese. Spread vegetables over cheese. Spoon sauce evenly over vegetables. Top with remaining cheese. Cover with top of loaf. Wrap loaf completely in aluminum foil.

Bake at 350° for 20 minutes. Remove loaf from foil and let stand 2-3 minutes before cutting. Slice loaf crosswise into 6 large pieces, then cut each piece in half crosswise. Serve immediately.

Makes 6 servings.

PER SERVING: 271 calories, 4.1 g fat, 47.3 g carbohydrate, 10.6 g protein, 452 mg sodium, 7 mg cholesterol
CALORIES FROM FAT: 13.9%

WHAT'S IN IT FOR ME?

Dieting is only wishful shrinking.

Canajun Rice & Beans

Sorta Canadian. Sorta Cajun. With a salad and a chunk of fresh bread, it's most definitely a hearty, filling, meatless meal.

**1-1/2 cups chopped onions
1 cup chopped green bell pepper
1/2 cup chopped celery
2 cloves garlic, minced
1 can (28 ounces) tomatoes, undrained, cut up
1-1/4 cups low-sodium, reduced-fat chicken broth
1 cup uncooked long grain white rice
2 tablespoons tomato paste
1 teaspoon *each* chili powder, dried oregano, and
   ground cumin
1/2 teaspoon *each* ground thyme and black pepper
1/4 teaspoon *each* cayenne pepper and salt
1 can (15 ounces) black beans, drained and rinsed
1/4 cup chopped fresh cilantro**

Spray a large saucepan with non-stick spray. Add onions, green pepper, celery, and garlic. Cook over medium heat until vegetables are softened, about 5 minutes. Stir in remaining ingredients, except beans and cilantro. Bring to a boil. Reduce heat to medium-low. Cover and simmer for 25 minutes, stirring occasionally.

Stir in beans and cilantro during last 5 minutes of cooking time.

Makes 4-6 servings.

WHAT'S IN IT FOR ME? ➡

PER SERVING (based on 6 servings):
244 calories, 0.8 g fat,
52.4 g carbohydrate, 9.3 g protein,
771 mg sodium, 0 mg cholesterol
CALORIES FROM FAT: 3%

Beans, Beans the Musical Fruit

You were probably sitting there wondering, "Why do beans cause gas?" The answer is fairly straightforward. All legumes (beans and peas) contain raffinose and stachyose, complex sugars that human beings cannot digest. The sugars sit in the gut and are fermented by intestinal bacteria, which then produces socially unacceptable hydrogen, methane, and carbon dioxide gases (Pee-yew!). One way to minimize bean-induced flatulence is to discard the water in which the beans were soaked. Another solution is to add a few drops of Beano to cooked beans. Beano is a natural food enzyme that helps digestion and helps you avoid the embarrassment of "breaking wind" at an inopportune time.

COOKING 101

Beans are an excellent source of hunger-satisfying complex carbohydrates, protein, vitamins, and fiber. An essential component of meatless cuisine, they are very low in fat.

Once you get the hang of it, soaking and cooking dried beans really isn't so difficult. All dried beans, except lentils and split peas, need to be soaked before cooking. Otherwise, the skins will burst before the beans are tender. Soaking beans first, then changing the water before cooking also helps alleviate the "social distress" associated with eating beans. Yup, you got it—good ol' flatulence.

Look for beans that are uniform in size and color, and that don't have any visible defects, like shriveled or cracked skin. Remove any debris that's mixed in with the beans. Give the beans a quick rinse in a colander. To soak the beans, you'll need a container that will allow the beans to expand roughly 2-1/2 times. Place the beans in the container, add enough cold water to cover by an inch, and let them stand at room temperature overnight.

Drain the soaked beans. Place them in a saucepan and add fresh water to reach two inches above the beans. Bring to a boil. Reduce heat to medium-low, partially cover the pot, and simmer until tender (until you can pierce them with a fork, 1-2 hours, depending on the type of bean).

As simple as it seems, some of us just can't be bothered with the extra preparation, and prefer to use canned beans. Luckily, they're a very acceptable alternative. Just make sure you give them a good rinse under cold running water to wash away the added sodium (unless the recipe calls for *undrained* beans).

Show me the WEIGH

You can't really put anything over on your body. If you skip breakfast, for instance, your body responds by slowing your metabolism in order to make the stored fat last as long as possible (and the more you starve yourself, the better your body gets at conserving the fat!) You can try using sneaky mealtime strategies to fool your stomach into thinking it has devoured a seven-course meal, like chewing each bite 4,675 times, or like eating with plates and utensils that you've borrowed from the Barbie Camper in order to disguise miniscule portions. You can try to dupe your stomach, but it won't work. Just remember that you can't fool your body, but you can certainly *fuel* it. Fill it up on low-fat, nutritious, healthy foods. Your stomach will think you're one smart cookie.

SAY IT AIN'T SO!

Ah! The smell of frying bacon—reason enough to haul yourself out of bed at the crack of dawn. Actually, you'd be doing your body a favor by staying in the sack! That's because four slices of bacon will pork you out with 16 grams of fat and 170 calories. With 85% calories from fat, you're better off taking cover!

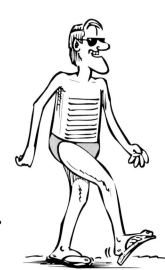

We all have a washboard stomach. It's just that some of us have a little extra laundry on top.

Lasagna with Mex Appeal

This dish is so "mexy" it's heating up kitchens all over the country. A great way to add a little spice to your life.

Ai Caramba! Eets Revolutionary!

2 cups chopped onions
2 cloves garlic, minced
1-1/2 cups chopped green
    bell pepper
1 can (28 ounces) tomatoes,
    undrained, cut up
1 cup salsa (mild, medium,
    or hot)
2 teaspoons ground cumin
1 can (15 ounces) black beans,
    drained and rinsed
1 can (15 ounces) red kidney
    beans, drained and rinsed
12 6-inch corn tortillas or
    8 7-inch flour tortillas
1-1/2 cups shredded reduced-
    fat Monterey Jack cheese
    (6 ounces)
2 small tomatoes, thinly
    sliced
1/3 cup chopped green onions
Low-fat sour cream (optional)

Spray a large saucepan with non-stick spray. Add onions, garlic, and green pepper. Cook and stir over medium heat until vegetables are softened, about 5 minutes. Add tomatoes, salsa, and cumin. Bring to a boil. Reduce heat to low and simmer, uncovered, for 10 minutes. Stir in black beans and kidney beans. Remove from heat.

Spray a 13 x 9-inch baking dish with non-stick spray. Spread 1/3 of the bean mixture over bottom. Cover with half the tortillas (overlapping as needed), and half the cheese. Spoon another 1/3 of bean mixture on top of cheese, followed by remaining tortillas, and last of the bean mixture. Sprinkle remaining cheese on top.

Cover and bake at 350° for 35 minutes. Let cool for 10 minutes before serving. Garnish with tomato slices and green onions. If desired, serve with a dollop of sour cream on top.

Makes 8 servings.

PER SERVING: 278 calories, 5.6 g fat, 43.7 g carbohydrate, 16.5 g protein, 763 mg sodium, 15 mg cholesterol
CALORIES FROM FAT: 17.2%

WHAT'S IN IT FOR ME?

"Not Nearly as Complicated as it Looks"
Veggie Lasagna

This one's definitely easier done than said. With a little practice, you'll be making it while blind-folded and standing on your head. (Warning: Use extreme caution while chopping vegetables in this position!)

Spray a large saucepan with non-stick spray. Add onions, garlic, mushrooms, carrots, red pepper, and zucchini. Cook and stir over medium heat until vegetables are softened, about 7-8 minutes.

Add tomatoes, tomato sauce, tomato paste, soy sauce, basil, oregano, brown sugar, black pepper, and red pepper flakes. Mix well. Bring to a boil. Reduce heat to medium-low, cover, and simmer for 15 minutes. Stir occasionally.

Meanwhile, prepare lasagna noodles according to package directions. Rinse under cold water and drain well.

In a medium bowl, combine cottage cheese, egg white, Parmesan cheese, and spinach. Set aside. In a separate bowl, toss mozzarella and cheddar cheeses together until well mixed.

To assemble lasagna, spray a deep 13 x 9-inch baking pan with non-stick spray. Spread 1 cup sauce over bottom of pan. Layer 3 noodles over top. Spread 2 cups sauce over noodles, followed by 1/2 of the cottage cheese/spinach mixture, and 1/3 of the cheese. Top with 3 more noodles, 2 cups sauce, 1/2 the cottage cheese/spinach mixture and 1/3 of the cheese. Layer final 3 noodles on top, followed by 2 cups sauce (you should be left with 1/3 of the cheese).

Cover with foil and bake at 375° for 30 minutes. Remove from oven, uncover, and sprinkle with remaining cheese. Return to oven, uncovered, for 10 minutes. Let lasagna cool for 10 minutes before slicing. (Be patient. It'll hold together much better if you wait!)

Makes 8 servings.

1 cup chopped onions
3 cloves garlic, minced
2 cups sliced mushrooms
1 cup *each* diced carrots, chopped
   red bell pepper, and thinly sliced zucchini
1 can (28 ounces) tomatoes, undrained, cut up
1 cup "Italian-style" tomato sauce
1 can (6 ounces) tomato paste
1 tablespoon reduced-sodium soy sauce
2 teaspoons dried basil
1 teaspoon dried oregano
2 teaspoons brown sugar
1/2 teaspoon *each* black pepper and crushed
   red pepper flakes
9 whole wheat or spinach lasagna noodles,
   uncooked
2 cups low-fat (1%) cottage cheese
1 egg white
1/2 cup grated Parmesan cheese
1 10-ounce package frozen spinach, thawed,
   squeezed dry, and chopped
1 cup shredded reduced-fat mozzarella
   cheese (4 ounces)
3/4 cup shredded reduced-fat sharp cheddar
   cheese (3 ounces)

WHAT'S IN IT FOR ME?

PER SERVING: 314 calories, 8.6 g fat, 41.1 g carbohydrate, 26.2 g protein, 956 mg sodium, 25 mg cholesterol
CALORIES FROM FAT: 22.3%

COOKING 101

When a recipe calls for cooked, chopped potatoes, an easy way to prepare them is in the microwave. Wash the potatoes, but don't dry them. Pierce the skins in several places with a fork. Wrap each potato in a paper towel and place on the floor of the microwave. Cook on high power for 5-6 minutes, rotate potatoes, and cook for another 5-6 minutes until tender. You may need to increase the cooking time if the potatoes are large, or if you're cooking several at a time. When cool enough to handle, peel off the skins and chop or mash as specified in the recipe.

D. I. E. T.

is a four-letter word that really means...

DON'T IMAGINE EATING TREATS

Because if you do, you would have "blown it," right? You feel like a guilt-ridden slug when you "cheat" and have one potato chip. When you go on a diet, so many foods are off limits, and of course, these will then become the foods that you crave. As soon as your diet is "over" you'll slip into your old habits again, eating all the treats you can get your hands on, and you'll end up weighing more than you did to begin with. Depriving yourself of occasional indulges in the foods you love is *not* the way to lose pounds and keep them off.

SAY IT AIN'T SO!

Basically, a baked potato is a healthful, low-fat food choice. It's the fat-soaked toppings that send your lipid levels to the moon. A good example is a baked potato with broccoli and cheese. Sounds ultra-healthy, but it actually carries 22 grams of fat and 530 calories! And that's not half as bad as topping your tater with bacon and cheese. Instead, inspire your spud by decorating it with physique-friendly toppings like salsa, dill, low-fat tzatziki, and low-fat sour cream.

One Fritatta, Two Fritatta

Overloaded with potatoes and fresh veggies, this hearty fritatta for two makes a great choice for Sunday brunch. Fat-free egg substitute is used in place of eggs to save on fat and cholesterol. Eggsactly what are you waiting for?

1/2 cup chopped onions
1 clove garlic, minced
1 cup broccoli florets
1/2 cup chopped red
    bell pepper
1 cup peeled and cubed
    potatoes, cooked (see
    Cooking 101)
1 cup fat-free egg substitute
2 tablespoons grated Parmesan cheese
1/4 cup shredded reduced-fat Swiss, cheddar,
    or mozzarella cheese (1 ounce)
3/4 teaspoon dried marjoram
1/4 teaspoon *each* salt and black pepper

Spray a medium non-stick skillet with non-stick spray. Add onions, garlic, broccoli, and red pepper. Cook over medium-high heat until tender-crisp, 4-5 minutes. Stir in cooked potatoes.

In a small bowl, combine egg substitute, Parmesan cheese, shredded cheese, marjoram, salt, and pepper. Mix well. Pour over vegetables. Tilt skillet to spread egg mixture evenly.

Reduce heat to medium-low. Cover and cook until set, about 10 minutes. If using an oven-proof skillet, place under broiler to brown top. Otherwise, slide fritatta onto a plate, then flip back into skillet to brown opposite side (2-3 minutes).

Makes 2 servings.

PER SERVING: 220 calories, 4.9 g fat, 24.4 g carbohydrate, 21.3 g protein, 589 mg sodium, 15 mg cholesterol
CALORIES FROM FAT: 24.4%

WHAT'S IN IT FOR ME?

Scentilentil Journey

Pack your bags! You're taking a trip to India on us! With an unforgettable blend of aromatic spices, this spectacular lentil and rice dish makes it possible to venture to a foreign country—even if it's just for dinner!

1/2 cup low-fat sour cream
1/2 teaspoon curry powder
1 tablespoon olive or canola oil
2 cloves garlic, minced
3 cups sliced mushrooms
1-1/2 cups chopped carrots
4 cups low-sodium, reduced-fat vegetable or chicken broth
1 cup uncooked long grain white rice
1 cup dried red lentils, sorted and rinsed
1 tablespoon grated ginger root
1-1/2 teaspoons *each* ground coriander and ground cumin
1 teaspoon ground turmeric
1/2 teaspoon salt
1/4 teaspoon pepper
1/2 10-ounce package frozen spinach, thawed, squeezed dry, and chopped (5 ounces total)
1/2 cup chopped green onions

In a small bowl, combine sour cream with curry powder. Cover and refrigerate until ready to use.

In a large saucepan, heat olive oil over medium-high heat. Add garlic, mushrooms, and carrots. Cook for 5 minutes, stirring often, until vegetables are softened.

Add broth, rice, lentils, ginger root, coriander, cumin, turmeric, salt, and pepper. Bring mixture to a boil. Reduce heat to low. Cover and simmer for 20 minutes, stirring occasionally.

Stir in spinach and green onions. Cover and simmer for 3-4 more minutes, until rice and lentils are tender. Remove from heat and serve immediately. Top each serving with a dollop of sour cream/curry mixture.

Makes 4 servings.

WHAT'S IN IT FOR ME? ➡ PER SERVING: 462 calories, 6.7 g fat, 81 g carbohydrate, 22.3 g protein, 819 mg sodium, 1 mg cholesterol CALORIES FROM FAT: 12.7%

Slim Pickin's

If you choose to eat a miniscule
4 OUNCES OF POLISH SAUSAGE,
you're choosing a remarkable
32 GRAMS OF FAT,
the equivalent of eating
128 CUPS OF JOLLY TIME POPCORN.
Which would fill you up more?

Go for quality *and* quantity!

Gotta MOVE It!

Other things being equal, a female of average build burns about 300 calories per hour by walking briskly, while a male of average build burns 440 calories. So for a woman, this means that it would take 30 minutes of brisk walking to burn off a frozen Margarita, 50 minutes of brisk walking to burn off a Kit Kat chocolate bar, 80 minutes of brisk walking to burn off a large order of fries, 2 hours of brisk walking to burn off a Personal Pan Pizza from Pizza Hut, and over 3 hours of brisk walking to burn off a Burger King Double Whopper with Cheese!

I'LL HAVE A MAMMOTH BURGER, LARGE FRIES, SHAKE AND A PAIR OF SNEAKERS TO GO

In 1950, vegetable farmers from all over the world held an important meeting. It went down in history as the first peas conference.

Aunt Chilada's Stuffed Tortillas

Aunt Chilada sure knows her stuff! She holds the family secret, originating in Mexico, for creatively stuffing tortillas with aromatic, flavorful ingredients. (If you're in a hurry, we're sure Aunt Chilada won't mind if you go ahead and cheat a little—substitute 3 cups prepared salsa for her enchilada sauce.)

Sauce
1 cup chopped onions
1 clove garlic, minced
1 can (28 ounces) tomatoes, undrained, cut up
1 can (6 ounces) tomato paste
1 jalapeño pepper, seeded and minced
1 tablespoon red wine vinegar
1 teaspoon *each* ground cumin and chili powder
1/2 teaspoon salt
1/4 teaspoon pepper
2 tablespoons chopped fresh cilantro

Enchiladas
1-1/4 cups chopped onions
1 cup *each* diced carrots and diced green
   bell pepper
3 cloves garlic, minced
1 jalapeño pepper, seeded and minced
1 tablespoon chili powder
2 teaspoons dried oregano
1 teaspoon ground cumin
2 cups canned black beans, drained and
   rinsed
1-1/2 cups whole kernel corn
2 tablespoons lime juice
2 tablespoons chopped fresh cilantro
12 7-inch flour tortillas (whole wheat or white)
1 cup shredded reduced-fat sharp cheddar
   cheese (4 ounces)
3/4 cup low-fat sour cream

Spray two 13 x 9-inch baking pans with non-stick spray and set aside.

To prepare sauce, spray a medium saucepan with non-stick spray. Add onions and garlic. Cook over medium heat until onions are softened, about 5 minutes.

Add remaining sauce ingredients, except cilantro. Bring to a boil. Reduce heat to low. Cover and simmer for 15 minutes, stirring occasionally. Remove from heat and stir in cilantro.

While sauce is simmering, prepare enchilada filling. Spray a large saucepan with non-stick spray. Add onions, carrots, green pepper, and garlic. Cook over medium heat until vegetables are softened, about 5 minutes. Add jalapeño pepper, chili powder, oregano, and cumin. Cook for 1 more minute. Remove from heat. Stir in beans, corn, lime juice, and cilantro. Mix well.

To assemble enchiladas, spread 3 heaping tablespoons of filling down center of tortilla. Sprinkle with 2 teaspoons of cheddar cheese. Fold tortilla to enclose filling and place seam-side down in baking dish. Repeat with remaining tortillas, leaving yourself with 1/4 cup shredded cheddar.

Pour sauce evenly over enchiladas, making sure each one is coated. Cover with aluminum foil and bake at 350° for 25 minutes. Uncover, sprinkle with remaining cheese, and return to oven for 5 more minutes. Serve enchiladas with a dollop of low-fat sour cream on top.

Makes 6 servings.

Note: These enchiladas use flour tortillas instead of corn tortillas because corn tortillas usually need to be softened by frying in oil before they're rolled (otherwise they'd break).

PER SERVING: 466 calories, 9.8 g fat, 86.3 g carbohydrate, 22.9 g protein, 1080 mg sodium, 14 mg cholesterol
CALORIES FROM FAT: 16.8%

WHAT'S IN IT FOR ME?

Luciano's Panzerotti

Our nextdoor neighbor, Luciano, swears that his vegetable garden is so bountiful because he sings opera music while tending to his plants. We borrowed some of his healthy, hearty veggies to really stuff our panzerotti with earthy goodness and flavor. Mmmm!

1 package (1/4 ounce) active dry yeast
1 teaspoon sugar
3/4 cup warm water
1-1/2 cups all-purpose flour
1/2 cup whole wheat flour
2 teaspoons sugar
1/2 teaspoon salt
1 tablespoon olive or canola oil
1 clove garlic, minced
1-1/2 cups sliced portobello mushrooms
1 cup sliced zucchini
1 cup chopped red or green bell pepper
1/2 cup sliced red onions
1 teaspoon dried oregano
2-1/2 cups low-fat spaghetti sauce
  (your favorite brand)
1 cup shredded part-skim mozzarella
  cheese (4 ounces)

In a large bowl, dissolve yeast and 1 teaspoon sugar in warm water. Let stand 10 minutes.

In a small bowl, combine flours, 2 teaspoons of sugar, and salt. Set aside.

Stir olive oil into yeast mixture. Add 1-3/4 cups of the flour mixture and stir until a soft ball forms. Turn dough out onto a lightly floured surface and knead for 3-4 minutes. Add some of the remaining flour mixture if dough is too sticky.

Spray a large bowl with non-stick spray and place dough inside. Cover and let rise in a warm place until double in size, about 1 hour.

Just before dough has finished rising, prepare filling. Spray a large skillet with non-stick spray. Add garlic, mushrooms, zucchini, red or green pepper, onions, and oregano. Cook and stir over medium-high heat until vegetables are tender, about 6-7 minutes. Remove from heat and set aside.

Punch down dough, form a ball, and place on a lightly floured surface. Cut dough into 4 equal pieces. Roll out each piece to a 6-inch diameter circle. Working one at a time, place crust on a large non-stick baking sheet. Spread 2 tablespoons spaghetti sauce over one half of crust, leaving a 1/2-inch border. Top with 1/4 vegetable mixture and 1/4 cheese. Fold opposite half over toppings and pinch seam closed. Repeat with remaining crusts.

Bake at 425° for 12-15 minutes, until dough is golden brown. Meanwhile, heat remaining spaghetti sauce over medium-high heat. Remove panzerotti from oven and transfer to serving plates. Pour 1/2 cup sauce over each and serve immediately.

Makes 4 servings.

WHAT'S IN IT FOR ME? → PER SERVING: 393 calories, 10 g fat, 63.1 g carbohydrate, 17.7 g protein, 784 mg sodium, 16 mg cholesterol CALORIES FROM FAT: 21.7%

He's on such a strict diet, he can't even listen to dinner music.

USING YOUR NOODLE

When ya hasta have pasta

A Penne Yearned

The name says it all. Those who taste it will have a yen for it and demand a repeat performance. A zesty combination of chicken, zucchini, spinach, mushrooms, and tomatoes, this pasta makes a super supper and great leftovers, too!

1 10-ounce package fresh spinach, washed, stems removed
1 cup chopped onions
3 cloves garlic, minced
3 cups sliced zucchini
2 cups sliced mushrooms
1/4 cup plus 1 tablespoon all-purpose flour
2 cups 2% milk
1 can (28 ounces) tomatoes, undrained, cut up
1-1/2 teaspoons *each* dried basil and dried oregano
3/4 teaspoon *each* salt and black pepper
1/2 teaspoon crushed red pepper flakes
18 ounces tri-color penne pasta, uncooked
(about 6 cups dry)
3 cups chopped cooked chicken breast
(about 1-1/4 pounds)
1 cup grated Parmesan cheese

EXCUSE ME—MAY I HAVE MY PENNE BACK ?

Blanch spinach in pot of boiling water for 1 minute. Drain. Squeeze out excess water and chop. Set aside.

Spray a large saucepan with non-stick spray. Add onions, garlic, zucchini, and mushrooms. Cook over medium-high heat until vegetables are tender, about 7 minutes. Mix the flour and milk together until smooth. Add to vegetables. Cook for 7-8 minutes, stirring often, until sauce is bubbly and thickened.

Stir in tomatoes (with liquid), spinach, basil, oregano, salt, pepper, and crushed red pepper flakes. Cook for 3 more minutes. Remove sauce from heat.

Meanwhile, cook penne in large pot of boiling water until slightly *underdone* (about 8 minutes). Drain and rinse with cold water. Return to pot. Add cooked chicken and sauce. Mix well.

Spray an extra-large baking dish with non-stick spray (a small roasting pan with a lid works well). Layer 1/2 the pasta mixture in the pan. Top with 1/2 the Parmesan cheese. Repeat layering. Cover and bake in a 350° oven for 35 minutes, until heated through. Remove from oven. Let sit for 5 minutes, uncovered, before serving.

Makes 8 servings.

WHAT'S IN IT FOR ME? ➡

PER SERVING: 463 calories, 8 g fat, 63.4 g carbohydrate, 32.2 g protein, 733 mg sodium, 51 mg cholesterol
CALORIES FROM FAT: 15.9%

COOKING 101

Spinach is undoubtedly one of the most healthful vegetables to include in our diets. Many studies have shown that iron-rich spinach is a regular feature on the dinner table of groups of people who have a low incidence of both heart disease and cancer.

If you like, you can substitute frozen spinach for the fresh spinach in this recipe. Remove the spinach from its carton and place it in a glass pie plate. Microwave on low power in 2-minute intervals until thawed. Using a fork, break up the block as it thaws. Transfer spinach to a strainer and press out the liquid, then chop.

Gotta MOVE It!

If you're the type of person who would sooner part with your right kidney than even entertain the thought of exercising, couldn't you, at the very least, consider taking up walking as your *one* form of exercise, as your fat-burner? Now don't get all excited! It's just a suggestion—and a good one, at that. Bet you didn't know that brisk walking burns 300 calories or more per hour (even slow walking uses 120 to 150 calories per hour). It's also easier on your back, knees, and other joints than jogging. (Jogging! Ugghh!) All you need is half an hour three or four

times a week, a decent pair of shoes, an interesting route to follow, and perhaps a friend who can tag along for a "Walkie-Talkie" session.

Pasta Schmasta!

Do recipes that call for 12 ounces of uncooked pasta leave you scrambling? It's pretty tough to figure out exactly how much dry pasta equals 12 ounces, especially when you don't have a food scale. The following guide will help you estimate the actual measure of the dry pasta you'll need for a particular recipe. The chart is based on the standard pasta serving of 85 grams or 3 ounces of uncooked pasta per person.

Approx. Measure Needed to Equal 3 oz or 85 g Dry	Pasta Shape
3/4 cup	Macaroni, Tiny Shells, Tubetti
1 cup	Penne, Radiatore, Rotini Fusilli, Wagon Wheels, Small Bows
1-1/3 cups	Medium and Large Shells
1-2/3 cups	Rigatoni, Fine, Medium, and Broad Egg Noodles, Medium Bows
Bunch, 3/4-inch thick diameter	Spaghetti, Linguini, Fettuccine, Capelli d'Angelo, Vermicelli

WE'VE GOT A PIG-OUT IN PROGRESS DOWN AT THE DRIVE-THRU... SOME JOKER DOING 60 GRAMS OF FAT IN A 20 GRAM ZONE

Dieting: The penalty for exceeding the feed limit.

♪Thou Shell Eat Beans

Here's a recipe you'll want to carve in stone! Create a sin-free supper by teaming shell-shaped pasta and black beans with a heavenly, spicy tomato sauce. Miraculous taste!

1 cup diced green bell pepper
1/2 cup chopped onions
2 cloves garlic, minced
1 teaspoon dried oregano
1/2 teaspoon *each* ground cumin
and crushed red pepper flakes
2 cups tomato sauce
2 cups canned black beans, drained and rinsed
8 ounces uncooked medium-sized shell-shaped pasta (about 3 cups dry)
1/2 cup shredded reduced-fat Monterey Jack cheese (2 ounces)

Spray a large saucepan with non-stick spray. Add first 6 ingredients and cook over medium heat for 5 minutes, until vegetables are softened. Add tomato sauce and black beans. Bring to a boil. Reduce heat to medium-low. Cover and simmer for 5 minutes.

Meanwhile, prepare pasta shells according to package directions. Drain. Add shells to sauce and mix well. Ladle into individual serving bowls and sprinkle with cheese.

Makes 4 servings.

Hint: If you're trying to reduce your sodium intake, look for low-sodium tomato sauce and make sure you rinse the canned beans well before using.

PER SERVING: 405 calories, 4.7 g fat, 76.3 g carbohydrate, 19.7 g protein, 1238 mg sodium, 10 mg cholesterol
CALORIES FROM FAT: 9.9%

WHAT'S IN IT FOR ME?

Legumania

The American Diabetic Association recommends a diet high in beans and other legumes because they help stabilize blood glucose. Beans are also thought to help in lowering blood cholesterol and several studies have found that beans help fight cancer. So eat your beans!

Unsurpasta Pizza

You just can't top this "pizza made of pasta"—unless, of course, you're topping it with a dizzying array of great-tasting stuff. Because it looks so fun and tastes even better, this might be a sneaky way to get your kids to eat their vegetables!

**6 ounces uncooked fettuccine
   (regular or spinach)**
1 egg
2 egg whites
1/4 cup skim milk
**2 tablespoons grated Parmesan
   cheese**
**1/4 teaspoon *each* salt and
   black pepper**
**1 cup *each* broccoli florets (cut
   small) and sliced mushrooms**
1/2 cup thinly sliced red bell pepper
1/2 cup pizza or spaghetti sauce
1/4 teaspoon dried oregano
3 ounces lean cooked ham slices, chopped
1/2 cup shredded part-skim mozzarella cheese (2 ounces)

Prepare fettuccine according to package directions. Drain. Rinse with cold water and drain again.

In a medium bowl, whisk together egg, egg whites, milk, Parmesan cheese, salt, and pepper. Add fettuccine and mix well. Spray a 9-inch pie plate with non-stick spray. Pour fettuccine mixture over bottom and spread evenly.

Combine broccoli, mushrooms, red pepper, and 1/4 cup water in a small, microwave-safe dish. Microwave on high power for 3 minutes. Drain.

Stir together pizza sauce and oregano, then spread evenly over fettuccine. Top with chopped ham, vegetables, and mozzarella. Bake in a 350° oven for 30 minutes, until set. Remove from oven and let stand 5 minutes before slicing.

Makes 4 servings.

PASS ME A PIECE OF PASTA PIZZA PLEASE!

WHAT'S IN IT FOR ME? ➡ PER SERVING: 297 calories, 6.7 g fat, 38.8 g carbohydrates, 19.9 g protein, 749 mg sodium, 74 mg cholesterol
CALORIES FROM FAT: 20.4%

Show & Tell

Pasta is a complex carbohydrate that supplies six of the eight essential amino acids. Although it's loaded with B vitamins and iron, it's not loaded with fat—one cup of cooked pasta has only 1 gram of fat and 210 calories! But like a salad or a baked potato, inherently low-fat pasta can be "corrupted" by what you put on it. Beware of oil-drenched sauces, cheese sauces, and creamy "Alfredo-style" sauces which can add significant fat content to pasta dishes. Alfredo sauces are typically made with whipping cream, which has 5 grams of fat per *tablespoon*! Look for tomato-based sauces or ones that specifically indicate that they are lower in fat. Being choosy about pasta sauces and how they are prepared is a very simple way to slice away unnecessary fat—a small investment that pays big health dividends!

Slim Pickin's

If you choose to eat a paltry
1 OUNCE OF COLBY CHEESE,
you'll be choosing a whopping
9 GRAMS OF FAT,
the equivalent of eating
30 BOWLS OF KELLOGG'S CORN FLAKES
with skim milk.
Which would fill you up more?

Go for quality *and* quantity!

Before the first macaroni factory could officially be opened, it had to pasta inspection.

Show me the WEIGH

People are used to eating fat. It has a pleasing mouth feel that's hard to resist, even though most people are coming to realize the health benefits of cutting back. But making healthy, low-fat food choices doesn't mean you have to sacrifice the pleasures of eating. No siree! There are a million ways to make delicious and extremely flavorful low-fat foods —foods that your taste buds will fancy and foods that you will start to crave instead of fat-laden choices. Mouth feel is something that can change gradually. Just because you want to be a healthy eater doesn't mean you want to enjoy your food any less, right?

SAY IT AIN'T SO!

"Alfredo" must have flipped his lid when he concocted the traditional recipe for his creamy fettuccine. He flipped the lid of his pot, that is, added whipping cream and tons of butter, and presto! He created a pasta sauce that derives 80% of calories from fat! Mama Mia would roll over in her grave if she only knew the truth.

Trivial Tidbit

Alfredo di Lellio, a Roman restaurant owner, is the "Alfredo" who in 1920, created the popular fettuccine dish. When movie fans discovered that Douglas Fairbanks and Mary Pickford patronized Alfredo's every day on their honeymoon in the Eternal City, the dish became very popular in the United States.

Eenie Meenie Fettuccine

Eenie Meenie Minie Mo!
Fet-tuc-ci-ne Al-fre-do!

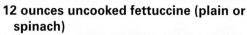

We're justifiably proud of our low-fat rendition of this popular classic. Its velvety Alfredo sauce is sheer RAPture! Yo!

12 ounces uncooked fettuccine (plain or spinach)
2 tablespoons butter
1-2 cloves garlic, minced (depending on your taste)
1-1/2 cups 2% milk
1-1/2 tablespoons all-purpose flour
1/3 cup grated Parmesan cheese
1/2 teaspoon dried basil
1/4 teaspoon *each* salt and black pepper
1 can (6 ounces) water-packed tuna, drained
1/4 cup low-fat sour cream
3/4 cup frozen peas, thawed
2 tablespoons chopped fresh parsley

Cook fettuccine according to package directions. Drain and return to pot.

While pasta is cooking, prepare sauce. Melt the butter in a medium saucepan over medium heat. Add the garlic and sauté for 1 minute. Mix the milk and flour together until smooth. Add to garlic. Increase heat to medium-high. Cook and stir until mixture is bubbly and thickened, about 4-5 minutes.

Reduce heat to low. Stir in Parmesan cheese, basil, salt, and pepper. Cook for 1-2 more minutes, until cheese is melted. Stir in tuna, sour cream, and peas. Cook until heated through, about 2 minutes.

Pour sauce over fettuccine and toss to coat. Sprinkle parsley over top. Serve with extra Parmesan cheese and black pepper, if desired. Best if served immediately.

Makes 4 servings.

Hint: For a tasty variation, try replacing the canned tuna with canned, skinless salmon, chopped cooked chicken breast, or cooked shrimp. Yum-o-rama!

PER SERVING: 554 calories, 13.7 g fat, 72.5 g carbohydrate, 31.6 g protein, 531 mg sodium, 41 mg cholesterol, CALORIES FROM FAT: 22.8%

WHAT'S IN IT FOR ME?

Thai It! You'll Like It!

Kin Khoa! In Thailand, this expression is an invitation to a meal. It translates as "come and eat rice." Well, there's no rice in this Thai creation, but why not come and eat a peanutty-pasta-shrimp dish instead?

12 ounces uncooked fettuccine or linguini
2 cups sliced red bell pepper
  (sliced in thin, long strips)
1 cup snow peas, trimmed and halved
1/3 cup chopped green onions
1/2 cup low-sodium, reduced-fat
  chicken broth
2 teaspoons sesame oil
2 tablespoons reduced-fat
  peanut butter
1-1/2 tablespoons reduced-
  sodium soy sauce
1 tablespoon white or rice
  vinegar
1 teaspoon grated ginger root
1 clove garlic, minced
1/2 teaspoon crushed red pepper
  flakes
1 pound cooked peeled shrimp (thaw first if using frozen)

Tonight's Special: Tie Food

Cook pasta according to package directions. Drain and keep warm.

While pasta is cooking, prepare sauce. In a large saucepan, combine all ingredients except shrimp. Mix well. Bring to a boil. Reduce heat to medium. Cook and stir for 3-4 minutes, until vegetables are tender-crisp and sauce is bubbly and slightly thickened.

Stir in shrimp and cook just until heated through, 1-2 minutes. Do not overcook or shrimp will be rubbery. Toss hot shrimp sauce with pasta and serve immediately.

Makes 4 servings.

Hint: If you're not a seafood lover, you can substitute chopped cooked chicken breast for the shrimp in this recipe. Add it to the sauce at the same time you would add the shrimp.

WHAT'S IN IT FOR ME?

PER SERVING: 436 calories, 7.8 g fat, 70.6 g carbohydrate, 23.5 g protein, 338 mg sodium, 86 mg cholesterol
CALORIES FROM FAT: 15.7 %

What the heck is "sesame oil" and where can I buy it?

Expressed from sesame seeds, Asian sesame oil is dark in color and has a distinct toasted sesame flavor and aroma. Don't substitute other oils for the sesame oil in recipes, or the dishes will have an entirely different taste. Most supermarkets carry a variety of different brands in the foreign foods section, or you can pick some up at any specialty or natural food store.

Nuttin' Butter To Do

The motto "everything in moderation" may be sticky business for those who just go nuts over the creamy, smooth taste of peanut butter. There's no hiding the fats. Yes, peanut butter is fattening—a mere 2 tablespoons pack in 16 grams of fat.

But fat aside, peanut butter is a nutritional superstar, supplying significant amounts of protein, fiber, zinc, and niacin. Besides, peanut butter is inexpensive and is the de facto standard in lunch pails across North America. It's no wonder that peanut butter ranks right up there as one of the most frequently purchased supermarket items.

Here's where things can get sticky: The calories in peanut butter are derived primarily from monounsaturated fats— better for you than saturated fat. However, in order to extend the shelf life of peanut butter, hydrogenated vegetable oil is added as a stabilizer. This process converts an unsaturated fat into a saturated fat—yup, a healthy fat is changed into an unhealthy fat.

If you want peanut butter to stick to the roof of your mouth and not to your arteries, your best bet is to practice moderation. Two tablespoons on a sandwich is okay. Half a jar with a box of crackers is *not* okay. Many varieties of reduced-fat peanut butter are now available at grocery stores. If you look for these products and use common sense, you won't have to "skippy" the peanut butter when hunger strikes.

In a hurry? Instead of making the sauce from scratch as indicated in the recipe, you can cheat a little and substitute your favorite brand of low-fat spaghetti sauce. No rigatoni on hand? No problem. Just use rotini or penne instead.

Gotta MOVE It!

Exercise is the ultimate healer, both physical and mental. That's because through aerobic activity you're giving your body what it craves the most—oxygen. Oxygen is a vital ingredient for good health. We need oxygen to live. It's the fuel that feeds every cell and muscle in our bodies and without the proper fuel, our engines will come to a grinding halt. Physical activity is a way to get the blood pumping and the oxygen coursing through our veins, and that's why we gain strength, energy, and a sense of well-being after exercising. Getting enough oxygen will give you the energy you need to do what you've got to do. Getting enough oxygen will give you the physical and emotional strength to overcome obstacles like illness, injury, stress, anxiety, depression, and fatigue. Getting enough oxygen is essential for life. So get enough oxygen! Just move it!

SLOW DOWN, YOU MOVE TOO FAST ♪

♪ Totally Tubular Pasta

Like, the taste of this pasta dish is sooo—you know—awesome! As *if*! Rigatoni tubes with *four* kinds of cheese! It's like, totally radical.

12 ounces uncooked rigatoni (about 7 cups dry)
1/2 cup chopped onions
2 cloves garlic, minced
3 cups tomato sauce
2 tablespoon reduced-sodium soy sauce
2 teaspoons brown sugar
1 teaspoon *each* dried oregano and dried basil
1/2 teaspoon crushed red pepper flakes
1/4 teaspoon black pepper
3/4 cup low-fat (1%) cottage cheese
1/2 cup part-skim ricotta cheese
1/4 cup grated Parmesan cheese
1 egg white
1 10-ounce package frozen spinach, thawed, squeezed dry, and chopped
1/2 cup shredded part-skim mozzarella cheese (2 ounces)
1 tablespoon chopped fresh parsley (optional)

Prepare rigatoni according to package directions, shortening cooking time by 1-2 minutes. Pasta should be slightly undercooked. Drain. Rinse with cold water and drain again. Set aside.

Spray a medium saucepan with non-stick spray. Add onions and garlic. Cook and stir over medium heat for 3-4 minutes. Add tomato sauce and next 6 ingredients. Bring to a boil. Reduce heat to low. Cover and simmer 5 minutes, stirring occasionally. Remove from heat.

Mix together cottage cheese, ricotta cheese, Parmesan cheese, and egg white in a large bowl. Add chopped spinach and stir until well blended. Add rigatoni and mix well.

Spray a large casserole dish with non-stick spray. Spread 1/2 cup sauce over bottom of casserole, followed by 1/2 the rigatoni mixture. Pour 1/2 the remaining sauce over rigatoni, followed by 1/2 the shredded cheese. Repeat layering: rigatoni, sauce, cheese. Sprinkle top with parsley, if using. Cover and bake for 30 minutes at 350°. If desired, serve with additional Parmesan cheese.

Makes 6 servings.

PER SERVING: 378 calories, 7.3 g fat, 58.7 g carbohydrate, 21.8 g protein, 1119 mg sodium, 17 mg cholesterol
CALORIES FROM FAT: 16.9%

WHAT'S IN IT FOR ME?

Manicotti Overboard

Help! Help! I'm drowning in a magnificent blend of crabmeat, cheese, dill, and spinach! All hands on deck...should grab a fork and try some of this! Save me! Save me! Save me some leftovers!

10 manicotti shells, uncooked
1-1/2 tablespoons reduced-fat butter or margarine
   (not fat-free)
1 clove garlic, minced
3 tablespoons all-purpose flour
1-1/2 cups 2% milk
1 can (14-1/2 ounces) tomatoes, drained, cut up
1 cup shredded reduced-fat Swiss cheese (4 ounces)
1 tablespoon chopped fresh dill or 3/4 teaspoon dried dillweed
1/2 teaspoon crushed red pepper flakes
1/4 teaspoon *each* salt and black pepper
10 ounces lump crabmeat, chopped (imitation crabmeat
   works well)
1 cup low-fat (1%) cottage cheese
1/2 10-ounce package frozen spinach, thawed, squeezed dry,
   and chopped (5 ounces total)
1/4 cup grated Parmesan cheese
1 egg white

Prepare manicotti according to package directions, undercooking slightly. Drain. Rinse with cold water and drain again. Set aside.

Melt butter in a medium saucepan. Add garlic and cook over medium heat for 1 minute. Mix the flour and milk together until smooth. Add to garlic. Continue to cook, stirring often, until sauce is thick and bubbly, about 7 minutes. Stir in tomatoes, 1/2 cup of the Swiss cheese, dill, red pepper flakes, salt, and pepper. When cheese has melted, remove from heat.

To prepare filling, combine crabmeat, cottage cheese, spinach, remaining Swiss cheese, Parmesan cheese, and egg white in a large bowl. Mix well.

Spray a 13 x 9-inch baking dish with non-stick spray. Using a teaspoon, spoon filling into manicotti shells. Place filled shells in baking dish in a single layer. Pour sauce evenly over top. Cover and bake in 350° oven for 30 minutes. Remove from oven, uncover, and let cool for 5 minutes before serving.

Makes 5 servings.

WHAT'S IN IT FOR ME? ➔ PER SERVING: 425 calories, 11.1 g fat, 49 g carbohydrate, 32.5 g protein, 1125 mg sodium, 45 mg cholesterol
CALORIES FROM FAT: 23.5%

Show me the WEIGH

Contrary to popular opinion, the concept of "healthy eating" is *not* about dieting. Simply put, it's about changing the way you think about food—permanently! Healthy eating means choosing to eat less fat more often, enjoying more of the sensible, nutritious foods that will help build a leaner, stronger you—foods like grains, pasta, potatoes, rice, vegetables, fruit, cereals, etc. The healthy eating school of thought suggests learning to love the foods that contribute to your overall well-being and that help you to look and to feel great. With a little practice, you'll find that sensible eating decisions become second nature.

SAY IT AIN'T SO!

Want to clog your arteries really fast? Just order a full breakfast from the local diner or family restaurant. A typical order sounds like this: 2 fried eggs, 1 sausage, hash browns, 2 pieces of toast with butter. And the richter scale says... 55 grams of fat! Tack on another 1.7 grams for the cream you just added to your coffee. Now you know why they call it a "greasy spoon."

Greasy Spoon

Used extensively in dishes of the Far East, fresh ginger or ginger root is completely different from dry ginger powder both in appearance and flavor. Store the fresh, tan-colored, gnarled root in a plastic bag in the refrigerator crisper for up to 2 weeks. Powdered dry ginger is often used to flavor baked goods, but shouldn't be substituted for fresh ginger.

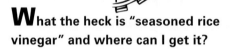

What the heck is "seasoned rice vinegar" and where can I get it?

Rice vinegar is made from soured and fermented rice wines, and is a versatile, mildly acidic vinegar. It's popular in Asian cooking, where it's used in sauces, dressings, and marinades. It's available both seasoned and unseasoned. Seasoned rice vinegar has sugar and salt added. You'll find it next to the other varieties of vinegar at the supermarket, or in the aisle where ethnic foods are sold.

IF YOUR FATHER COULD SEE YOU NOW HE'D TURN OVER IN HIS GRAVY!

Orient Express

Whether you're oriented or disoriented, you're just gonna love this one! Linguini, chicken, and vegetables are tossed in a far-out, Far East dressing. Quick and delicious!

12 ounces uncooked linguini
1 cup chopped onions
2 cloves garlic, minced
1 cup low-sodium, reduced-fat chicken broth
1/4 cup *each* reduced-sodium soy sauce and ketchup
3 tablespoons seasoned rice vinegar
1 tablespoon *each* lemon juice, sesame oil, and grated ginger root
2 teaspoons honey or brown sugar
1 teaspoon hot pepper sauce
1/2 teaspoon black pepper
2 tablespoons cornstarch
2 large chicken breast halves, cooked and cut into thin strips
1-1/2 cups broccoli florets
1 cup thinly sliced red bell pepper
1 cup carrots, cut into thin strips

Prepare linguini according to package directions. Drain and keep warm.

While pasta is cooking, prepare sauce. Spray a large saucepan with non-stick spray. Add onions and garlic. Cook and stir over medium heat until tender, about 5 minutes. Add broth, soy sauce, ketchup, vinegar, lemon juice, sesame oil, ginger root, honey or brown sugar, hot pepper sauce, and black pepper. Bring mixture to a boil, stirring often. Blend cornstarch with an equal amount of water until smooth. Add to sauce. Cook and stir until sauce thickens, about 1 minute.

Add cooked chicken strips, broccoli, red pepper, and carrots to sauce. Stir well. Cook for 3-4 minutes, until vegetables are tender-crisp. Pour sauce over warm linguini and toss to coat evenly. Serve immediately.

Makes 4 servings.

Hint: Give the cooked linguini a quick rinse with very hot water before adding sauce if the linguini has stuck together. Drain linguini well before mixing with sauce. Using low-sodium ketchup will help reduce the sodium content.

PER SERVING: 533 calories, 7.5 g fat, 88 g carbohydrate, 27 g protein, 902 mg sodium, 36 mg cholesterol
CALORIES FROM FAT: 12.8%

WHAT'S IN IT FOR ME?

On Top of Old Smokey

Not covered in cheese
I lost my poor meatball
When somebody... suggested that ground turkey would make meatballs that were just as scrumptious and yet much lower in fat than hamburger meatballs. So we use turkey here in our famous spaghetti and meatballs recipe.

To prepare meatballs, preheat oven to 375°. Combine all meatball ingredients in a large bowl. Mix well using your hands. Shape turkey mixture into 30 meatballs. Spray a shallow baking pan with non-stick spray and arrange meatballs in a single layer. Bake for 20-25 minutes, until lightly browned and no longer pink inside.

To prepare sauce, spray a large saucepan with non-stick spray. Add garlic, onions, green pepper, and celery. Cook over medium heat until tender, about 5-6 minutes, stirring often. Stir in remaining sauce ingredients and cooked meatballs. Cover and simmer for 30 minutes.

Meanwhile, cook spaghetti according to package directions. Drain. Serve meatball sauce over pasta. Sprinkle with Parmesan cheese, if desired.

Makes 6 servings.

Hint: Dip your hands frequently into cold water when forming meatballs or meat patties to prevent the ground meat from sticking.
Use no-salt-added tomatoes and a salt substitute if you're concerned about your sodium intake.

Turkey Meatballs

1-1/4 pounds lean ground turkey (skinless)
1/3 cup unseasoned dry bread crumbs
2 tablespoons *each* minced onions and chopped
   fresh parsley
3/4 teaspoon Italian seasoning
1/2 teaspoon *each* salt and black pepper
1 egg white
2 tablespoons skim milk

Sauce

3 cloves garlic, minced
1 cup chopped onions
1 cup chopped green bell pepper
3/4 cup chopped celery
3 cups tomato sauce
1 can (14-1/2 ounces) tomatoes, drained, cut up
1 can (6 ounces) tomato paste
1/3 cup dry red wine (optional)
1 tablespoon reduced-sodium soy sauce
1 teaspoon *each* dried oregano and
   dried basil
1/2 teaspoon *each* dried marjoram, salt,
   and black pepper
1/4 teaspoon crushed red pepper flakes
18 ounces uncooked spaghetti
Grated Parmesan cheese (optional)

WHAT'S IN IT FOR ME? ➤ PER SERVING: 541 calories, 3.4 g fat, 87.3 g carbohydrate, 39.4 g protein, 988 mg sodium, 46 mg cholesterol
CALORIES FROM FAT: 5.7%

When the first hamburger press was made, the inventor got a real patty on his back.

Show me the WEIGH

Men and women are not created equal when it comes to burning calories. The more lean muscle mass you have, the faster your metabolism, which explains why a man, who has the help of testosterone to build muscle, can burn more calories at rest than a woman. The average female has a higher fat-to-lean-muscle ratio, and fat cells require fewer calories than protein-rich muscle tissue to function and survive. A man of average build burns approximately 1900 calories a day sitting still, while a woman of average build burns about 1430 calories a day. So when a man and a woman are put on the same diet, the man usually starts dipping into his stored supplies of fat a lot sooner. Go figure!

SAY IT AIN'T SO!

You may think that popcorn is good for you. "It's corn, right? It's a low-fat carbohydrate, isn't it?" Besides the fact 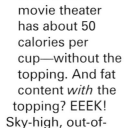 that popcorn offers little nutritional value, the typical popcorn cooked in fat at the movie theater has about 50 calories per cup—without the topping. And fat content *with* the topping? EEEK! Sky-high, out-of-this-world, beyond belief! Now 50 calories doesn't sound too bad, but when you add the topping and consider that a large box is nearly as big as a fire bucket, we're looking at almost a day's worth of calories and fat crammed into one sitting! Your best bet is to bring your own air-popped popcorn or light microwave popcorn along for the show.

Motivation is what gets you started, but habit is what keeps you going.

Pasta Point of No Return

There's just no going back to the old way of making the perennial favorite, Pasta Primavera, once you've tried this revamped version from the "Try-Light Zone!"

2 cups whole button mushrooms
2 cups cubed zucchini (cut into 1-inch cubes)
2 cups coarsely chopped tomatoes
1 cup *each* sliced red and yellow bell pepper
1 tablespoon olive oil
2 cloves garlic, minced
3 tablespoons chopped fresh basil *or* 1-1/2 teaspoons dried basil
1/4 teaspoon freshly ground black pepper
12 ounces uncooked tri-color rotini (about 4 cups dry)
1-1/2 cups broccoli florets
1/2 cup frozen peas, thawed
2 tablespoons *each* grated Parmesan cheese and chopped fresh parsley

I'M SORRY SIR. ONCE YOU'VE TASTED THE PASTA, THERE'S NO GOING BACK.

NO RETURN POLICY

Preheat oven to 400°.

Spray a 13 x 9-inch baking pan with non-stick spray. Set aside.

In a large bowl, combine mushrooms, zucchini, tomatoes, sweet peppers, olive oil, garlic, basil, and pepper. Toss until vegetables are evenly coated with oil and seasonings. Transfer vegetables to prepared baking pan. Bake, uncovered, for 25 minutes. Stir once, halfway through cooking time.

Meanwhile, prepare pasta according to package directions. About 4 minutes before pasta is ready, add broccoli and peas to the boiling water (yup, right along with the rotini). When pasta is cooked, drain pasta and vegetables, then return them to the pot. Stir in roasted vegetables, Parmesan cheese, and parsley. Serve with extra freshly ground black pepper, if desired.

Makes 4 servings.

PER SERVING: 432 calories, 6.9 g fat, 77.9 g carbohydrate, 16.4 g protein, 101 mg sodium, 2 mg cholesterol
CALORIES FROM FAT: 14.1%

WHAT'S IN IT FOR ME?

Gringo's Star

While travelling aimlessly through Mexico, our friend Gringo discovered this spicy and ultra-hearty Spanish-style pasta dish that was the star attraction at a local eating house called the Obla Di Obla Diner. He loved it so much that he took a job there drumming up business for the owners.

12 ounces uncooked Scoobi-Do (spiral macaroni) or medium shell pasta (about 4 cups dry)
1 pound lean ground turkey or chicken (skinless)
1 cup chopped onions
2 cloves garlic, minced
3/4 cup *each* diced red and green bell pepper
2 jalapeño peppers, seeded and minced
2 cups low-fat spaghetti sauce (your favorite)
3/4 cup salsa (mild, medium, or hot)
1 teaspoon *each* dried oregano, ground cumin, and chili powder
1/4 teaspoon black pepper
1 cup low-fat (1%) cottage cheese
1/2 cup shredded reduced-fat Monterey Jack or cheddar cheese (2 ounces)
1 tablespoon chopped fresh cilantro or parsley

Prepare pasta according to package directions. Drain. Rinse with cold water and drain again. Set aside.

Spray a large skillet or saucepan with non-stick spray. Add turkey or chicken, onions, garlic, green and red peppers, and jalapeños. Cook and stir over high heat until turkey is no longer pink, about 5 minutes. Drain off any fat. Add spaghetti sauce, salsa, oregano, cumin, chili powder, and pepper. Bring to a boil. Reduce heat to medium-low. Cover and simmer for 5 minutes, stirring occasionally. Remove from heat.

Spray a 13 x 9-inch baking dish with non-stick spray. Spread 1/2 the pasta over bottom, followed by 1/2 the sauce. Spread cottage cheese evenly over sauce. Pour remaining pasta over cottage cheese, followed by remaining sauce. Top with shredded cheese and cilantro or parsley.

Cover and bake at 350° for 30 minutes, until completely heated through. Let stand 5 minutes before serving.

Makes 6 servings.

Hint: For a milder version of this dish, omit the jalapeño peppers and use mild salsa.

WHAT'S IN IT FOR ME?

PER SERVING: 406 calories, 5.9 g fat, 54.8 g carbohydrate, 34.5 g protein, 831 mg sodium, 47 mg cholesterol
CALORIES FROM FAT: 12.9%

D. I. E. T.

is a four-letter word that really means...
DEFINITELY INVITING ETERNAL TORMENT

Dieting is torture. Counting every morsel of food that goes into your mouth is ridiculous. Who has time to weigh their portions? You ask yourself, "If I have one cookie, does that mean I've blown it? What happens when I go to a restaurant? What about having dinner at a friend's place? What can I eat at the office?" Too many questions are left unanswered and you end up a tormented "failure." You'll have much more success by making small, gradual changes to your eating habits rather than attempting a drastic, self-defeating overhaul.

Slim Pickin's

If you choose to eat a trifling
1/2 CUP OF DRY-ROASTED PISTACHIOS,
you'll be choosing an unbelievable
34 GRAMS OF FAT,
the equivalent of eating
34 COBS OF CORN.
Which would fill you up more?

Go for quality *and* quantity!

The first drive-in restaurant was opened for people who wanted to curb their appetites.

Sun-dried tomatoes (which are actually dried in ovens) provide concentrated flavor and a chewy texture to enliven savory dishes. They're available packaged dry or in oil. Stay clear of the oil-packed version, and buy them dried and in plastic. Sun-dried tomatoes are easily softened by pouring boiling water over them and letting them soak for 5 minutes. You can find them in the produce section of the supermarket or on the shelf with the other Italian specialty items.

Show me the WEIGH

The question: What can add inches to your physique even though it's empty? The answer: "Empty" calories like the ones in alcohol. Alcoholic beverages provide calories and nothing else (except the occasional great beer commercial).

If you drink regularly—two beers or two glasses of wine per day—that's about 1400 calories per week, or more than 73,000 calories in a year, enough to create approximately 20 excess pounds of unsightly flab! Yikes! And it's highly unlikely you'll burn off any of those extra calories by doing the serious bicep curls that go hand in hand with beer drinking. Just remember to enjoy your vices in moderation.

Rich, fatty foods are like destiny: they too, shape our ends.

A Penne For Your Thoughts

Too good for words! The zest and zing of this pasta dish will be stored in your memory bank forever.

1 cup sun-dried tomatoes (see Cooking 101 on left)
3 cups sliced mushrooms
12 ounces uncooked penne pasta (about 4 cups dry)
4 slices raw bacon, cut crosswise into 1/2-inch sections
3 cloves garlic, minced
1 cup sliced red onion rings
2 cups chopped fresh spinach
2 tablespoons chopped fresh basil *or* 1 teaspoon dried basil
1/2 teaspoon crushed red pepper flakes
Freshly ground black pepper (to taste)
2 tablespoons grated Parmesan cheese
2 tablespoons chopped fresh parsley

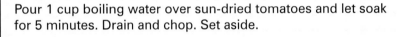

Pour 1 cup boiling water over sun-dried tomatoes and let soak for 5 minutes. Drain and chop. Set aside.

Place mushrooms in a medium bowl with 1/4 cup water. Microwave on high power for 5 minutes. Drain and set aside.

Cook penne according to package directions. Drain and keep warm.

Cook bacon in a large skillet over medium-high heat until crisp. Add garlic and cook 1 more minute. *Do not discard drippings!* Add onions, spinach, sun-dried tomatoes, cooked mushrooms, basil, and red pepper flakes. Cook and stir for 4-5 minutes, until onions are tender.

Toss bacon/vegetable mixture with hot pasta until evenly distributed. Divide pasta between 4 serving dishes. Top each with freshly ground black pepper and 1/4 of the Parmesan cheese. Sprinkle with parsley. Serve immediately.

Makes 4 servings.

PER SERVING: 476 calories, 11.8 g fat, 74 g carbohydrate, 18.2 g protein, 468 mg sodium, 18 mg cholesterol
CALORIES FROM FAT: 22.3%

WHAT'S IN IT FOR ME?

Mac Attack

A revamped macaroni and cheese that's sure to please your lips *and* your hips.

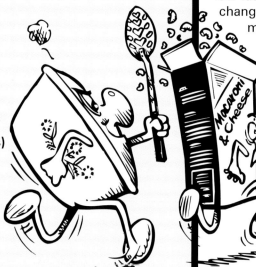

2-1/2 cups 1% milk
1/4 cup all-purpose flour
1/2 teaspoon *each* dry mustard and salt
1/4 teaspoon *each* paprika and black pepper
1-1/2 cups shredded reduced-fat sharp cheddar cheese (6 ounces)
2 ounces "light" cream cheese
1/4 cup minced onions
3 tablespoons grated Parmesan cheese
6 cups cooked elbow macaroni (about 3 cups dry)

Topping
1/4 cup unseasoned dry bread crumbs
1 tablespoon grated Parmesan cheese.

In a medium saucepan, combine the milk and flour until smooth. Cook over medium-high heat until mixture is bubbly and thickened, about 7-8 minutes.

Stir in dry mustard, salt, paprika, pepper, all cheeses, and onions. Continue to cook until cheeses are completely melted.

Combine cheese sauce with cooked macaroni. Transfer to a large casserole dish that has been sprayed with non-stick spray.

Mix bread crumbs and Parmesan cheese. Sprinkle over macaroni. Bake at 350°, uncovered, for 30 minutes. Serve immediately.

Makes 8 servings.

WHAT'S IN IT FOR ME? ➡ PER SERVING: 296 calories, 7.7 g fat, 40.4 g carbohydrate, 17.3 g protein, 462 mg sodium, 23 mg cholesterol CALORIES FROM FAT: 23%

*N*othing tastes as good as being fit feels.

COOKING 101

When you don't have the time or the ingredients to prepare homemade macaroni and cheese, you can at least transform the boxed variety into a creamy low-fat version by making the following changes (use the cheese packet and macaroni as directed): Instead of 1/4 cup butter plus 1/4 cup 2% milk, try 1/4 cup low-fat sour cream plus 2 tablespoons skim milk.

No one will know the difference and you'll save an incredible 375 calories and 45 grams of fat!

SAY IT AIN'T SO!

And now, the "oh, so painful" truth! One package of the old standby, the beloved and economically appealing macaroni and cheese, prepared as directed on the box (Come on, admit it! You've polished off a box all by yourself many, many times!) weighs in at an unthinkable 1230 calories and 60 grams of fat (49% of its calories are derived from fat). Mac and cheese may be easy on the wallet, but prepared in the usual manner, it's obviously tough on the waistline!

In a
FOWL MOOD?

Poultry dishes to cheer you up

Wowie Maui Chicken

This pineapple chicken dish may not be volcanic, but it's definitely erupting with a luscious, tropical flavor that'll have you dreaming of Hawaii's ocean breezes, white sands and luaus. A-lo-fat!

4 boneless, skinless chicken breast halves, cut into 1-inch cubes
2-1/2 cups low-sodium, reduced-fat chicken broth
1-1/2 cups canned pineapple tidbits in juice, undrained
1-1/2 cups uncooked long grain white or brown rice (see hint below)
3/4 cup finely chopped carrots
1/2 cup *each* chopped red and green bell pepper
1/3 cup ketchup
2 tablespoons *each* brown sugar, reduced-sodium soy sauce, and white vinegar
2 cloves garlic, minced
3/4 cup chopped green onions

Spray a large saucepan with non-stick spray. Add chicken. Cook over medium-high heat until no longer pink.

Add remaining ingredients, except green onions. Stir well. Bring to a boil. Reduce heat to medium-low. Cover and simmer for 25 minutes, until rice is tender. Stir occasionally.

Stir in green onions during last five minutes of cooking time. Serve immediately.

Makes 4 servings.

Hint: If using brown rice, make sure it's the quicker-cooking variety (cooks in 25 minutes), but not instant rice.

WHAT'S IN IT FOR ME?

PER SERVING: 546 calories, 4.2 g fat, 89.7 g carbohydrate, 35.2 g protein, 718 mg sodium, 73 mg cholesterol CALORIES FROM FAT: 7.1%

Show & Tell

Pineapples contain a protein-dissolving enzyme called bromelain. Bromelain breaks down the fibers of meat, so a pineapple's juice can be used as a natural meat tenderizer. This enzyme also acts as an anti-inflammatory, which may be why it's soothing to a sore throat. So the next time your throat's sore, stop whining and start "pining"!

SAY IT AIN'T SO!

And now the really bad news. A large chocolate shake prepared in the traditional manner (without low-fat frozen yogurt) has approximately (brace yourself) 990 calories! And fat content? Yikes! It's better left unsaid. Up the straw, your taste buds craving. To burn it off, you'll be slaving!

May the Best Beast Win

If there were such a thing as the "Barnyard Olympics," which of these two finalists would win the 100-yard dash: the chicken or the pig? Well sports fans, it would be a close race, right down to the chicken wire, but the gold medal would go to the underdog, or in this case, the "under*pig*." Yes, the pig wins! Despite its unappealing diet of slop, its passion for lethargy, and its rotund physique, the domestic pig actually clocks in at an average maximum speed of 11 miles per hour compared to a chicken's 9 miles per hour. Apparently, chicken feed does not constitute the "breakfast of champions"!

What the heck is "Chinese five-spice powder" and where can I get it?

Five-spice powder is a seasoning commonly used in Chinese cooking. It's a blend of cumin, cloves, fennel, Szechuan peppercorns, and star-anise. You can find it at Asian specialty stores and some well-stocked supermarkets.

D. I. E. T.

is a four-letter word that really means...
DECEPTIVE INDUSTRY EATING TRAP

Diets that promise next-to-impossible, immediate or don't-lift-a-finger results are all a big fat lie. If it sounds too good to be true, then it probably is. Over 95% of us who lose weight by starving and depriving ourselves—dieting, that is—will gain the weight back. With a failure rate that high, why do we continue to support the industry which has taken advantage of and profited from the desperation of dieters? A healthy, low-fat lifestyle is realistic, sensible, and affordable, unlike "miracle" diet fads and gimmicks which are effectively a form of "high weigh robbery."

Skinful is Sinful

Removing the skin from chicken reduces fat content by approximately 50%. That's a lot of fat! Chicken wings (mostly skin) and fried chicken (skin left on to give crispness) are absolute fat fiends and should be enjoyed in moderation.

Ancient Chinese Secret, Huh?

My husband! Some hotshot! Here's his ancient Chinese secret—Chinese five-spice powder! Chicken and rice never tasted so nice. And your plates will be sparkling clean when you polish off every last morsel!

4 boneless, skinless chicken breast halves, cut into 1-inch cubes
1 teaspoon Chinese five-spice powder
1 cup trimmed and halved snow peas
1 cup thinly sliced red bell pepper
2 cloves garlic, minced
2 teaspoons grated ginger root
3 cups low-sodium, reduced-fat chicken broth
1-1/2 cups uncooked long grain white rice
1/2 cup chopped green onions
2 tablespoons lime juice
2 tablespoons reduced-sodium soy sauce
1 tablespoon honey
2 teaspoons sesame oil
1/4 teaspoon *each* crushed red pepper flakes and black pepper

Combine chicken and five-spice powder in a large bowl. Toss or stir to coat chicken evenly with spice.

Spray a large saucepan with non-stick spray. Add chicken and cook over medium-high heat, stirring often, until no longer pink.

Add snow peas, red pepper, garlic, and ginger root. Cook and stir over medium heat for 2-3 minutes.

Add all remaining ingredients and bring to a boil. Reduce heat to medium-low. Cover and cook for 20-25 minutes, until liquid is absorbed by rice and chicken is very tender.

Makes 4 servings.

PER SERVING: 514 calories, 7.2 g fat, 69.4 g carbohydrate, 40.3 g protein, 673 mg sodium, 88 mg cholesterol
CALORIES FROM FAT: 12.8%

WHAT'S IN IT FOR ME?

Chicken and Rice and Everything Spice

That's what health-conscious folks are made of! Since snakes and snails and puppy dog tails aren't considered low-fat ingredients, they're not included in the recipe.

1 cup coarsely chopped onions
1 clove garlic, minced
3 cups chopped cooked chicken breast
 (about 1-1/4 pounds)
1 can (28 ounces) tomatoes, undrained,
 cut up
1 can (15 ounces) chickpeas, drained and
 rinsed
1 can (6 ounces) tomato paste
1 cup *each* sliced zucchini and chopped yellow bell pepper
3/4 cup *each* chopped carrots and chopped celery
2 bay leaves
1 cinnamon stick (about 5 inches long)
1 teaspoon *each* grated ginger root and chili powder
3/4 teaspoon ground cumin
1/4 teaspoon *each* crushed red pepper flakes and
 black pepper
4 cups cooked brown rice

Spray a large saucepan with non-stick spray. Add onions and garlic. Cook over medium heat for 5 minutes, stirring often, until onions are tender.

Add chicken and all remaining ingredients except rice. Stir well. Bring mixture to a boil. Reduce heat to medium-low. Cover and simmer for 25 minutes. Stir every once in a while.

To serve, remove cinnamon stick and bay leaves. Divide hot rice among six plates and ladle chicken and vegetables on top.

Makes 6 servings.

Hint: See page 95 for tip on preparing chicken.

WHAT'S IN IT FOR ME? ➤

PER SERVING: 396 calories, 5.1 g fat, 58.1 g carbohydrate, 32.1 g protein, 746 mg sodium, 59 mg cholesterol
CALORIES FROM FAT: 11.3%

COOKING 101

Brown rice has a pleasant nutty flavor and contains more fiber than white rice. It also takes longer to cook—about 45 minutes. Look for quicker-cooking varieties of brown rice that are ready in 25-30 minutes, but not *instant* rice, which is far inferior in both texture and taste. Uncle Ben's Whole-grain Brown in a box is a good choice. Since cooked brown rice will keep for up to 1 week in the refrigerator, why not make extra and simply steam or reheat the leftovers for a subsequent meal?

Show me the WEIGH

It's great that you meet your friends a few times a week at the local pub for a couple of brews and a bite to eat—sort of like having your own Cheers, a place where everyone knows your name. But have you ever considered exactly how fattening it is to sit around, drink alcohol, and eat the usual high-fat foods that are served in pubs? Someone who eats the typical North American high-fat diet and also drinks regularly will often consume an average of 3100 to 3600 calories each week more than a moderate drinker who eats a low-fat diet. Eeeeek! It wouldn't take much of that before you'd start looking like Norm Peterson. Just remember to temper your occasional splurges with healthy, low-fat choices.

The best remedy for forgetfulness is drinking milk of amnesia.

Show & Tell

Because cabbage is loaded with fiber, it helps lower the risk of certain cancers, particularly of the esophagus, stomach, and colon. Cabbage is low in sodium, low in calories, and high in vitamin C—good for you! If that's not enough to put cabbage at the head of its class, it's cheap and can grow just about anywhere, even in cold climates.

Cabbage, in fact, played a significant role in history. During Captain James Cook's second great voyage to explore the Pacific in 1772, he ordered thousands of pounds of sauerkraut (cabbage fermented and pickled in a salt solution) for its healthy properties. Over a period of more than 1,000 days, he lost only one of his 118 men to scurvy, thanks to the abundant supply of vitamin C in the virtuous cabbage.

Gotta MOVE It!

"It's easy to start an exercise program. I've done it a hundred times!" Sound familiar? Well, you don't have to follow the conventional notions of exercise anymore to reap the physical benefits. The "new" fitness rules stress enjoyment, everyday activity, and moderation. Gardening, walking, tennis, and golf are all excellent forms of exercise. And besides, none of them call for a swanky, skin-tight Spandex leotard as mandatory attire!

Choose your words with taste. You may have to eat them later.

Unrolled Cabbage Rolls

This recipe was transported across the Atlantic in the late 1940's by our mother, Alfreda, who felt that North America deserved a taste of authentic Polish cuisine. Finally, a recipe that unravels the mystery behind creating ultra-flavorful cabbage rolls without a lot of fuss. (Actually, we've *unrolled* them to make it even easier!)

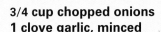
DEEZ ARE DA GREATEST!

3/4 cup chopped onions
1 clove garlic, minced
1-1/2 cups low-sodium, reduced-fat chicken broth
3/4 cup uncooked long grain white rice
1 medium head cabbage (about 3-4 pounds)
1-1/2 pounds lean ground turkey (skinless)
1 egg white
1/4 cup chopped fresh parsley
1 teaspoon dried marjoram
1/2 teaspoon *each* salt and black pepper
2 cans (10-3/4 ounces each) low-fat condensed tomato soup (Campbell's Healthy Request)

Spray a medium saucepan with non-stick spray. Add onions and garlic. Cook over medium heat for 2 minutes, stirring often. Add broth and rice. Bring to a boil. Reduce heat to medium-low. Cover and cook for 20-25 minutes, until rice is tender and liquid has been absorbed. Stir occasionally.

Meanwhile, bring a large pot of water to a boil. Cut cabbage into 8 wedges. Boil cabbage wedges for 5 minutes. Drain. Remove tough inner pieces. Separate individual leaves and set aside.

Combine cooked rice with turkey, egg white, parsley, marjoram, salt, and pepper. Mix well (using your hands works best).

Spray a 13 x 9-inch baking pan with non-stick spray. Line bottom with 1/2 the cabbage leaves. Spread rice/turkey mixture evenly over cabbage. Top with remaining cabbage leaves.

Empty both cans of soup into a medium bowl. Add 1 can water and mix well. Pour soup evenly over cabbage. Cover and bake for 1 hour at 350°. Reduce heat to 325° and cook another 45 minutes. Let cool for 5 minutes before serving.

Makes 8 servings.

PER SERVING: 258 calories, 3.3 g fat, 33.5 g carbohydrate, 24.9 g protein, 492 mg sodium, 41 mg cholesterol
CALORIES FROM FAT: 11.4%

WHAT'S IN IT FOR ME?

Loafstyles of the Rich & Famous

Enquiring minds want to know: What's the secret behind this low-fat loaf that "everyone who's a someone" is raving about? Well, according to the Psychic to the Stars, the secret ingredient is ground turkey, of all things, and apparently it has a very bright future ahead of it. First, loaves. Then, the world! You'll just fall in loaf with it!

1 teaspoon butter or margarine
2 cups chopped, unpeeled Granny
Smith apples
3/4 cup chopped onions
1-1/2 pounds lean ground
turkey (skinless)
1/2 cup *each* **quick-cooking rolled oats and**
chopped fresh parsley
1/3 cup skim milk
2 egg whites
1 teaspoon Dijon mustard
1 clove garlic, minced
3/4 teaspoon dried marjoram
1/2 teaspoon *each* **ground sage, salt, and black pepper**

Preheat oven to 350°.

Melt butter in a non-stick skillet over medium heat. Add apples and onions. Cook and stir for about 5 minutes, until onions are tender. Let cool.

In a large bowl, mix together apples, onions, and all remaining ingredients.

Spray a 9 x 5-inch loaf pan with non-stick spray. Pat turkey mixture into pan. Bake for 1 hour, or until no longer pink in center. Pour off any liquid from pan. Invert onto a platter and serve.

Makes 6 servings.

WHAT'S IN IT FOR ME? ➡ PER SERVING: 198 calories, 3 g fat, 13.7 g carbohydrate, 30.3 g protein, 300 mg sodium, 57 mg cholesterol CALORIES FROM FAT: 13.3 %

COOKING 101

Ground turkey from the supermarket often contains ground turkey skin, which can increase fat content substantially. For the leanest ground turkey around, grind skinless turkey breast yourself. Remove all visible fat before grinding. If you don't have a meat grinder, cut the turkey breast into cubes and finely chop in a food processor. Or better yet, ask the butcher to grind the skinless turkey breast for you.

Slim Pickin's

If you choose to eat
1 BURGER KING DOUBLE WHOPPER,
you'll be choosing a whopping
53 GRAMS OF FAT,
the equivalent of eating
5,300 GRAPES.
Which would fill you up more?

Go for quality *and* quantity!

"I think my wife is getting tired of me. She keeps wrapping my lunches in roadmaps."

Show & Tell

To store fresh dill, wrap the bunches in damp paper towels, then place them in a plastic bag and refrigerate. Or better yet, grow your own! Dill will grow quite easily in a bright, sunny spot in your garden. (By the way, rumor has it that a speckled toad, when dragged around the garden by its hind leg, will make your herbs grow abundantly!) No need to fret, however, if you don't have any fresh dill on hand. Dried dill is an acceptable substitute in most recipes. Simply use 1/3 of the amount specified for the fresh herb.

SAY IT AIN'T SO!

Any way you slice it, deli counters just don't cut it when it comes to keeping the fat out of sandwiches. For example, the typical tuna sandwich made with mayonnaise on buttered bread (what you'd get at many deli counters) weighs in at 40 grams of fat, 600 calories, and 60% calories from fat! When they asked you take a number, did you think it would be this big?

Dillicious Lemon Chicken

A chicken dish that's slimply dillightful, positively dillectable! Won't find this in a dillicatessen. Don't dilly dally! Just dilliver it to your dinner table!

1 cup low-fat sour cream
1 tablespoon minced fresh dill
1 teaspoon lemon pepper seasoning
1 teaspoon lemon zest
4 boneless, skinless chicken breast halves

Preheat oven to 425°.

Combine sour cream, dill, lemon pepper, and lemon zest in a small bowl.

Spray a medium casserole dish with non-stick spray. Spoon 1/4 of the lemon-dill sauce over bottom. Arrange chicken breasts on top in a single layer. Pour remaining sauce over chicken. Spread evenly.

Bake uncovered for 30-35 minutes, until chicken is tender and no longer pink.

Makes 4 servings.

PER SERVING: 218 calories, 4.4 g fat, 6.2 g carbohydrate, 35.6 g protein, 401 mg sodium, 90 mg cholesterol
CALORIES FROM FAT: 19.2%

WHAT'S IN IT FOR ME?

My best friend made a gravy I'll never forget. One quart of vodka, two quarts of rum, and three quarts of brandy. I asked him, "Where did you get this recipe?" He said, "From a cookbook." I said, "Who wrote it?" He said, "Betty Crocked!"

Slimply Orange Chicken

Attention all citrus lovers! This deliciously sweet chicken is the pick of the crop when you're short of time but searching for gourmet flavor.

**4 boneless, skinless chicken breast
  halves
1 can (11 ounces) mandarin
  oranges in light syrup
1-1/2 tablespoons brown sugar
1-1/2 tablespoons cornstarch**

Spray a large skillet with non-stick spray. Add chicken and cook over medium-high heat for 3-4 minutes on each side, until no longer pink. Remove chicken from skillet and keep warm.

Add mandarin oranges with their syrup to a food processor or blender. Pulse on and off once or twice until oranges are coarsely puréed (still slightly chunky). You should end up with about 1-1/2 cups puréed oranges.

Whisk together puréed oranges, brown sugar, and cornstarch in a small bowl. Add to skillet that chicken was cooked in. Return skillet to medium-high heat and cook orange mixture for 1-2 minutes, until bubbly and thickened.

Return chicken to skillet. Reduce heat to low. Cover and simmer for 5-7 minutes, until chicken is very tender. Serve chicken with orange sauce spooned over top.

Makes 4 servings.

WHAT'S IN IT FOR ME? ➡ PER SERVING: 235 calories, 4.2 g fat, 16.6 g carbohydrate, 32 g protein, 322 mg sodium, 88 mg cholesterol CALORIES FROM FAT: 16.2%

Trivial Tidbit

In the 1840's, mandarin oranges were shipped to Britain from the port of Tangier, Morocco, which is believed to be the origin of the name "tangerine."

Show me the WEIGH

Although most of the big fast food chains are offering a glimmer of hope with their nutritional efforts (switching to low-fat mayonnaise, low-fat milk, and leaner burgers), fast food still hits the waistline with a triple whammy: 1. Fast food is still high in sodium, calories, and despite the recent efforts, FAT; 2. Fast food tends to be eaten quickly, which means more of it is consumed; 3. All of it tends to get eaten, even if it's enough to feed King Kong and his family. Even some fish and chicken entrées, touted as healthful alternatives to traditional hamburgers, get up to 50% of their calories from fat. Remember the 80/20 rule: 80% of the time, make low-fat choices and 20% of the time, allow yourself an indulgence, like a trip to the fast food joint if that's what you crave.

She's been on a coconut and banana diet. She hasn't lost any weight, but you should see her climb trees.

An easy method of preparing chicken for this recipe and others calling for pre-cooked chicken is "poaching," cooking slowly in simmering liquid. For your poaching liquid, choose from water, broth, fruit juice, wine, or a combination of your choice. Poach the chicken until tender, about 15-20 minutes, then chop or slice as specified in the recipe.

Gotta MOVE It!

We all know that exercise develops muscle tissue. Yeah, yeah. What's the big deal about that? The big deal is that muscle tissue is more metabolically active than fat—it actually burns more calories at rest than does fat. For instance, an average-sized person burns approximately 70 calories per hour at rest. If this same person were physically fit, he/she would burn up to 10 more calories per hour, or over 14% more calories! An active, fit body is a fuel-burning body and fuel-burning means fat-burning! So burn, baby, burn!

Did you hear about the boy who drank 8 Cokes? He burped 7-Up.

Grocery Cart Chicken Chili

One man's junk is another man's treasure! This super-spicy creation is based on a recipe that was found in an abandoned grocery cart at the side of a dirt road. Yes, we're serious, and no, we're not garbage pickers.

**1-1/2 cups chopped red onions
3 cloves garlic, minced
1-1/2 cups chopped green bell pepper
3 jalapeño peppers, seeded and minced
3 cups chopped cooked chicken breast (about 1-1/4 pounds)
1 can (14-1/2 ounces) tomatoes, undrained, cut up
1 cup tomato-based chili sauce
1-1/2 cups low-sodium, reduced-fat chicken broth
1-1/2 tablespoons chili powder
1 tablespoon *each* Dijon mustard and "lite" Worcestershire sauce
2 teaspoons ground cumin
1 teaspoon dried oregano
1/4 teaspoon *each* cayenne pepper and black pepper
1 can (15 ounces) red kidney beans, drained and rinsed
1 can (15 ounces) white kidney beans, drained and rinsed
1/2 cup shredded reduced-fat cheddar cheese (2 ounces)**

Spray a large saucepan with non-stick spray. Add onions, garlic, green peppers, and jalapeños. Cook over medium heat until tender, about 7 minutes.

Add remaining ingredients, except kidney beans and cheese. Bring to a boil. Reduce heat to medium-low. Cover and simmer for 20 minutes, stirring occasionally. Add kidney beans and cook 5 more minutes. Ladle chili into individual bowls and top each with a sprinkle of cheese.

Makes 6 servings.

Hint: Reduce the sodium content by using no-salt-added tomatoes and reduced-sodium chili sauce. Try canned black beans in place of the red kidney beans for a nice variation.

PER SERVING: 308 calories, 5.8 g fat, 36.1 g carbohydrate, 33.8 g protein, 1190 mg sodium, 66 mg cholesterol
CALORIES FROM FAT: 15.7%

WHAT'S IN IT FOR ME?

Miss American Thigh

Bye bye Miss American Thigh! Don't waste your time driving your Chevy to the levee. Stay home and savor the delectable taste of these baked chicken thighs— they won't last long!

1 cup grape jelly
3/4 cup ketchup
1/2 cup minced onions
2 tablespoons white vinegar
1 teaspoon dry mustard
3 pounds chicken thighs,
   skin removed

Preheat oven to 350°.

In a small saucepan, stir together grape jelly, ketchup, onions, vinegar, and dry mustard. Heat over medium-high heat until mixture comes to a boil and jelly is melted. Remove from heat.

Arrange chicken pieces in a 13 x 9-inch baking dish. Pour sauce evenly over chicken and turn pieces to coat both sides. Bake uncovered for 1 hour, until chicken is very tender.

Makes 4-6 servings.

WHAT'S IN IT FOR ME? → PER SERVING (based on 6 servings): 379 calories, 6.1 g fat, 44.8 g carbohydrate, 32.6 g protein, 587 mg sodium, 140 mg cholesterol CALORIES FROM FAT: 15.1%

The Conscientious Nibbler

Are you an Amnesia Eater? Do you nibble all day long without being able to account for what you ate later on? Well, if you're unconsciously nibbling on high-fat snacks, you'd better drop the automatic eating motion like a hot potato (hold the sour cream, please)! Small doses of fat taken all day long can add up to just as much as having one big, fat-drenched shot at mealtime. Be reminded that a mere handful of regular potato chips has a shocking 10 grams of fat, about the same as eating 10 slices of bread! If you're accustomed to polishing off a large bag on your own (pretty easy to do if you're a seasoned couch potato), you will have consumed 63 grams of fat and about 954 hip-hugging calories.

When you feel a snack attack coming on, simply try to make smarter choices. Despite what you may have heard, that doesn't mean you're stuck chomping on carrot and celery sticks. There are plenty of healthy, tasty snacks to choose from—really! Here are a few:

pretzels
air-popped popcorn
bagels
fruits and veggies
angel food cake
low-fat crackers
cinnamon toast

skim milk pudding
baked tortilla chips
low-fat granola bars
ginger snap cookies
low-fat frozen yogurt
flavored rice cakes
baked potato chips

raisins
low-fat yogurt
low-fat muffins
applesauce
cereal with skim milk
shakes made with
   yogurt and fruit

Trivial Tidbit

The expression "to get a lucky break" is believed to have originated nearly 2,500 years ago from the familiar custom of two people making a wish, then tugging on a dried chicken "wishbone" (actually the clavicle) until it breaks in two. Even today, many still believe that the wish made by the person who ends up with the larger piece will come true.

Show me the WEIGH

Slow down. What's the big rush? You didn't put those extra 20 pounds on overnight, so why are you killing yourself by trying to lose them in record-setting time? If you need to lose weight, do it slowly—1 or 2 pounds per week is good. Any more than that and you end up losing more water and lean muscle tissue than fat. Loss of muscle can account for up to 30% of any rapid weight loss, and reduced muscle tissue lowers your metabolic rate. In the end, you'll have more fat, less muscle, and a slower metabolism. Is that what you had in mind when you bought those diet pills? Fat chance! Instead, try the sensible approach: eating nutritious, low-fat foods and putting your muscles to work on a regular basis. C'mon! Give it a try! You might be amazed at the way your body responds.

∫The Thigh's the Limit

Marinated chicken thighs that soar to new flavor heights. Remember: Removing the skin means you won't blimp out. And that's not a bunch of hot air!

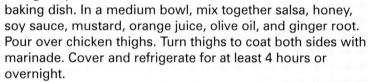

12 skinless chicken thighs
   (about 3 ounces each)
3/4 cup salsa (mild,
   medium, or hot)
1/3 cup honey
1/4 cup *each* **reduced-**
   sodium soy sauce and
   orange juice
2 tablespoons Dijon mustard
2 teaspoons olive oil
1-1/2 tablespoons grated
   ginger root
1 tablespoon cornstarch

Arrange chicken thighs in a single layer in 13 x 9-inch baking dish. In a medium bowl, mix together salsa, honey, soy sauce, mustard, orange juice, olive oil, and ginger root. Pour over chicken thighs. Turn thighs to coat both sides with marinade. Cover and refrigerate for at least 4 hours or overnight.

Bake chicken and sauce, covered, in a 400° oven for 40 minutes. Transfer chicken thighs to a serving platter and keep warm. Carefully pour sauce into a small saucepan. Bring to a boil over medium-high heat. Mix cornstarch with 2 tablespoons water until smooth. Add to sauce and stir until mixture thickens, about 1 minute. Pour thickened sauce over chicken and serve immediately.

Makes 4-6 servings.

PER SERVING (based on 6 servings): 310 calories, 8.1 g fat, 21.4 g carbohydrate, 32.1 g protein, 787 mg sodium, 140 mg cholesterol
CALORIES FROM FAT: 25.3%

WHAT'S IN IT FOR ME?

Waiter: A man who believes that money grows on trays.

Starvin' Guy Chicken Pie

Our version of the hungry man dinner is a chicken pot pie that's so jammed with hearty goodness, you might have to solicit the help of a few family members to stuff it into the oven! Topped off with an innovative biscuit crust, this one's sure to please the whole clan!

1 cup chopped onions
1 clove garlic, minced
1 cup low-sodium, reduced-fat chicken broth
1-1/2 cups peeled, cubed potatoes
1-1/2 cups chopped carrots
1 cup sliced green beans (cut into 1-inch pieces)
1 can (10-3/4 ounces) reduced-fat Cream of Mushroom Soup
   (Campbell's Healthy Request), undiluted
1-1/2 tablespoons all-purpose flour
2 cups chopped cooked chicken breast (about 3/4 of a pound)
2 tablespoons chopped fresh parsley
1/2 teaspoon *each* dried basil and ground thyme
1/4 teaspoon black pepper

Biscuit Crust
1 cup all-purpose flour
2 teaspoons baking powder
1/2 teaspoon ground sage
1/4 teaspoon salt
2 tablespoons butter or margarine
1/3 cup skim milk

Spray a large saucepan with non-stick spray. Add onions and garlic. Cook over medium heat until tender, about 5 minutes. Add broth, potatoes, carrots, and beans. Bring to a boil. Reduce heat to medium-low. Partially cover and simmer for 12 minutes. The potatoes should be slightly undercooked. Remove from heat.

In a small bowl, stir together mushroom soup and flour. Add to vegetables, along with chicken, parsley, basil, thyme, and pepper. Stir well. Pour into a medium casserole dish.

To prepare crust, combine flour, baking powder, sage, and salt in a large bowl. Using a pastry blender, cut in butter or margarine until mixture resembles coarse crumbs. Stir in milk. Form a ball with the dough. Add a bit more flour if dough is too sticky. Roll out on a floured surface to fit top of casserole. Place dough over chicken mixture. Prick several times with a fork. Bake at 400° for 25 minutes, until crust is golden brown. Let cool for 5 minutes before serving.

Makes 4 servings.

PER SERVING: 355 calories, 11.2 g fat, 34.4 g carbohydrate, 29.6 g protein, 918 mg sodium, 85 mg cholesterol
CALORIES FROM FAT: 28.2 %

WHAT'S IN IT FOR ME?

Show & Tell

Why is a chicken leg "dark meat" and a chicken breast "white meat"? Well, meat is actually muscle, and the muscle requirements of the chicken leg and breast are different. The more active the muscle, the more oxygen it stores from the blood, and this makes it darker than meat from muscles that are not used as frequently. Chickens use their legs quite often, roaming around the barnyard looking for insects and other food, and that makes their leg meat dark. But they hardly use their wings except for balance, which is why the breast meat is so pale. By the way, dark meat is higher in fat and calories than white meat.

Gotta *MOVE* It!

Flab-u-less Recipe for Fitness and Good Health (this *is* a cookbook, after all):

1. Combine large muscle groups into an active unit.
2. Stir in a variety of enjoyable activities. Mix them up.
3. Blend moderately and continuously for at least 30 minutes. (Caution: Extending the time to 45 minutes to one hour may result in severe burning—*of fat!*)
4. Store leftover energy for use the next day, as process should be repeated at least 3 times a week, preferably 4 or 5.

Flab-u-less Fajitas

"Liar, liar, pan's on fire!" That's probably what you'd say if we told you that these fajitas have only a fraction of the fat and double the flavor of regular fajitas. But it's really true! Cross our hearts, hope to die, great fajitas—that's no lie!!

Guacamole

1/2 medium avocado
1-1/2 teaspoons lime juice
1 clove garlic, minced
2 tablespoons finely chopped seeded tomatoes
1 tablespoon minced onions

4 boneless, skinless chicken breast halves,
   cut into 1/2-inch wide strips
1 tablespoon fajita seasoning
1 large red bell pepper, seeded and cut
   into 1/2-inch wide strips
1 large green bell pepper, seeded and
   cut into 1/2-inch wide strips
1 medium zucchini, cut in half crosswise,
   each half cut into 4 wedges
1 large onion, cut into thick rings
1 tablespoon *each* lime juice and chopped
   fresh cilantro
8 7-inch flour tortillas
1/2 cup salsa
1/2 cup low-fat sour cream
1 cup shredded lettuce

To prepare guacamole, scoop out the flesh from the avocado. Place in a small bowl along with lime juice and mash with a fork. Stir in garlic, tomatoes, and onions. Cover and refrigerate until ready to use.

Spray a large skillet or wok with non-stick spray. Place over medium-high heat. Add chicken and cook, stirring often, until lightly browned. Sprinkle with fajita seasoning. Stir until chicken is evenly coated with seasoning. Remove from skillet and keep warm.

To same skillet, add peppers, zucchini, onions, and 1/4 cup water or chicken broth. Cook and stir until vegetables are tender-crisp, about 8-10 minutes. Stir in lime juice and cilantro, then transfer to serving dish.

Ten minutes before serving time, wrap tortillas in aluminum foil and place in 350° oven to warm.

To serve, spread 1 teaspoon guacamole in center of tortilla. Top with 1/8 of the chicken, 1/8 of the vegetables, 1 tablespoon salsa, 1 tablespoon sour cream, and 1/8 of the lettuce. Roll up tortilla to enclose filling. Repeat with remaining tortillas and filling.

Makes 4 servings.

PER SERVING: 461 calories, 12.1 g fat,
53.9 g carbohydrate, 41.8 g protein,
630 mg sodium, 89 mg cholesterol
CALORIES FROM FAT: 22.1 %

WHAT'S IN IT FOR ME?

COOKING 101

It's easier to thinly slice uncooked boneless chicken breasts if they're partially frozen. Thaw frozen breasts slightly in the refrigerator or, if fresh, place breasts in the freezer for about 45 minutes before slicing.

Sizzling Rivalry

It's the hottest ticket in town! Potatoes vs. chicken in a battle to clinch top flavor honors in a skillet already overcrowded with delicious contenders. Non-stop sizzlin' action!

**4 medium red potatoes,
 unpeeled, cut into cubes**
**1 pound boneless, skinless
 chicken or turkey breasts,
 cut into 1-inch cubes**
1 tablespoon vegetable oil
**1 cup *each* whole kernel corn
 and canned black beans (drain and
 rinse the beans)**
3/4 cup chopped green onions
1-1/2 cups salsa (mild, medium, or hot)
1/4 cup chopped fresh cilantro

Steam the cubed potatoes until tender, about 15 minutes. (Alternatively, cook them in the microwave with a small amount of water, covered with plastic wrap, for about 10 minutes.)

While potatoes are cooking, spray a wide non-stick skillet or wok with non-stick spray. Add chicken and cook over high heat until no longer pink, about 5 minutes. Continue to cook until chicken is lightly browned. Remove chicken from skillet. Add vegetable oil and steamed potatoes to same skillet. Cook until potatoes are lightly browned, stirring often.

Stir in cooked chicken, corn, beans, onions, and salsa. Reduce heat to medium and cook until heated through, 4-5 minutes. Stir in cilantro. Remove from heat and serve immediately.

Makes 4 servings.

WHAT'S IN IT FOR ME? ➡ PER SERVING: 510 calories, 6.5 g fat, 78.9 g carbohydrate, 35.5 g protein, 718 mg sodium, 64 mg cholesterol CALORIES FROM FAT: 11.4%

After dieting for a while, you get obsessed with the idea of eating. For instance, we're sitting here with our drumsticks crossed, but what we really have our minds on is food.

SAY IT AIN'T SO!

A triple cheeseburger from a "classic" leading fast food franchise is absolutely choking with 68 grams of fat and 1040 calories. It's bad enough that one patty has a day's worth of fat, but they actually endorse a "three-tiered burger" that packs in a thigh-enlarging, gut-enhancing 59% of calories from fat! Look for the healthier alternatives that they do cook up, like grilled chicken sandwiches without mayo, and feel free to splurge at the salad bar (but beware of the fatty salad dressings, croutons, and cheese toppings).

Show & Tell

Cilantro is also known as coriander or Chinese parsley. Popular in the cuisines of Africa, Asia, India, and Latin America for some time, its widespread use in North American kitchens is relatively new. Try using it sparingly at first—its unique flavor is somewhat of an acquired taste, but once it's acquired, you may become addicted! It looks similar to parsley and is usually found right beside parsley at the supermarket.

COOKING 101

Whole bulbs of garlic can be stored for up to 2 months in a cool, dark place, and keep for about 1 week once the individual cloves have been separated from the bulb. Try to use them within a month, however, because they tend to dry out. To peel garlic cloves quickly, trim off the ends and crush the cloves with the bottom of a heavy saucepan or the flat side of a large knife. The peels should slide right off.

Gotta MOVE It!

Like the booster shots your school nurse gave you as a kid, exercise can be considered another form of "immunization" against illness and disease. Studies show that moderate and consistent exercise, such as walking for a minimum of 30 minutes a day at least four or five days a week, protects us against cardiovascular disease, high blood pressure, depression, and anxiety. It reduces body fat and the risk of diabetes and colon cancer, boosts immune system functioning, and increases bone mass. Your school nurse would have needed to use a Mighty Mammoth-Sized Hypodermic Needle to rival the enormous health benefits derived from exercise.

The only exercise some people get is jumping to conclusions, running down their friends, side-stepping responsibility, and pushing their luck.

ʃ Chicken Catcha Tory

In this recipe title, **Tory** could refer to (a) a member of the British Conservative Party, (b) a certain "Tory" of the **Beverly Hills 90210** gang (okay, okay, we know our **Spelling** is wrong—it's "Tori"), or (c) a spectacular low-fat version of a popular chicken entrée. Choose "c" and enjoy!

4 boneless, skinless chicken
   breast halves, cut into
   1-inch cubes
1 cup *each* **chopped**
   onions and chopped
   green bell pepper
3 cups sliced
   mushrooms
1 can (14-1/2 ounces) tomatoes,
   undrained, cut up
1 cup tomato sauce
1 can (6 ounces)
   tomato paste
1/2 cup dry white wine
1-1/2 teaspoons *each*
   dried basil and dried
   oregano
2 cloves garlic, minced
1/2 teaspoon salt
1/4 teaspoon black pepper
12 ounces uncooked spaghetti or linguini

Preheat oven to 350°.

Combine all ingredients in a large bowl and mix well. Transfer mixture to a small roasting pan or large casserole dish. Cover and bake for 1 hour, until chicken is very tender.

Ten minutes before cooking time has ended, prepare pasta according to package directions. Serve chicken and sauce over hot pasta.

Makes 4 servings.

Hint: To reduce the sodium content of this recipe, use no-salt-added tomatoes and low-sodium tomato sauce.

PER SERVING: 604 calories, 5.7 g fat, 84.4 g carbohydrate, 47.8 g protein, 1066 mg sodium, 88 mg cholesterol
CALORIES FROM FAT: 8.6%

WHAT'S IN IT FOR ME?

A Curried Affair

Extra! Extra! Read all about it! Enticing curried chicken creation takes culinary world by storm! A true epicurean event in the making! You read it here first!

1 tablespoon reduced-fat butter or margarine (not fat-free)
1 cup *each* **chopped onions and chopped celery**
1-1/2 teaspoons curry powder
2 cans (10-3/4 ounces each) reduced-fat Cream of Mushroom Soup (Campbell's Healthy Request), undiluted
3 cups chopped cooked chicken breast (about 1-1/4 pounds)
1-1/2 cups canned pineapple tidbits and their juice
1 tablespoon low-sodium chicken bouillon powder
1/2 teaspoon ground cumin
1/4 teaspoon *each* **crushed red pepper flakes and black pepper**
3 cups cooked white or brown rice

Preheat oven to 350°.

Melt butter in a large non-stick saucepan over medium heat. Add onions, celery, and curry powder. Cook and stir for 2-3 minutes, until onions begin to soften.

Stir in undiluted soup, chicken, pineapple (with juice), bouillon powder, cumin, black pepper, and red pepper flakes. Mix well.

Transfer mixture to a medium casserole dish. Cover and bake for 30 minutes. Serve over hot rice.

Makes 4 servings.

WHAT'S IN IT FOR ME? ➔ PER SERVING: 459 calories, 8.1 g fat, 61.3 g carbohydrate, 32.6 g protein, 718 mg sodium, 82 mg cholesterol
CALORIES FROM FAT: 16.3%

SAY IT AIN'T SO!

No need to feel like a coward if you "chicken out" of All-You-Can-Eat Wing Night at your favorite restaurant, because wings are flying high with fat-laden calories! Just five chicken wings (and who eats just five?) contain 33 grams of fat, 500 calories, and 59% calories from fat. Up to two-thirds of the fat comes from the skin. Will removing the skin help trim the fat content? Yup, but you'll just end up with Chicken Little.

Slim Pickin's

You'd have to oink out on
37 CUPS OF FRESH PINEAPPLE
to consume the
26 GRAMS OF FAT
found in a mere
1/2 CUP OF PEANUT BUTTER CHOCOLATE ICE CREAM.
Which would fill you up more?

Go for quality *and* quantity!

Trivial Tidbit

Airline food doesn't deserve the bad rap it's been getting. The fact is, taste buds are actually dulled by high altitude and cabin pressure, so as the plane goes up, our sense of taste goes down.

Show & Tell

The dark meat of a turkey is higher in fat than the white meat. But turkey is actually slightly lower in calories, total fat, and cholesterol than the other favorite sources of meat protein: chicken, beef, and pork. So go ahead and gobble it up guilt-free.

Show me the WEIGH

Whoa, big eater! That bag of cookies may be labelled "fat-free," but that doesn't mean you should shovel down the entire package in one sitting! A common misconception about low-fat eating is that it gives you free reign to devour unlimited amounts of carbohydrates and proteins, eating with reckless abandon because these are the "good" foods. But can you get too much of a good thing? The truth is, low-fat foods still provide calories, and if you consume more calories than you burn off through activity, these excess calories will be stored as fat. Simple, isn't it? Yes, it's true that the amount of fat we eat often plays a larger role in affecting our weight than the number of calories we consume. Fat is the most easily stored food source and the most concentrated source of calories (9 calories per gram versus 4 calories per gram for carbohydrates and protein). Although it's much harder to overeat complex carbohydrates because they're so filling, that doesn't seem to stop some people from trying! Let's clear this up right here and now. A label reading "fat-free" or "reduced fat" is *not* a license to pig out. Eat enough to satisfy your hunger and then move on. Once again, moderation and common sense are key ingredients in developing and maintaining a healthy, fit body.

I served turkey for dinner and my guests were tickled. I forgot to take off the feathers.

8-Hour Turkey Stew (What a Crock!)

Step 1: Dig through basement and find that crockpot you received as a wedding gift but have never used. Step 2: Prepare turkey stew as directed. Step 3: Eat it. Step 4: Like it. Step 5: Find space in kitchen cupboards for your suddenly favorite cooking appliance. Step 6: Repeat steps 2 to 4 over and over again.

3 cups peeled, cubed potatoes
2 cups quartered mushrooms
1-1/2 cups chopped carrots
1 cup coarsely chopped onions
2 cloves garlic, minced
1 teaspoon *each* ground thyme and dried basil
1/2 teaspoon black pepper
2 pounds boneless, skinless turkey breast, cut into 1-inch cubes
2 tablespoons all-purpose flour
1/2 cup dry white wine
1/2 cup low-sodium, reduced-fat chicken broth
1-1/2 tablespoons tomato paste
1 teaspoon "lite" Worcestershire sauce
1/4 cup chopped fresh parsley

Combine first 8 ingredients in a 3-quart or larger slow cooker.

Pat turkey cubes dry and coat with flour. Arrange over top of vegetables.

Mix wine, broth, tomato paste, and Worcestershire sauce in a small bowl. Pour over turkey.

Cover and cook on low setting for approximately 8 hours. During last hour of cooking, stir once or twice, breaking apart any turkey cubes that have stuck together. Be careful not to remove lid for more than a minute or so, as lots of heat will escape. Stir in parsley just before serving.

Makes 6 servings.

PER SERVING: 384 calories, 4.4 g fat, 24.8 g carbohydrate, 57 g protein, 182 mg sodium, 136 mg cholesterol
CALORIES FROM FAT: 10.5 %

WHAT'S IN IT FOR ME?

Always a Dill Moment

But never dull. How can dill be dull? Impossible! In fact, dill makes this fish a *dill*ectable dish!

1/2 cup low-fat sour cream
2 teaspoons prepared horseradish
Juice of 1/2 a lemon
1/2 teaspoon dried dill weed
1/4 teaspoon black pepper
1/2 cup unseasoned dry bread crumbs
2 tablespoons grated Parmesan cheese
3/4 teaspoon dried oregano
1/4 teaspoon paprika
4 fish steaks or fillets, 1/2 to 1 inch thick
  (try halibut, salmon, cod, or haddock)
1/4 cup buttermilk

Preheat oven to 425°.

To prepare dill sauce, combine sour cream, horseradish, lemon juice, dill weed, and pepper in a small bowl. Cover and refrigerate until ready to serve.

To prepare crumb coating, mix bread crumbs, cheese, oregano, and paprika in a small bowl. Spread mixture evenly on a dinner-size plate.

Rinse the fish and pat dry. Dip the fish in buttermilk and then in crumb coating (both sides).

Place fish in shallow baking pan sprayed with non-stick spray. Cook according to thickness of fish, 10 minutes per 1 inch of thickness. Fish should be browned on outside but moist and slightly opaque in thickest part. Remove from pan and spoon dill sauce over top.

Makes 4 servings.

Hint: You'll get more juice out of a lemon by microwaving it on high power for 30 seconds before squeezing it.

WHAT'S IN IT FOR ME? → PER SERVING: 235 calories, 4.1 g fat, 14.5 g carbohydrate, 34 g protein, 326 mg sodium, 76 mg cholesterol CALORIES FROM FAT: 16%

If you choose to eat a measly **1 TABLESPOON OF MAYONNAISE**, you'll be choosing a whopping **11 GRAMS OF FAT**, the equivalent of eating **157 CUPS OF RASPBERRIES**. Which would fill you up more?

Go for quality *and* quantity!

Show & Tell

Most fish fats and oils are higher in unsaturated fatty acids than the fat in beef, pork, or lamb. The exact proportion of fat and saturated fatty acids varies with the kind of fish as well as when and where it is caught. For example, fat content usually decreases in relation to the depth of a fish's living environment. Bottom-dwelling fish like sole and cod are usually leaner than those that dwell near the surface, like tuna or herring. And any given fish will be leaner after it has spawned or experienced a food shortage. In addition, the most important nutrient in fish, the healthful, cholesterol-lowering Omega-3 fatty acids, are most prevalent in oils from fatty fish that live in cold water—herring, mackerel, and salmon. These oils stay liquid at cold temperatures, and may help insulate the fish against the cold.

HOW'S THE FOOD?

I COULD GET MORE NOURISHMENT BITING MY LIP

COOKING 101

Something smell fishy? When preparing fresh fish, rub the fish with lemon juice, then rinse it under cold running water. Since lemon juice is an acid, it will convert the nitrogen compounds that make fish smell "fishy" to compounds that break apart and can be rinsed off the fish with cool running water. Rinsing your hands in lemon juice and water will get rid of the fishy smell after you've been preparing fresh fish. Caution: Be wary of fresh fish that has a strong or foul-smelling odor. This is a sure sign that the fish has been sitting around for too long.

SAY IT AIN'T SO!

Olive Oyl a narcissist? Heck no! She may have cut a sleek and svelte figure next to her muscular Sailor Man, but she probably didn't get that way by actually pigging out on olives. Ten green Manzanilla olives have only 50 calories, but they pack in a staggering 77% of calories from fat (5 grams)! Wasn't it Olive Oyl who said, "I eats me spinach and that's why I've got buns of steel"?

WHAT ARE WE HAVING FOR DESSERT TONIGHT DEAR?

SPONGE CAKE. I SPONGED THE FLOUR FROM MRS BROWN, THE EGGS FROM MRS JONES, AND THE MILK FROM MRS SMITH

Sweet & Sour Fish Dish

It was fishful thinking that led us to create an unforgettable fish dish that's both sweet and sour. No need to fish for compliments when you make this one—those who eat it will praise the fact that it's both delectable and gillt-free!

SWEET
SOUR

1 pound monkfish, shark, or tuna steaks or fillets, cut into 1-inch cubes
2 teaspoons vegetable oil
1 teaspoon grated ginger root
1 clove garlic, minced
3 cups broccoli florets
1 cup sliced red bell pepper
1-1/2 cups canned pineapple chunks in juice
2 tablespoons *each* **brown sugar, ketchup, reduced-sodium soy sauce, and orange juice**
1-1/2 tablespoons *each* **white vinegar and cornstarch**
3 cups cooked white or brown rice

Spread fish in a single layer in a microwave-safe dish. Cook on high power for 2 minutes. Gently stir fish, then cook another 2 minutes, until fish is opaque. Drain off liquid and set aside.

Heat oil in a large saucepan over medium heat. Add ginger root and garlic. Cook for 1 minute. Add broccoli and red pepper. Cook and stir until vegetables are tender-crisp, about 5-6 minutes.

Drain pineapple, reserving 1/2 cup juice. Set pineapple aside. To reserved juice add brown sugar, ketchup, soy sauce, orange juice, vinegar, and cornstarch. Stir until smooth. Add to pan with vegetables. Cook until sauce is thick and bubbly, about 2 minutes. Add fish and pineapple chunks. Cook for 2 more minutes, until completely heated through.

Serve over hot, cooked rice.

Makes 4 servings.

Hint: Make sure you select a firm fish for this recipe, otherwise the fish will fall apart when you're stirring it.

PER SERVING: 367 calories, 5.5 g fat, 60.9 g carbohydrate, 21 g protein, 456 mg sodium, 28 mg cholesterol
CALORIES FROM FAT: 13.2%

WHAT'S IN IT FOR ME?

Pita the Great

Can't decide what to serve the Russian emperor for lunch? (He's so fussy!) Rumor has it that tuna-packed pita pockets czar his favorite!

2 cans (6 ounces each)
   water-packed tuna,
   drained and flaked
1/2 cup diced red bell pepper
2 tablespoons chopped fresh
   cilantro
1 tablespoon *each* honey, lime
   juice, and low-fat mayonnaise
1/2 teaspoon black pepper
4-5 drops hot pepper sauce
1/4 teaspoon *each* ground cumin
   and salt
2 6-inch pitas, each cut in half
1 cup thinly sliced, unpeeled
   English cucumber
2 cups alfalfa sprouts (unpacked)

Combine first 10 ingredients in a medium bowl. Mix well. Open pita pockets and line each with 1/4 of the cucumber slices and 1/4 of the alfalfa sprouts. Fill each pocket with 1/4 of the tuna mixture.

Makes 4 stuffed pita pockets.

WHAT'S IN IT FOR ME? ➡ PER SERVING: 217 calories, 1.8 g fat, 22.1 g carbohydrate, 28.5 g protein, 626 mg sodium, 15 mg cholesterol CALORIES FROM FAT: 7.2%

You know you're over-weight when you're living beyond your seams.

Show & Tell

Tune in to tuna! While a can of tuna packed in oil weighs in at approximately 15 grams of fat, a can of water-packed tuna contains roughly 220 calories and a mere .8 grams of fat—not to mention a healthy supply of protein, iron, phosphorous, iodine, and vitamins A, B, and D! Albacore, Bigeye, Bluefin, Skipjack, and Yellowfin are five of the most popular species in North America (there are 13 species in total).

D. I. E. T.

is a four-letter word that really means...
DESPERATELY IMPOSSIBLE EATING TARGETS

Fad diets that call for unbelievably low daily caloric intake are impossible to sustain and often do more harm than good. And diets with catchy-sounding names often lure the gullible and the desperate into absurd, unrealistic eating programs that don't provide the nutrients or the variety to keep them going. Ever-hoping, dieters over the years have confined themselves to the likes of The Grapefruit Diet, The Popcorn Diet, The Hollywood Pineapple Diet, The Peanut Butter and Banana Diet, and The Cider Vinegar Diet, just to name a few. While these restrictive eating plans may have produced the immediate results that dieters were striving for, you can bet that these results were temporary and unhealthy (rapid weight loss usually means loss of lean muscle tissue and water). Why choose to live in "diet desperation" when you can simply eat sensibly when you're hungry? Choosing a variety of nutritious, low-fat foods is a realistic and healthy way to lose weight slowly and to stay slim for years to come.

Slim Pickin's

You'd have to oink out on
15 CANS OF WATER-PACKED TUNA
to consume the
12 GRAMS OF FAT
found in a paltry
3 SLICES OF BACON.
Which would fill you up more?

Go for quality *and* quantity!

Gotta MOVE It!

Do you look forward to exercise with the same air of expectation and excitement that is typically reserved for a dental appointment? Does the mere thought of the word "exercise" cause beads of sweat to drip from the end of your nose?

You most likely feel this way because you really don't enjoy the activities that you've chosen as exercise. Remember, the best aerobic activity is the one you enjoy doing. Try putting in 30-45 minutes of enjoyable activities four or five days a week. Walking, biking, gardening, dancing, washing the car, and playing with the kids all qualify. Choose activities that you think are fun and you'll probably stick with them.

There must be a destiny to shape our ends, but our middles are of our own chewsing.

Scalloping Gourmet

Don't let the number of ingredients in this super-savory one-dish wonder scare you off. The combination of spices is what gives this meal a triple thumbs-up (friend needed to do this stunt!).

- 1 cup *each* chopped onions, chopped celery, and chopped green bell pepper
- 2 cloves garlic, minced
- 2-1/2 cups low-sodium, reduced-fat chicken broth
- 1 can (14-1/2 ounces) tomatoes, undrained, cut up
- 1 tablespoon tomato paste
- 1 teaspoon *each* chili powder, ground cumin, ground thyme, and dried basil
- 1/4 teaspoon *each* salt, black pepper, and crushed red pepper flakes (add a bit more red pepper if you like it hot!)
- 1-1/4 cups uncooked long grain white rice
- 1/4 cup chopped fresh parsley
- 3/4 pound bay scallops

Combine onions, celery, green pepper, garlic, and 1/4 cup of the chicken broth in a large saucepan. Sauté vegetables over medium-high heat for about 5 minutes, until softened.

Add remaining chicken broth, tomatoes, tomato paste, chili powder, cumin, thyme, basil, salt, black pepper, and crushed red pepper flakes. Bring to a boil. Stir in rice. Reduce heat to low. Cover and simmer for 20 minutes or until rice is almost tender, stirring occasionally.

Add parsley and scallops. Cover and cook an additional 5-6 minutes, until scallops are tender and opaque. Stir well before serving.

Makes 4 servings.

Hint: This dish tastes just as great with shrimp or cooked chicken in place of the scallops. To reduce the sodium content, use no-salt-added tomatoes and omit the salt or use a salt substitute.

PER SERVING: 407 calories, 4.6 g fat, 64.3 g carbohydrate, 25.5 g protein, 907 mg sodium, 33 mg cholesterol
CALORIES FROM FAT: 10.4%

WHAT'S IN IT FOR ME?

I'm a Sole Man

Or is the proper term "sole person"? For the politically correct and the politically incorrect too, here's a soleful creation that's lavishly presented on a bed of delicious, herb-coated vegetables.

1-1/2 cups sliced zucchini
   (cut about 1/4 inch thick)
1-1/2 cups chopped tomato
1 cup *each* chopped green and
   red bell pepper
1/2 cup coarsely chopped onions
1 teaspoon olive oil
3/4 teaspoon *each* dried oregano
   and dried basil
1/4 teaspoon black pepper
1 pound sole fillets
Salt and pepper (to taste)
Juice of 1/2 a lemon

Preheat oven to 425°.

Combine zucchini, tomatoes, green and red pepper, onions, olive oil, oregano, basil, and black pepper in a large bowl. Stir to distribute seasonings evenly. Transfer to a 13 x 9-inch baking dish that has been sprayed with non-stick spray. Bake, uncovered, for 35 minutes.

Remove baking dish from oven and layer fish fillets over vegetables. Sprinkle fish lightly with salt and pepper. Squeeze lemon juice over fish. Return to oven. Bake an additional 5-7 minutes, until fish turns opaque and flakes easily. Remove from oven and serve immediately.

Makes 4 servings.

WHAT'S IN IT FOR ME? ➡ PER SERVING: 156 calories, 2.8 g fat, 10.4 g carbohydrate, 23.1 g protein, 101 mg sodium, 52 mg cholesterol CALORIES FROM FAT: 15.9%

SAY IT AIN'T SO!

Fish is usually a healthy choice for a dinner entrée, but when you opt for fish and chips you're opening up a whole new can of worms. Two pieces of fish deep-fried in batter along with fries has a cod-awful amount of fat! Forty to 50 grams is common at most fish houses. Feeling a little gillty?

Show & Tell

Those on low-sodium diets needn't worry about eating fish. It's actually quite low in sodium, with a 3-ounce serving containing only 100 milligrams (experts recommend that we consume no more than 2400 milligrams of sodium per day). You'd think that saltwater fish would have a higher sodium content than freshwater fish, but that isn't the case. Saltwater fish aren't any saltier than freshwater fish because their physiology prevents them from becoming as salty as the water they inhabit.

My grandmother started walking five miles a day when she was sixty-five. Today she's ninety and we don't know where the heck she is.

I SHOULD'VE TAKEN THAT RIGHT TURN AT ALBUQUERQUE

Anchors A-weigh Seafood Lasagna

This super-creamy, rich-tasting lasagna is a seafood lover's dream that *won't* weigh you down. Go on! Sea for yourself!

9 whole-wheat lasagna noodles
1 cup trimmed and halved snow peas
1 cup thinly sliced red bell pepper
1-1/2 cups part-skim ricotta cheese
1/4 cup grated Parmesan cheese
1 egg white
1 tablespoon butter
2 cloves garlic, minced
1/4 cup plus 1 tablespoon all-purpose flour
2-1/2 cups skim milk
2 teaspoons low-sodium chicken bouillon
   powder
1/2 teaspoon *each* dry mustard and black
   pepper
1/4 teaspoon salt
3/4 pound bay scallops
3/4 pound lump crabmeat, chopped or broken
   into bite-sized pieces
3/4 cup shredded reduced-fat sharp cheddar
   cheese (3 ounces)
1/4 cup chopped fresh parsley

Prepare lasagna noodles according to package directions. Drain. Rinse with cold water and drain again. Set aside.

Place snow peas and red pepper in a microwave-safe dish with 1/4 cup water. Cook on high power for 3 minutes. Drain vegetables and set aside.

In a medium bowl, mix together ricotta cheese, Parmesan cheese, and egg white. Set aside.

To prepare sauce, melt butter in a large saucepan over medium heat. Add garlic. Cook for 1 minute. Mix the flour and milk together until smooth. Add to garlic. Increase heat to medium-high. Stir using a whisk. Cook until mixture is thickened and bubbly, about 6-7 minutes.

Stir in bouillon powder, dry mustard, pepper, and salt. Add scallops. Cook until scallops are opaque, about 5 minutes. Stir in crabmeat, 1/2 cup cheese, parsley, snow peas, and red pepper. Cook for 1 more minute, until cheese is completely melted. Remove sauce from heat.

Spray a 13 x 9-inch baking dish with non-stick spray. To assemble lasagna, cover bottom of baking dish with 3 noodles. Pour 1/3 sauce over top. Layer 3 more noodles over sauce. Spread all of the ricotta/Parmesan mixture over noodles, followed by 1/3 sauce. Top with 3 more noodles and remaining sauce. Sprinkle remaining 1/4 cup cheese over top.

Cover and bake at 350° for 40 minutes. Let stand for 5 minutes before serving.

Makes 6-8 servings.

PER SERVING (based on 8 servings):
345 calories, 9.9 g fat,
38.6 g carbohydrate, 31.1 g protein,
744 mg sodium, 53 mg cholesterol
CALORIES FROM FAT: 24.3%

*H*ave you ever really noticed what the first three letters of the word "diet" spell?

Happily Marri-nated Salmon Steaks

Dearly beloved, we are gathered here at the dinner table to joyfully unite deliciously herbed salmon steaks with eagerly anticipating taste buds. Be sure to say "I do" when asked "Who wants a second helping?" Eat now, or forever cold your piece.

4 salmon steaks or fillets,
   (5-6 ounces each)
1/2 cup lemon juice
1/4 cup chopped fresh dill
2 cloves garlic, minced
2 teaspoons sugar
1/2 teaspoon paprika
1/4 teaspoon *each* salt and black pepper

Arrange salmon over bottom of a 13 x 9-inch baking dish. Combine remaining ingredients in a small bowl and pour over salmon. Turn salmon to coat with marinade. Cover and refrigerate for 30 minutes.

Meanwhile, preheat oven to 425°. Drain off excess marinade from salmon. Bake for 10-12 minutes, depending on thickness of fish. Fish will flake easily and be opaque in center.

Makes 4 servings.

WHAT'S IN IT FOR ME? ➡ PER SERVING: 255 calories, 7.9 g fat, 5.4 g carbohydrate, 40.6 g protein, 235 mg sodium, 149 mg cholesterol CALORIES FROM FAT: 27.9%

Show & Tell

In order to make salmon look acceptably pink, beta-carotene is added during the canning process. This is actually a healthful addition—beta-carotene is a powerful antioxidant that plays a role in strengthening the immune system and in fighting off a wide range of diseases. Incidently, if you drink a lot of alcohol, you'll reduce the healthful effects of beta-carotene. You booze, you lose!

Gotta MOVE It!

With more and more conveniences in our everyday lives, we're doing less and less manual work. From elevators and garage door openers to remote control and drive-through windows, technological advances are driving us towards a future where saving time and energy is of paramount importance. But we'd better be careful that technology's conveniences don't end up detouring us down Lipid Lane on a direct route to Cellulite City! It's in your body's best interest that you throw technology out the window at least a few times a week, and just get up and MOVE! Take the stairs, walk to the grocery store, use a push lawnmower, use a shovel instead of a snowblower. Exercise contributes to overall health in many more ways than technology ever will. It's physical activity that will steer you clear of Cellulite City.

COOKING 101

To keep fresh herbs longer in the refrigerator, try treating them like a bouquet of flowers. Immerse the stems of dill, parsley, cilantro, or basil in a jar containing 2-3 inches of water. Cover the "bouquet" loosely with a plastic bag. This way, the herbs will stay fresh for several days.

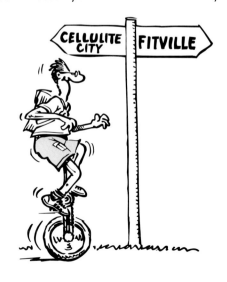

Canned pink salmon contains soft bones which are rich in calcium, and these should not be removed before eating. Remove any large, hard bones, then mash the small bones with a fork. By the way, pink salmon is a good source of Omega-3 fatty acids, which experts believe have a positive effect in reducing the risk of blood clots and reducing blood pressure.

Show me the WEIGH

When you try fasting (starving, that is), what you're really doing is slowing (your metabolism, that is). When you eat under 1000 calories in a day, your body believes that starvation is occurring, and accommodates by 1) slowing down its metabolic rate; 2) craving high-calorie, high-fat foods (must have barbeque chips!); and 3) efficiently storing the fuel that will last the longest during the great famine: FAT! So if you don't want fasting to slow the progress you've been making towards a fit and healthy body, try eating low-fat, nutrition-loaded food instead.

He's been eating so much fish, he's breathing through his cheeks.

Salmon Spy Rolls

I spy with my little eye... savory salmon that is elegantly rolled in a delicious dough to create sophisticated spirals. Perfect for fancier fare!

Filling
2 cans (7-1/2 ounces each) skinless, water-packed pink salmon, drained
1/2 cup *each* grated carrot, finely chopped celery, and chopped green onions
2 tablespoons *each* lemon juice and low-fat sour cream
1 tablespoon white wine vinegar
1/2 teaspoon dry mustard
1/4 teaspoon black pepper

Dough
2 cups all-purpose flour
1 tablespoon baking powder
1/2 teaspoon salt
1/4 teaspoon cayenne pepper
2 tablespoons canola oil
7 ounces skim milk (roughly)

Combine salmon, carrots, celery, and green onions in a medium bowl. In a small bowl, combine lemon juice, sour cream, vinegar, mustard, and pepper. Stir until smooth. Add sour cream mixture to salmon mixture. Mix well. Set aside.

In a large bowl, sift together flour, baking powder, salt, and cayenne pepper. Set aside.

Add canola oil to a measuring cup. Add enough skim milk to oil to make 1 cup. Blend well. Add liquid to dry ingredients. Mix until a ball forms. Knead on a lightly floured surface 10 times. Roll out dough into a 12-inch square (or as close as you can get to a square!) Make sure rolling surface is sprinkled with enough flour to prevent sticking.

Spread salmon mixture over dough to within 1/4 inch of edges. Roll up like a jelly roll. Pinch seams to seal. Using sharp knife, cut into 10 slices.

Spray a large baking sheet with non-stick spray. Place salmon spirals on baking sheet without overlapping. Bake at 400° for 20 minutes, or until golden brown. Best if served immediately.

Makes 10 salmon spirals.

PER SPIRAL: 167 calories, 4.7 g fat, 20.5 g carbohydrate, 10.8 g protein, 467 mg sodium, 23 mg cholesterol
CALORIES FROM FAT: 25.2%

WHAT'S IN IT FOR ME?

Steak It Up, Baby

Twist and trout! Hey, these are *TUNA* steaks, not trout steaks. Darn! Trout fit in so nicely with the song. Oh well. These grilled tuna steaks with a delicious "twist o' chili and lime" marinade are a really tasty alternative for the barbeque-aholic.

YA KNOW YA GOT ME GOIN' BABY ♪♪

4 tuna steaks, about 6 ounces each and 1 inch thick
2 tablespoons *each* lime juice, reduced-sodium soy sauce, honey, and tomato-based chili sauce
2 teaspoons olive oil
1/2 teaspoon cornstarch

Rinse tuna steaks and pat dry. Arrange tuna in a 13 x 9-inch baking dish. Mix lime juice, soy sauce, honey, chili sauce, and olive oil in a small bowl. Pour over tuna. Turn fish to coat with marinade. Cover and refrigerate for 1-2 hours.

Prepare grill (medium-high setting). Remove tuna from marinade. Pour remaining marinade into a small saucepan and set aside. Cook tuna over hot coals for 4-5 minutes on each side. Fish should be lightly browned on outside and pale pink in thickest part. Remove from heat.

Bring reserved marinade to a boil over medium-high heat. Mix cornstarch with 2 tablespoons water until smooth. Add to marinade. Cook and stir until sauce thickens, about 1 minute. Spoon sauce over tuna steaks and serve immediately.

Makes 4 servings.

As long as it isn't overcooked, tuna is a tender and moist fish that's great for broiling, baking, and grilling. You could substitute other types of fish steaks, such as halibut or shark, for the tuna in this recipe. Too cold for a barbeque in the winter? No problem. Bake the tuna for 10-12 minutes in a preheated 425° oven.

Slim Pickin's

You'd have to oink out on
500 BOILED SHRIMP
to consume the
25 GRAMS OF FAT
found in
1 SAUSAGE EGG McMUFFIN.
Which would fill you up more?

Go for quality *and* quantity!

WHAT'S IN IT FOR ME? ➡

PER SERVING: 248 calories, 4.4 g fat, 11.8 g carbohydrate, 40.1 g protein, 474 mg sodium, 75 mg cholesterol
CALORIES FROM FAT: 15.9%

A poet's favorite food is rhyme bread.

ROSES ARE RED, VIOLETS ARE BLUE, I LOVE RYE BREAD AND SOURDOUGH, TOO

Hips Ahoy! Wolf down only one Chewy Chocolate Chip Cookie and you'll direct 3 grams of fat to your hips (and thighs and middle and...). Can you eat just one? Not likely. But you might think twice about hoovering half the bag when you come to realize that each cookie is 46% fat. Remember, everything in moderation.

Show & Tell

If you're hooked on shrimp, the good news is that it's no longer considered a no-no for those on low-cholesterol diets. Yes, shrimp does have a higher cholesterol content than other commonly eaten shellfish (such as oysters, clams, scallops, and mussels), but the fact is that all shellfish, even those with higher cholesterol levels, are low in saturated fat. (Shrimps are about 78% water by weight and contain less than 1% fat.) It's the saturated fat in a food rather than its cholesterol content that ultimately has a greater impact on blood cholesterol levels. Shrimp and other shellfish are also an excellent source of Omega-3 fatty acids, which are thought to lower the risk of cardiovascular disease. It's important to keep in mind that blood cholesterol levels are influenced not so much by eating a single food, but by your total diet, as well as many other factors like your age, weight, and heredity. So when it boils down to eating shrimp, there's no need to skimp—just practice moderation.

Seafood Galore
OUR FISH COME FROM THE BEST SCHOOLS

SCHOOL CROSSING

Mission Shrimpossible

It took a top-secret undercover operation and some heavy-duty espionage to unravel the mystery behind this unparalleled Greek-style shrimp dinner: There's nothin' betta than shrimp 'n feta!

2 teaspoons olive oil
1 cup chopped red onions
1 clove garlic, minced
3 cups sliced zucchini
1 can (28 ounces) tomatoes, drained, cut up
1/4 cup dry white wine
2 teaspoons dried oregano
1/2 teaspoon black pepper
1/4 teaspoon *each* salt and crushed red pepper flakes
1 pound large shrimp, peeled and deveined
1/2 cup crumbled feta cheese (2 ounces)
3 cups cooked white or brown rice

OK I CONFESS — IT WAS ME AND THE FETA!

Heat oil in a large skillet or saucepan over medium heat. Add onions and garlic. Cook for 2 minutes, stirring often. Add zucchini and cook for 5 more minutes, until zucchini is softened.

Add tomatoes, wine, oregano, black pepper, crushed red pepper flakes, and salt. Bring to a boil. Reduce heat to medium. Cook, uncovered, for 10 minutes.

Add shrimp and feta cheese. Increase heat to medium-high. Cook until shrimp turns pink, about 5 minutes. Stir often.

Serve over hot, cooked rice.

Makes 4 servings.

Hint: Instead of cooking the feta cheese with the sauce, you can sprinkle it over the shrimp and rice once they're on the serving plates.

PER SERVING: 320 calories, 7.1 g fat, 48.9 g carbohydrate, 16 g protein, 794 mg sodium, 88 mg cholesterol
CALORIES FROM FAT: 19.1%

WHAT'S IN IT FOR ME?

Square Dancin' Salmon

Yeeeehaaa! Swing yer partner round and round, these salmon squares you'll wolf right down! We're not joshin' ya—this here's a dang tasty meal that's so chock-full of flavor, you'll "doh see doh" right back to the kitchen for more!

1/2 cup chopped onions
1/3 cup chopped celery
1-1/2 tablespoons
   all-purpose flour
3/4 cup skim milk
1/2 teaspoon *each* salt,
   celery seeds, dry mustard,
   and ground thyme
1/4 teaspoon black pepper
1 tablespoon lemon juice
2 tablespoons chopped
   fresh parsley
3 cans (6 ounces each)
   skinless, water-packed pink
   salmon, drained
1/2 cup quick-cooking rolled oats
2 egg whites

Preheat oven to 350°.

Spray a medium saucepan with non-stick spray. Add onions and celery. Cook over medium heat until vegetables are softened, about 5 minutes.

Sprinkle flour over onions and celery. Mix well. Add skim milk and continue to cook until mixture is bubbly and thickened, stirring often.

Remove sauce from heat and stir in celery seeds, dry mustard, thyme, salt, pepper, lemon juice, and parsley. Set aside.

In a large bowl, combine salmon, oats, and egg whites. Add the sauce and mix well.

Spray a 8 x 8-inch baking pan with non-stick spray. Pat salmon mixture into pan. Spread evenly. Bake for 45 minutes. Cut into squares and serve immediately.

Makes 4-6 servings.

WHAT'S IN IT FOR ME? ➡

PER SERVING (based on 6 servings):
157 calories, 4 g fat,
9.6 g carbohydrate, 20.1 g protein,
673 mg sodium, 50 mg cholesterol
CALORIES FROM FAT: 23.1%

Show me the WEIGH

Researchers say that it takes an average of 21 days of practice to develop a new habit. In your effort to permanently change your eating and exercise routines, keep a positive attitude. Instead of focusing on how terribly you used to eat, and how out of shape you are, concentrate on how happy, fit, and energetic you'll feel once you've shed your old attitudes towards diet and exercise. If you can dream it, you can do it!

SAY IT AIN'T SO!

Message on fortune cookie: "Beware of seemingly harmless chow mein noodle!" This little culprit can sneak up on you with its partially hydrogenated vegetable oil and shocking 57 percent of calories from fat! Chopsticks and stones may break my bones, but chow mein can really hurt me!

NO! NO! NOT THE CHOW MEIN NOODLES!

Trivial Tidbit

In a 25-year study of 13,000 people, moderate exercisers had a death rate at least 50% lower than those who were sedentary. Isn't that enough motivation to get you off of the couch and into your walking shoes?

It's a
MEAT MARKET

**Beef, veal & pork
that's light on the fork**

Reggae Gumbo

We're jammin'
Pork and veggies in our stew
We're jammin'
Caribbean flavor—good for you!

1 teaspoon canola oil
1 pound boneless pork
  tenderloin, cut into 1-inch
  cubes
2 cups sliced mushrooms
1 cup chopped onions
2 cloves garlic, minced
1/2 cup chopped celery
1 can (28 ounces) tomatoes,
  undrained, cut up
1 can (6 ounces) tomato paste
2 cups peeled, cubed sweet potatoes
1 teaspoon *each* ground cumin and grated ginger root
3/4 teaspoon dried oregano
1/4 teaspoon *each* salt, black pepper, and crushed red
  pepper flakes
1 cup sliced okra or zucchini
1/4 cup chopped fresh cilantro

Heat oil in a large saucepan over medium-high heat. Add pork cubes and cook until browned, about 8-10 minutes.
Add mushrooms, onions, garlic, and celery. Cook and stir until vegetables are tender, about 5 minutes.

Stir in tomatoes, tomato paste, cumin, ginger root, oregano, salt, pepper, and crushed red pepper flakes. Bring to a boil. Reduce heat to medium-low. Cover and simmer for 45 minutes, stirring occasionally.

Stir in sweet potatoes and okra or zucchini. Cover and simmer another 30-35 minutes, until pork and potatoes are very tender. Stir in cilantro during last 5 minutes of cooking time. Remove from heat and serve.

Makes 4 servings.

**WHAT'S
IN IT
FOR ME?** ➡ PER SERVING: 325 calories, 5.8 g fat,
38.1 g carbohydrate, 30.2 g protein,
617 mg sodium, 74 mg cholesterol
CALORIES FROM FAT: 15.9%

What the heck is "okra" and where can I buy it?

Okra, the mild-flavored green pods of a tropical plant, is a typical ingredient of Caribbean cookery. Okra is usually 2-1/2 to 5 inches long, and resembles a tiny zucchini with longitudinal ridges. If you can't find okra hosting a popular daytime talk show, then you can look for it in the produce section of a well-stocked supermarket or you can buy it at just about any fruit and vegetable market. If you have trouble finding okra, use zucchini in its place.

SAY IT AIN'T SO!

When you need a helping hand in preparing a quick dinner, there's no doubt that Hamburger Helper does the trick. And you'll certainly be helping your waistline to grow larger—one cup of Hamburger Helper has 15 grams of fat! So let's be realistic and say that a serving is more like 2 cups. That's 30 grams of fat down your tube. Fat-drenched ground beef is the real culprit here. Why not change the name to Ground Turkey Helper? Skinless ground turkey tastes just as good as beef, and with far less fat, you can really gobble it up.

Did you hear about the hockey player who was kicked out of cake-decorating class? He was always called for icing.

Slim Pickin's

If you choose to eat a miniscule
1 OUNCE OF PEPPERONI,
you'll be choosing a remarkable
12 GRAMS OF FAT,
the equivalent of eating
60 RED BELL PEPPERS.
Which would fill you up more?

Go for quality *and* quantity!

D. I. E. T.

is a four-letter word that really means...
DOOMED INVESTMENT EVERY TIME

Millions of dollars are spent each year on "diet" programs and "diet" products, all for temporary results. Weight is almost always regained. In fact, the chances of staying svelte after dieting are only slightly better than winning the lottery. You're not only volunteering for starvation, but you're paying for it, even though it's been proven that you'll end up failing 95% of the time. Those are pretty bad odds, don't you think? It's difficult enough to handle the deprivation that dieting involves, but the indignity of paying for it makes it seem even worse.

When the inventor of the first elastic girdle was asked if it worked he replied, "Of corset does!"

Veal of Fortune

Veal Scall_pini is about to turn over a new letter. This version of a traditionally higher-fat favorite has no oil and uses low-fat sour cream to keep the fat count in check.

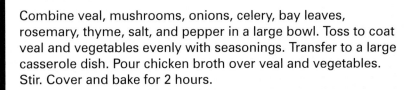

- **1 pound stewing veal, cut into 1/2-inch strips**
- **3 cups sliced mushrooms**
- **1 cup chopped onions**
- **1/2 cup chopped celery**
- **2 bay leaves**
- **1/2 teaspoon ground rosemary**
- **1/4 teaspoon *each* ground thyme, salt, and black pepper**
- **2 cups low-sodium, reduced-fat chicken broth**
- **3 tablespoons cornstarch**
- **1/2 cup low-fat sour cream**
- **1/4 cup chopped fresh parsley**
- **4 cups cooked brown or white rice**

Preheat oven to 350°.

Combine veal, mushrooms, onions, celery, bay leaves, rosemary, thyme, salt, and pepper in a large bowl. Toss to coat veal and vegetables evenly with seasonings. Transfer to a large casserole dish. Pour chicken broth over veal and vegetables. Stir. Cover and bake for 2 hours.

Remove casserole from oven and place on stove-top element over medium-high heat (make sure it's a heat-proof dish). Mix cornstarch with an equal amount of water and stir until smooth. Add to casserole. Stir until bubbly and thickened, 1-2 minutes. Remove from heat. Stir in sour cream and parsley. Serve veal and vegetables over hot, cooked rice.

Makes 4 servings.

PER SERVING: 360 calories, 6 g fat, 57.5 g carbohydrate, 24.3 g protein, 449 mg sodium, 58 mg cholesterol
CALORIES FROM FAT: 14.2%

WHAT'S IN IT FOR ME?

The Way We Stir

This beef stir-fry becomes a cherished memory pretty quickly. From wok to plate and poof—it's gone in an instant!

Memories... of the contents of my wok ...spicy beefy, snow pea Memories Of the way we stir

1 pound lean sirloin steak, cut into thin strips (about 1/4-inch thick)
1 cup thinly sliced red bell pepper
2 cups trimmed snow peas
1 cup chopped green onions
1 cup low-sodium, reduced-fat chicken broth
2 tablespoons reduced-sodium soy sauce
2 teaspoons reduced-fat peanut butter
1 tablespoon grated ginger root
1 tablespoon cornstarch
1 teaspoon sesame oil
1/2 teaspoon crushed red pepper flakes
4 cups cooked brown rice

Spray a large non-stick wok or skillet with non-stick spray. Add the beef and cook over high heat until beef is no longer pink, about 4 minutes. Remove beef from wok and set aside.

Add red pepper, snow peas, and green onions to wok. Cook and stir until vegetables are tender-crisp, about 3-4 minutes.

Whisk together broth, peanut butter, soy sauce, ginger root, cornstarch, sesame oil, and red pepper flakes. Add to vegetables, along with beef. Cook and stir until sauce is bubbly and thickened, about 2 minutes.

Serve beef and vegetables over hot, cooked rice.

Makes 4 servings.

Hint: You can replace the sirloin steak with strips of boneless, skinless chicken or turkey breast. The sesame oil adds a distinct flavor to the stir-fry, so don't leave it out of this recipe.

WHAT'S IN IT FOR ME?

PER SERVING: 446 calories, 12.4 g fat, 57.6 g carbohydrate, 31.7 g protein, 407 mg sodium, 68 mg cholesterol
CALORIES FROM FAT: 23.8%

Show me the WEIGH

A switch in time saves nine! Nine calories, to be exact. If you want to lose weight, switching to low-fat food choices is definitely the *weigh* to go. That's because fat contains more than twice as many calories as protein and carbohydrates (fat has 9 calories per gram, compared to 4 calories per gram for carbohydrates and proteins). So cutting back on fat means you'll automatically cut back on calories.

Gotta MOVE It!

"The moment I decide to stop lifting weights, my muscle will start turning to fat!" We've all heard this comment before. Yet surprisingly none of us have reported the news to Merlin the Magician, because he'd surely want to incorporate this impossible feat into his magic act! Let's get it straight. Muscle is muscle, fat is fat. Muscles can turn into fat just like apples can turn into oranges and dogs can turn into cats. So don't be afraid to add weight training to your exercise regimen as a way to tone and strengthen your body. Hey! Maybe Merlin *can* turn muscle into fat. Ever heard of "Flabra-cadabra"?

Flabra Cadabra

What you do today is very important. After all, you're exchanging a day of your life for it.

Roast Feast

Feast your eyes and your taste buds on this! It's the roast with the most—the most succulent flavor, the most tasty roasted veggies ever, and the most eye-appealing, mouthwatering platter ever to be served to a hungry crowd. Beauty and a feast!

1 boneless top sirloin roast (4 pounds)
1 teaspoon salt
1 tablespoon all-purpose flour
1 teaspoon canola oil
1-1/2 cups *each* barbeque sauce and
   low-sodium, reduced-fat beef broth
1/4 cup "lite" Worcestershire sauce
3 cloves garlic, minced
1 teaspoon dry mustard
1/4 teaspoon black pepper
2 tablespoons lime juice
2 small heads cabbage, each cut into 4 wedges
25 pearl onions, peeled
4 medium white potatoes, peeled and cut in
   half lengthwise
4 medium sweet potatoes, peeled and cut in
   half lengthwise

Preheat oven to 350°.

Sprinkle roast lightly on all sides with salt and flour. Heat oil in large non-stick skillet over medium-high heat. Add roast and brown on all sides. Remove roast from skillet and place in a large roasting pan.

In a medium bowl, combine barbeque sauce and next 6 ingredients. Mix well. Pour over roast. Cover and cook for 1 hour. Reduce heat to 325° and cook 1 more hour. Baste roast with sauce every 1/2 hour.

Remove roasting pan from oven. Arrange vegetables around roast, starting with cabbage on the bottom, followed by onions, white potatoes, and sweet potatoes. Baste roast and vegetables with sauce. Cover, return to oven, and cook for 1 hour (total cooking time for roast: 3 hours).

Remove roast from oven. Allow to stand 15 minutes before carving. Slice roast thinly. Arrange slices on a serving platter and surround roast with vegetables. Pour off as much fat as possible from sauce in pan. Pour 1/2 cup sauce over meat and serve immediately.

Makes 8 servings.

PER SERVING: 624 calories, 17.7 g fat, 61.2 g carbohydrate, 54.5 g protein, 655 mg sodium, 136 mg cholesterol CALORIES FROM FAT: 25.6%

A quick way of removing the smell of onions or garlic from your hands is to rinse them under running water, rub with baking soda, and rinse again.

Shepherdopoulos Pie

THE ONLY THING I LOVE MORE THAN THIS MEAT PIE IS MYSELF

We took your traditional Shepherd's Pie and gave it an exciting new twist with the addition of sleek, Greek ingredients like tomatoes, feta cheese, and oregano. Guess we didn't study "Greek Meatology" for nothin'!

4 medium potatoes, peeled and quartered
1/2 cup skim milk or buttermilk
1/2 teaspoon salt
1 pound extra-lean ground beef
1/4 cup unseasoned dry bread crumbs
1/4 cup minced onions
1 egg white
1 tablespoon ketchup
1 clove garlic, minced
1/4 teaspoon black pepper
1 large tomato, thinly sliced
1/2 teaspoon dried oregano
1/4 cup shredded reduced-fat Swiss cheese (1 ounce)
1/4 cup crumbled feta cheese (1 ounce)
1/2 10-ounce package frozen spinach, thawed, squeezed dry, and chopped (5 ounces total)

Cook potatoes in a large pot of boiling water until tender, about 20 minutes. Drain well. Add milk and salt. Mash until smooth. Set aside.

In a large bowl, combine beef, bread crumbs, onions, egg white, ketchup, garlic, and black pepper. Mix well (using your hands works best). Pat beef mixture over bottom and up sides of a 9-inch pie plate.

Layer tomato slices over beef. Sprinkle oregano over tomatoes. Spread Swiss and feta cheeses over tomatoes. Top cheese with chopped spinach. Spoon mashed potatoes over spinach. Spread evenly, leaving a 1-inch border around edges. (Meat and potatoes should not touch.) Smooth top.

Bake at 350° for 45 minutes. Let cool 5 minutes. Slice into wedges and serve.

Makes 4-6 servings.

Hint: Try it with ground turkey instead of beef.

WHAT'S IN IT FOR ME?

PER SERVING (based on 6 servings):
339 calories, 9.6 g fat,
41.9 g carbohydrate, 21.9 g protein,
386 mg sodium, 56 mg cholesterol
CALORIES FROM FAT: 25.2%

Here's a tip that will save you a pile of fat grams when preparing casseroles or sauces that contain ground beef: After browning the meat, transfer it to a colander to drain off the fat. Give the ground beef a quick rinse with warm water to wash away even more fat. Finally, blot the ground beef with paper towels to absorb any final traces of grease. Return beef to skillet and proceed according to recipe directions.

Slim Pickin's

You'd have to oink out on
150 CUPS OF HONEYDEW MELON
to consume the
30 GRAMS OF FAT
found in a mere
2 PIECES OF FRESH COCONUT
(2" x 2" x 1/2").
Which would fill you up more?

Go for quality *and* quantity!

HO HUM. I'M A DUD SPUD

A commentator is an undistinguished potato.

Show & Tell

Shakey, shakey. Wakey, wakey. What is Worcestershire sauce anyway? Worcestershire sauce is a commercially prepared condiment containing molasses, anchovies or sardines, sugar, garlic, soy sauce, tamarind (Indian date), vinegar, and spices. The chemists who invented the stuff, Lea and Perrins, named it after the Worcester shop where the concoction was created. A "lite" version is available for those who are concerned about reducing their sodium intake.

Show me the WEIGH

Diet Fads + Myths = Confusion
Even though modern science inevitably unveils the truth behind diet fads, the myths never seem to die. Here's one: *"Choice" and "prime" cuts of meat are the lowest in fat.* Just the opposite. These cuts are the most tender but they have the highest fat content. Funny that they're the most expensive, too! Meats marked "select" or "good" are typically lower in fat. How about this one: *Yogurt is a health food.* Ain't necessarily so! Some fruit-on-the-bottom yogurts and frozen yogurts contain more sugar than a chocolate bar, and whole-milk yogurts are high in fat. Your best bet is plain, non-fat yogurt with fresh fruit. *Non-dairy creamers and whipped toppings are low-fat alternatives to cream.* Oops! Wrong again! Non-dairy does not mean low-fat. Often, these products contain highly saturated fats like palm and coconut oils (and many are loaded with sugar). The best choice for a coffee whitener is evaporated non-fat milk.

"Dressed to Grill" Pork Chops

HONEY, THE CHOPS WILL BE READY IN 007 MINUTES!

And grill you will! When you fire up the barbeque for succulent pork chops with a drop-dead delicious marinade, all the neighbors will be talkin'. Prepare for the grill of a lifetime!

6 pork loin chops, trimmed of fat (4-5 ounces each)
1 cup V8 juice
3 cloves garlic, minced
2 tablespoons brown sugar
1-1/2 tablespoons "lite" Worcestershire sauce
1-1/2 teaspoons *each* chili powder and ground cumin
3/4 teaspoon dried oregano
1/2 teaspoon black pepper
1 recipe La Rice-a Bon-eata, (page 136)

Arrange pork chops in a single layer in a shallow pan. Combine remaining ingredients and pour over pork chops. Turn pork chops to coat both sides with marinade. Cover and marinate in refrigerator for at least 8 hours or overnight.

One hour before serving time, prepare rice as directed. Keep warm. Preheat grill. Cook pork chops over hot coals for 6-7 minutes on each side, basting with any leftover marinade. Serve with Spanish rice (see page 136).

Makes 6 servings.

PER SERVING (with rice):
349 calories, 9.4 g fat,
37 g carbohydrate, 27.5 g protein,
489 mg sodium, 66 mg cholesterol
CALORIES FROM FAT: 24.6%

WHAT'S IN IT FOR ME?

SAY IT AIN'T SO!

They don't call it liverwurst for nothing! It really is one of the *wurst* choices you can make if you're attempting to cut down on fat. Over 80% of its calories are derived from fat, and in combination with the hidden fat in crackers, liverwurst makes a potent artery clogger.

Yabba Dabba Stew

A hit with modern Stone Age families, this hearty beef stew is sure to be equally popular with your modern 90's clan!

- 1-1/2 pounds boneless top sirloin steak, cut into 1-inch cubes
- 2 cups sliced leeks
- 2 cloves garlic, minced
- 2-1/2 cups low-sodium, reduced-fat beef broth
- 1 whole clove
- 1 bay leaf
- 3 cups *each* chopped carrots and sliced mushrooms
- 3 cups peeled, cubed potatoes
- 1 teaspoon ground thyme
- 1/3 cup tomato-based chili sauce
- 1 cup light beer
- 2 tablespoons cornstarch
- 1/4 cup chopped fresh parsley
- 1/2 teaspoon black pepper

Spray a large saucepan with non-stick spray. Add beef cubes and cook over medium-high heat until no longer pink, about 10 minutes. Add leeks and garlic. Cook and stir for 5 minutes. Stir in 1/2 cup of the beef broth. Reduce heat to medium and cook, uncovered, until liquid has evaporated, about 15 minutes. Stir occasionally.

Stir in remaining beef broth, clove, and bay leaf. Bring to a boil. Reduce heat to medium-low. Cover and simmer for 40 minutes (stir every once in a while).

Add carrots, mushrooms, potatoes, and thyme. Stir well. Cover and simmer another 40 minutes, until vegetables and meat are tender.

Stir in chili sauce. Combine beer and cornstarch in a small bowl. Add to stew. Cook and stir until sauce thickens, 1-2 minutes. Stir in parsley and pepper. Remove bay leaf and serve immediately.

Makes 6 servings.

WHAT'S IN IT FOR ME?

PER SERVING: 368 calories, 10 g fat, 39.8 g carbohydrate, 29 g protein, 328 mg sodium, 68 mg cholesterol
CALORIES FROM FAT: 24.1%

COOKING 101

Leeks look like giant scallions and are native to the Mediterranean countries. The leek is related to both the onion and garlic, although its flavor is more subtle. When buying leeks, choose those with bright green, unwithered leaves and an unblemished white portion. They can be stored in the refrigerator in a plastic bag for about 5 days. To prepare leeks for cooking, trim off the root and all but the first 3 inches of the green leaf ends. Discard any tough outer leaves. Cut the leeks in half lengthwise and rinse them under cold water to remove any grit caught between the layers. Shake dry and slice or chop as required.

Gotta MOVE It!

Bored with the same old dull exercise routine? Thought so. Boredom and burnout are two very common reasons why people quit exercising altogether. To broaden the benefits of exercise while avoiding boredom, burnout, and injury, maybe you should consider "cross training." (No. We're not talking about men jogging around in women's leotards—that's cross *dressing*!) Choose activities that you genuinely enjoy (if you really hate jogging or aerobics, don't do it) and then vary these activities over the week. For example, you might swim on Monday, walk on Wednesday, bike on Thursday, and play tennis on Saturday. This varied activity also balances the muscle strength that you'll begin building so the risk of injury is lessened. Exercise should be as much a part of your daily life as brushing your teeth. The only way that'll happen is if you make it fun!

Is the word tofu really short for *to fool you*? It seems that everyone has been fooled into thinking that tofu, made from soybeans, is low in fat. Despite its healthy characteristics, and the fact that it makes a great substitute for meat, tofu gets a whopping 55% of its calories from fat! Healthy? Yes. Low-fat? No. Flavorful? We're not sure.

This Little Piggy Lost His Potbelly

Despite persistent name-calling and stereotypes, the 90's pig is actually much slimmer than its ancestors. Decades ago, the pig was bred as much for its yield of lard (the fat used for cooking before vegetable oils were commercialized) as for its meat. But thanks to the pork industry's aggressive efforts, the health profile of most cuts has been dramatically improved, and fat has been reduced by more than 50%.

Pork tenderloin is about as slim as skinless chicken breast, with a 3-ounce serving containing just 4 grams of fat. Not all cuts score big points with the health conscious, though. Top loin chops are 50% leaner than they were in days gone by, but still contain 61% more fat than tenderloin. And spareribs? Lotsa bone, little meat, tons of fat! Three small ribs serve up a thigh-bulging 26 grams!

It *is* possible to eat pork as part of a healthful, low-fat dict. It just depends on what kind you eat, how much of it you eat, and how you prepare it.

DON'T JUST STAND THERE— SLAY SOMETHING !

Jurassic Pork Roast

On one of our many archaeological expeditions, we unearthed this prehistoric recipe for a spectacular and succulent pork roast. We later discovered that it was voted "best low-fat pork dish" by Cavemopolitan Magazine.

PORKASAURUS REX

1 boneless pork top loin roast (3 pounds)
2 cloves garlic, thinly sliced
2 tablespoons Dijon mustard
1 teaspoon red wine vinegar
3/4 teaspoon ground thyme
1/2 teaspoon ground sage
3/4 cup low-sodium, reduced-fat beef broth
3/4 cup unsweetened apple juice
1/4 cup apricot jam
1-1/2 cups peeled and chopped Granny Smith apples
1 tablespoon low-fat sour cream
1 tablespoon cornstarch

Cut 8 deep slits in the top of roast using a very sharp knife. Insert garlic into slits.

Mix mustard, vinegar, thyme, and sage in a small bowl. Using a pastry brush, coat roast with all of the mustard mixture. Place roast in roasting pan.

Warm the broth, apple juice, and jam in a small saucepan over medium-high heat until jam melts. Pour over roast. Arrange chopped apples around roast. Cover. Roast at 350° for 1-1/4 to 1-1/2 hours, basting every 30 minutes or so.

Remove roast from pan and keep warm. Reserve 1/2 cup pan juices. Pour remaining pan juices and apples into a medium saucepan. Skim off as much fat as possible. Into reserved 1/2 cup pan juices, add sour cream and mix well. Add cornstarch and blend again until smooth.

Bring pan juices and apples (in saucepan) to a boil. Whisk in sour cream mixture and cook over medium-high heat for 2 minutes, until bubbly and thickened. Serve apple gravy over thin slices of pork roast.

Makes 8 servings.

PER SERVING: 302 calories, 9 g fat, 11.6 g carbohydrate, 39.4 g protein, 186 mg sodium, 93 mg cholesterol
CALORIES FROM FAT: 29.8%

WHAT'S IN IT FOR ME?

Tube Beef or Not Tube Beef

That is the question. This extraordinary meal of rigatoni tubes with stewed beef is meant to be shared, but it's only human nature to want to keep something so delicious all to yourself (especially since it makes great leftovers!).

1-1/4 pounds stewing beef
1 can (28 ounces) tomatoes,
    undrained, cut up
1 can (6 ounces) tomato paste
3 cups sliced mushrooms
1 cup chopped onions
2 tablespoons *each* reduced-
    sodium soy sauce, brown sugar,
    and white vinegar
2 teaspoons low-sodium beef
    bouillon powder
2 cloves garlic, minced
1 teaspoon *each* dry mustard
    and dried oregano
1/2 teaspoon black pepper
1/4 teaspoon crushed red pepper flakes
10 ounces uncooked rigatoni (about 6 cups dry)

Preheat oven to 350°.

Trim all visible fat from beef. Cut into 1-inch cubes. Arrange beef in a small roaster or a large casserole dish.

Combine remaining ingredients, except rigatoni, in a large bowl. Mix well. Pour over beef. Cover and bake for 1 hour and 45 minutes to 2 hours, until beef is very tender. Stir halfway through cooking time.

During last 15 minutes of cooking time, prepare rigatoni according to package directions. Drain. Serve hot beef and sauce over rigatoni.

Makes 4 servings.

Hint: Using no-salt-added tomatoes will help lower the sodium content.

WHAT'S IN IT FOR ME? ➤ PER SERVING: 642 calories, 14.3 g fat, 78.8 g carbohydrate, 47 g protein, 1019 mg sodium, 105 mg cholesterol
CALORIES FROM FAT: 20.4%

COOKING 101

Bake, broil, grill, boil, poach, roast, or microwave your food. Never, never fry foods. (If you do fry something, that's okay...just don't eat it!) Be on the alert for Unidentified Frying Objects and when you see one...run!

Show me the WEIGH

The diets of North American children are engorged with fat, and it's not surprising to see their waistlines beginning to reflect that kind of diet. With time pressures created by the hectic, frenetic lifestyles of the '90s, frazzled parents are feeding their children unbalanced, overprocessed meals that are loaded with fat. Plop them in front of the television set for a couple of hours, throw in a bag of Cheetos, some chocolate bars, and a pizza, and hocus-pocus—there you have it—chubby chunky children. The way to fight flab in children, besides upping their activity level, is to moderate trips to the fast food joint and gradually introduce lower-fat, healthier foods into the family diet. In order to do this, parents need to do some planning ahead. For instance, if there's very little time to eat in the morning, parents could put together a brown-bag meal for their kids to eat in the car (a bagel, some fruit, and some juice will do the trick). For quick and healthy dinners, large quantities of soup, pasta, stews, or casseroles can be prepared on weekends and frozen, to be served during the week. Planning and preparing nutritious meals should be high on the priority list, even for extremely busy parents. After all, it really boils down to your kid's health and that has to be important to you.

Television is like a steak— a medium rarely well done.

Slim Pickin's

If you choose to eat a feeble
2 SLICES OF BOLOGNA,
you'll be choosing a mammoth
16 GRAMS OF FAT,
the equivalent of eating
16 CUPS OF RIGATONI.
Which would fill you up more?

Go for quality *and* quantity!

D. I. E. T.

is a four-letter word that really means...
DETERMINED INITIALLY ENTHUSIASM TEMPORARY

Have you ever found yourself saying, "This time I'm really gonna lose the weight—once and for all"? Unfortunately, restricted eating is impossible and unrealistic for any prolonged period of time, and more often than not you surrender to your cravings and end up gaining back any weight that was lost *and then some*. This pattern of losing and gaining weight over and over again is referred to as "yo-yo dieting." When weight cycles up and down, the ratio of fat to muscle increases progressively and your metabolic rate is lowered, so that each time you start your diet again, you start from a harder place. Your dieting plan has actually backfired! No wonder your enthusiasm has waned—you now have more fat and a sluggish metabolic rate!

LOSING WEIGHT SHOULD BE A CINCH THIS TIME

♪ Pork-u-Pine Kabobs

For "picky" eaters, here's a treat. You won't be able to resist these sweet and sour kabobs, even if you have amazing quill-power!

**3 tablespoons reduced-sodium
    soy sauce
2 tablespoons brown sugar
2 tablespoons apricot or peach jam
1 tablespoon *each* minced onions
    and lemon juice
1/4 teaspoon salt
1/8 teaspoon black pepper
1 pound boneless pork tenderloin,
    trimmed of fat, cut into
    16 1-inch cubes
16 slices zucchini (1/2-inch thick)
16 chunks red bell pepper
16 chunks fresh pineapple**

Mix first 7 ingredients together in a medium bowl. Add pork cubes and stir to coat. Cover and marinate in refrigerator for 1 hour.

Thread the pork, zucchini, red pepper, and pineapple alternately onto 8 metal skewers. Reserve marinade for basting kabobs.

Prepare grill. Cook kabobs for about 15 minutes, basting and turning frequently, until pork is done.

Makes 4 servings.

PER SERVING: 213 calories, 4.3 g fat, 18.2 g carbohydrate, 24.9 g protein, 645 mg sodium, 74 mg cholesterol
CALORIES FROM FAT: 18.2%

WHAT'S IN IT FOR ME?

***T**he best way to break a bad habit is to drop it.*

Grand Slam Ham

A good ham recipe is an essential and popular item for a complete cooking repertoire. It just means that you've covered all the bases, you know. Guests who just can't get enough ham won't be standing out in left field at your dinner parties. No siree! This tangy ham's a major league, BIG, BIG hit!

1 fully-cooked lean ham (2 pounds)
1 cup apricot or peach jam
1-1/2 tablespoons *each* white vinegar
   and Dijon mustard
1 tablespoon orange zest
1/4 teaspoon ground allspice

Preheat oven to 350°.

Slice ham into 1/2-inch thick slices. Arrange slices in a 13 x 9-inch baking dish.

Combine jam, vinegar, mustard, orange zest, and allspice in a small saucepan. Cook over medium heat until bubbly, 2-3 minutes. Spoon sauce over ham. Make sure each slice is coated with sauce. Cover and bake for 30-35 minutes, until ham is heated through.

Makes 6-8 servings.

WHAT'S IN IT FOR ME? → PER SERVING (based on 8 servings): 211 calories, 6.5 g fat, 7.8 g carbohydrate, 28.2 g protein, 1564 mg sodium, 62 mg cholesterol CALORIES FROM FAT: 28.9%

 The expression "high on the hog" originated from the way meat was once portioned out in the British army. Officers received the tender cuts "high on the hog," while the lower ranks shared the remains.

SAY IT AIN'T SO!

It's no wonder that Fred and Wilma's car tipped over when the waitress delivered their order of Brontosaurus Ribs! Spareribs are heavyweight fat contenders, with one pound registering in at a whopping 805 calories and 56 grams of fat! Yabba Dabba Do not eat these regularly, unless you're hoping to have Fred's physique!

Gotta MOVE It!

Don't just sit there! Just move it! It's easy to incorporate fuel-burning movement into your daily life. Just move every chance you get. Feel like reading? Why not read while on a stationary bike? Try a recumbent bike—it's easier on the back and on the butt, so you'll be able to pedal comfortably and for a longer time. Do stretching exercises while watching your favorite TV show. In the office, get up when the phone rings, walk over to a co-worker's desk instead of using the telephone, or walk during lunch hour. Early for an appointment? Why not walk around the block a few times rather than read magazines in the waiting room? Whatever you do, don't just sit there! Remember, any kind of movement is better than no movement at all.

The SUPPORTING CAST

Complementing the main attraction

The Rice is Right

Come on down! Vegetarian fried rice is the next concoction on "The Rice is Right!" When it comes to savory side dishes to serve your guests, this is undoubtedly Showcase Number One!

1/2 cup fat-free egg substitute
1/2 teaspoon sesame oil
1 teaspoon olive oil
1 cup chopped onions
3 cloves garlic, minced
3/4 cup *each* diced carrots and
    diced celery
1/2 cup chopped green onions
1 teaspoon grated ginger root
1/4 cup reduced-sodium soy sauce
1 tablespoon honey
4 cups cooked brown rice

Whisk together egg substitute and sesame oil in a small bowl. Set aside.

Add olive oil to a large non-stick skillet and place over medium heat. Pour egg mixture over bottom of skillet. Cook until set, about 3 minutes. Remove from skillet and cut into bite-sized pieces. Set aside.

Spray same skillet with non-stick spray. Add onions, garlic, carrots, celery, green onions, and ginger root. Cook and stir over medium heat for about 5 minutes, until vegetables are softened. Add soy sauce, honey, cooked egg, and cooked rice. Mix well. Cook for 2-3 more minutes, until heated through.

Makes 8 servings.

WHAT'S IN IT FOR ME?

PER SERVING: 140 calories, 2.2 g fat, 28.6 g carbohydrate, 4.3 g protein, 358 mg sodium, 0 mg cholesterol
CALORIES FROM FAT: 13.2%

SAY IT AIN'T SO!

Expect to start looking like Homer Simpson if you eat too many chocolate glazed donuts. Mmmmm! Chocolaty! Homer's favorite snack has 324 calories and 21 grams of fat (56% calories from fat). And that's just one DOH! nut! Remember, everything in moderation. So don't be a cow, man!

Show & Tell

Soy sauce is a dark brown liquid seasoning made by fermenting soybeans and wheat. It's a versatile flavoring for soups, sauces, marinades, meat, fish, and vegetables. In North America, there's essentially one type of soy sauce made widely available, but in China and Japan a number of varieties are produced, ranging from light to dark and from thin to thick. Appearing more frequently as an ingredient on restaurant menus, "tamari sauce" is a Japanese sauce that's similar to soy sauce (also made from soybeans), but it's richer, darker, and thicker. Keep in mind that soy sauce is very high in sodium (1000 milligrams of sodium per tablespoon!). Luckily, "lite" brands are available at any supermarket and are a good choice for those trying to reduce their salt intake.

What you eat in private shows up in public.

Green-tinged potatoes and those with sprouts should be left behind at the grocery store. The green surface blemishes are caused by overexposure to light, resulting in a bitter taste. The tainted areas will contain some level of toxic solanine, a chemical also present in potato sprouts. While the level of solanine may not be enough to harm you, why eat a tainted tater when you don't have to?

Show me the WEIGH

In addition to supplying "empty" calories (no nutritional value whatsoever), another problem that alcohol causes for those trying to lose weight is that, since it is absorbed quickly into the blood, blood sugar rises rapidly. To compensate, the body secretes insulin. Insulin is a fat-hoarding compound. It actually makes less fat available for the body to burn as fuel. So if you feel like a guilt-ridden slug after gulping down your sixth brew in two hours, you should! Because in the Battle to Lose Lard, you've just helped out the competition—you've assisted on the goal scored by The Mighty Fats!

An old Transylvanian remedy for easing the pain and swelling of inflamed joints calls for applying a cooked onion directly on the sore spot. Strange how garlic was never suggested?

Slim, Trim, and Scalloped Spuds

These luscious scalloped potatoes seasoned with dill may fall into the lightweight category as far as fat content goes, but they're serious heavyweight contenders when it comes down to *dill*ectable, unsurpassed flavor.

1-1/2 cups sliced mushrooms
3/4 cup sliced onion rings
1/4 cup all-purpose flour
2 cups skim milk
1 tablespoon minced fresh dill, *or* 1/2 teaspoon dried dillweed
1 teaspoon "lite" Worcestershire sauce
1/4 teaspoon *each* salt and black pepper
1/2 cup shredded reduced-fat Swiss cheese (2 ounces)
4 large potatoes, peeled and sliced into 1/4-inch thick rounds

Preheat oven to 350°.

Spray a medium saucepan with non-stick spray. Add onions and mushrooms. Cook and stir over medium-high heat until vegetables are tender, about 5 minutes.

Sprinkle flour over vegetables. Stir until vegetables are evenly coated with flour. Gradually stir in milk. Cook until mixture is thick and bubbly, about 5-6 minutes, stirring frequently.

Add dill, Worcestershire sauce, salt, pepper, and shredded cheese. Cook for 1 more minute, until cheese is melted. Remove from heat.

Spray a medium casserole dish with non-stick spray. Spread 1/3 of potatoes over bottom, followed by 1/3 cheese sauce. Repeat layering two more times. Cover and bake for 1-1/2 hours. Let potatoes stand for 10 minutes before serving.

Makes 6 servings.

PER SERVING: 272 calories, 2.3 g fat, 53.3 g carbohydrate, 11.1 g protein, 164 mg sodium, 9 mg cholesterol
CALORIES FROM FAT: 7.4%

WHAT'S IN IT FOR ME?

Hail a Cabbage

You won't find better "fare" anywhere in town! Simple to prepare, this tremendously tasty cabbage will have the flavor-meter in a ticking tizzy.

1/2 cup sliced onion rings
1 clove garlic, minced
1/2 cup apple juice
1 cup peeled and grated apples
2 tablespoons red wine vinegar
1-1/2 tablespoons brown
  sugar
1 bay leaf
1/4 teaspoon black pepper
4 cups shredded red cabbage
2 tablespoons chopped fresh
  parsley

Spray a large saucepan with non-stick spray. Add onions and garlic. Cook and stir over medium heat until tender, about 5 minutes.

Dilute apple juice with 1/2 cup water to make 1 cup total. Add to onions and garlic, along with apples, vinegar, brown sugar, bay leaf, and pepper. Stir and bring mixture to a boil. Stir in cabbage. Cover and simmer over medium heat until cabbage is tender-crisp, about 12 minutes.

Discard bay leaf and stir in parsley before serving.

Makes 4 servings.

WHAT'S IN IT FOR ME? → PER SERVING: 89 calories, 0.5 g fat, 21.3 g carbohydrate, 1.5 g protein, 16 mg sodium, 0 mg cholesterol CALORIES FROM FAT: 4.7%

COOKING 101

The apples and vinegar in this recipe serve two purposes. The first and most obvious function is to add both flavor and aroma. The second purpose is to add acidity, which prevents the red cabbage from turning a bluish-purple when cooking.

SAY IT AIN'T SO!

Kiss me, you fool! That's precisely what you'll be—a fool—if you regularly overindulge on chocolate Kisses. Only 12 of the chocolaty little treats have 18 grams of fat and 300 calories (54% calories from fat! Ouch!) Human kisses are a better choice. They're fat-free and immensely more satisfying than chocolate!

Gotta MOVE It!

Those folks at Oil of Olay have really worked wonders by bottling the secret formula to "keep them guessing" about our age. But there's another secret formula for looking and feeling young, and it doesn't come in a bottle. It's called "exercise," and it can help protect against the slow but steady signs of aging. In most cases, we don't feel old because we are old. We feel old because we become sedentary, and this actually accelerates the deterioration of our bodies—stiffening joints, weight gain, wimpy muscles, heart straining to pump as much blood as usual, energy levels dropping. Imagine! Helping your body to grow old! Why not help the Forever Young Cause by making exercise a part of your everyday life? Oil of Olay may help you look better on the outside, but exercise will help you look better on the outside *and* the inside, and that'll definitely keep them guessing!

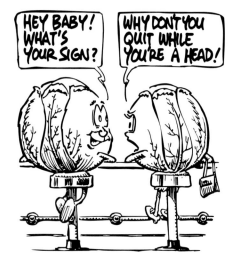

Show & Tell

There are hundreds of types of peppers, but for simplicity and cooking's sake, they can be divided into two main categories. Sweet, mild peppers include the more common green, red, yellow, orange, purple, and black bell peppers, which pack in a lot of nutrition (vitamin C, potassium, and fiber). Spicy, hot chili peppers, such as jalapeños, serranos, habañeros, cayenne, and Thai chilies contain the chemical capsaicin, which can often be volcanic enough to make every cell in your body do handsprings! Hot peppers have nutritional benefits as well, and some experts say that including these peppers in your diet can boost your after-dinner metabolism by as much as 25%.

Slim Pickin's

If you choose to nibble on
1 HONEY-DIPPED CRULLER,
you'll be choosing a walloping
11 GRAMS OF FAT,
the equivalent of eating
11 SLICES OF WHOLE WHEAT TOAST.
Which would fill you up more?

Go for quality *and* quantity!

I BOUGHT THIS GIRDLE TODAY FOR A RIDICULOUS FIGURE

I KNOW—BUT HOW MUCH DID IT COST?

Peter Piper's Packed Peppers

We're not quite sure who Peter Piper is, or what was in that pipe he was smoking (huh?), but he certainly picked a winning combination when he picked veggies, rice, and beans as a stuffing for colorful, spicy pepper cups.

2 cloves garlic, minced
1 cup chopped onions
1/2 10-ounce package frozen spinach, thawed, squeezed dry, and chopped (5 ounces total)
1 can (28 ounces) tomatoes, undrained, cut up
1 can (6 ounces) tomato paste
1 teaspoon "lite" Worcestershire sauce
1 teaspoon *each* dried oregano and dried basil
1/2 teaspoon *each* ground cumin and crushed red pepper flakes
1/4 teaspoon *each* salt and black pepper
6 large red or yellow bell peppers (or a combination of the two)
3 cups cooked brown rice
1 can (15 ounces) black beans, drained and rinsed
Fresh parsley for garnish

Spray a large saucepan with non-stick spray. Cook garlic and onions over medium heat until tender, about 5 minutes. Add next 10 ingredients. Stir and bring to a boil. Reduce heat to low. Cover and simmer for 10 minutes, stirring occasionally.

Meanwhile, prepare peppers for stuffing. Cut off tops with stem and remove seeds. Fill a stock pot 1/2 full with water and bring to a boil over high heat. Add peppers 2 or 3 at a time, and blanch for 2 minutes. Remove from water with tongs and place in sink full of cold water until cool.

Remove sauce from heat and stir in rice and beans. Stuff peppers evenly with filling. Stand upright in a small roasting pan. Cover and bake at 375° for 35 minutes. Let cool 5 minutes before serving.

Garnish tops with a sprig of fresh parsley. Serve any leftover filling on the side.

Makes 6 stuffed peppers.

PER SERVING: 255 calories, 2.5 g fat, 53.7 g carbohydrate, 11.2 g protein, 658 mg sodium, 2 mg cholesterol
CALORIES FROM FAT: 7.8%

WHAT'S IN IT FOR ME?

Mixed Medley Veggie Bake

Tired of the same old song and dance when it comes to vegetable side dishes? Well this tantalizing accompaniment is destined for the number one spot on the Dinner Time Hit Parade! A hearty, wholesome vegetable casserole that's brimming with flavor, it's likely to become a regular request at your kitchen table.

1 cup chopped onions
3 cups sliced mushrooms
1/4 cup all-purpose flour
1-1/2 cups skim milk
1/2 cup shredded reduced-fat sharp cheddar cheese (2 ounces)
1 tablespoon Dijon mustard
1 teaspoon "lite" Worcestershire sauce
1/4 teaspoon black pepper
4-5 dashes hot pepper sauce
6 cups frozen "California-style" mixed vegetables
** (broccoli, cauliflower, and carrots)**
1/2 cup unseasoned dry bread crumbs
1/2 teaspoon ground thyme
1 egg white

Spray a medium saucepan with non-stick spray. Add onions and mushrooms. Cook and stir over medium-high heat until vegetables are tender, about 6-7 minutes. Sprinkle flour over mushrooms and onions. Stir well. Gradually add milk, stirring constantly. Cook until mixture becomes thick and bubbly, 5-6 minutes. Remove from heat. Stir in cheese, Dijon mustard, Worcestershire sauce, black pepper, and hot pepper sauce.

Place frozen vegetables in a large casserole dish. Pour sauce over vegetables. Gently stir to coat vegetables with sauce.

In a small bowl, combine bread crumbs, thyme, and egg white. Stir until crumbs are moistened. Sprinkle crumb mixture evenly over vegetables. Cover and bake at 350° for 45 minutes. Uncover and bake 15 more minutes. Let stand 5 minutes before serving.

Makes 8 servings.

WHAT'S IN IT FOR ME? →

PER SERVING: 166 calories, 4.2 g fat, 25 g carbohydrate, 8.7 g protein, 544 mg sodium, 6 mg cholesterol
CALORIES FROM FAT: 22%

SAY IT AIN'T SO!

Some packaged "diet," "lite," or "lean" dinners have unrealistically small portion sizes to keep calories to a minimum, but that doesn't necessarily mean they're low in fat. For instance, a brand-name oven fried fish dinner (frozen) contains only 220 calories but 49% of those calories are derived from fat (12 grams per serving). Weight a minute! There's something wrong with this picture. Stock up on these "diet" entrées and the only thing you'll be watching grow thinner is your wallet. Read the label before you buy!

Show me the WEIGH

Holidays are often the time that willpower is weakest. When you have "visions of sugar cookies dancing through your head," who can think of eating anything low in fat? Most of the time, one little indulgence or mistake leads to the attitude, "Oh, who cares! I've blown it already, so I might as well really pig out!" It's very important to realize that one mistake or one high-fat, high-calorie occasion doesn't mean you've blown it. The next 2500 fat-laden calories do the most damage. It's easy to devour six "oh, what the heck" shortbread cookies and a cup of eggnog in less than two minutes, but they'll hang around on your waistline for a lot longer than that! Remember that eating well isn't all or nothing. It's what you do consistently, over the long haul, that counts.

HO, HO, HOLD THE EGGNOG

Trivial Tidbit

All culinary oils contain 120 calories and 14 grams of fat per tablespoon.

Show & Tell

Did you know that cooked carrots are actually better for you than raw carrots? The crisp texture of carrots comes from cell walls stiffened with the indigestible food fibers cellulose, hemicellulose, and lignin. Cooking dissolves some of the cellulose-stiffened cell walls, making the nutrients inside more readily available.

Carrots are an excellent source of the deep-yellow carotenoids from which we produce vitamin A. Interestingly enough, the carotenoids in carrots are fat-soluble, so if you were to eat large amounts of carrots day after day, these carotenoids would be stored in your fatty tissues, including the fat just under your skin. Eventually your skin would look yellow. So no matter how much you love this carrot recipe, it probably wouldn't be wise to make it *every* day!

Gotta MOVE It!

Having a bad day? If you feel like you're about to have a fit, maybe you should try *getting* fit instead! Obviously, if you look physically fit, you're probably going to feel better mentally, too. But there's more to it than that. Physical activity raises your body temperature slightly, which imparts a sense of relaxation. Add to that the fact that exercise can affect brain chemistry, actually heightening your feelings of well-being and self-esteem. It does this by increasing the levels of neurotransmitters such as serotonin, dopamine, and epinephrine, which can elevate your mood. This uplifting energy gives you the strength to conquer anxiety and stress, the motivation to take care of your nutritional needs, and the willpower to see yourself through the temptation of junk food. Life's lighter side may be easier to see after a heavy helping of physical activity.

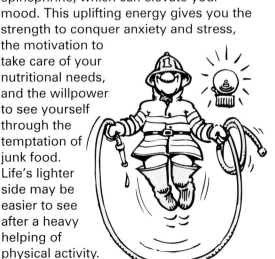

Glazed and Confused Carrots

Pardon the confusion, but you can't really blame the carrots. After all, they're about to undergo a rather dramatic transformation—from humdrum, run-of-the-mill carrots to zesty, zingy "carrots extraordinaire"! Quick and easy.

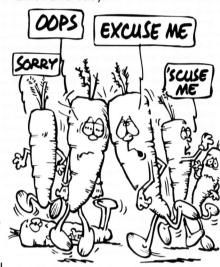

1 pound baby carrots
3 tablespoons peach jam
1 teaspoon *each* **grated orange zest and Dijon mustard**
1/4 teaspoon ground thyme

Steam or boil carrots until tender, about 15 minutes.

While carrots are cooking, prepare glaze. Combine jam, orange zest, mustard, and thyme in a small saucepan. Cook over medium heat until bubbly, about 2 minutes.

Toss cooked carrots with glaze and serve immediately.

Makes 4 servings.

PER SERVING: 76 calories, 1.1 g fat, 17.1 g carbohydrate, 1 g protein, 74 mg sodium, 0 mg cholesterol CALORIES FROM FAT: 12.3%

Menu Lingo Made Easy

If you're able to read between the lines, it's easy to pick up on menu language that cries out "FAT ALERT!" Be on the lookout for the following food descriptions when you're dining out:

The Good Words: Baked, broiled, boiled, steamed, poached, grilled, barbequed, roasted, tomato-based, broth, marinara, in white wine, au naturel

The Bad Words: Fried, deep-fried, stir-fried, battered, buttered, breaded, sautéed (unless in broth), creamy, cheesy, with garlic butter, Alfredo, au gratin, Hollandaise, Bernaise, marinated in oil, in pastry shells

La Rice-a Bon-eata

La chihuahua esta sombrero cerveza. Por favor no padre si Ponce de Leon. Speedy Gonzales bienvenido siesta. All right, all right—so maybe we don't know how to speak Spanish, but we sure know how to make a wickedly delicious Spanish rice!

1 cup chopped onions
1/2 cup diced green bell pepper
1 clove garlic, minced
2-1/3 cups low-sodium, reduced-fat chicken broth
1 cup uncooked long grain brown rice (the quicker-cooking variety, but not instant)
1 cup chunky-style salsa (mild, medium, or hot)
1/2 teaspoon *each* chili powder and ground cumin
1/4 teaspoon *each* salt and black pepper
2 tablespoons chopped fresh cilantro (optional)

Spray a medium saucepan with non-stick spray. Add onions, green pepper, and garlic. Cook over medium heat until vegetables are softened, about 5 minutes.

Add remaining ingredients, except cilantro, and stir well. Bring to a boil. Reduce heat to medium-low, cover partially, and cook for another 25-30 minutes, or until liquid has been absorbed and rice is tender.

Remove from heat, stir in cilantro (if using), and serve.

Makes 6 servings.

WHAT'S IN IT FOR ME? → PER SERVING: 124 calories, 1.1 g fat, 27.2 g carbohydrate, 3.6 g protein, 370 mg sodium, 0 mg cholesterol CALORIES FROM FAT: 7.6%

You can't turn back the clock, but you can certainly wind it up again.

A Word from the Rice Squad

Low in fat, very filling, easy to prepare, cholesterol-free, inexpensive, and nutritious. Rice is, indeed, the perfect food for health-conscious folks who are watching their weight. Problem is, with so many different varieties out there, we tend to get a little confused. Here's a brief run-down to help us get our rices right.

Rice is divided into three classifications, based on the length of its grain. **Long grain rice** is the most popular. When cooked, the grains stay separate and fluffy, making them perfect for casseroles, salads, and pilafs. **Medium grain rice** is plumper, shorter, and a bit stickier when cooked. **Short grain rice** is almost round in shape—kind of stubby, actually. It's sticky when cooked. **Arborio** is a popular Italian short grain with a creamy texture that's used for making risotto.

Brown rice gets top honors as far as nutrition goes because it's undergone very little processing. In fact, brown rice has three times as much fiber as white rice. Only its inedible outer hull has been removed, with the valuable bran left intact. It takes longer to cook brown rice than other types of rice, but its nutty flavor and chewy texture are worth it. You can buy it in long, medium, and short grains. Save on cooking time by using Uncle Ben's Wholegrain Brown Rice—it's ready in 25 minutes.

White rice, while not as nutritionally valuable or as full-flavored as whole-grain rice (both the hull and bran are removed), is still an important staple in healthy diets worldwide. It cooks in a relatively short time (20 minutes) and comes in long, medium, and short grains. **Instant rice** has been fully cooked, then dehydrated. The end product is a rice that is usually inferior in both flavor and texture.

Wild rice is not truly a rice, but the grain of an aquatic grass native to North America. It's difficult to produce and therefore more expensive. Wild rice is usually combined with other rices for use in stuffings, side dishes, and salads.

Basmati and **Texmati** are known as aromatic rices because they have a faint smokey aroma when they're cooking. They have slender, long grains and are most often served as side dishes.

Slim Pickin's

If you choose to eat
1 MEDIUM ORDER OF FRIES,
you'll be choosing a gut-busting
16 GRAMS OF FAT,
the equivalent of eating
80 CUPS OF YAMS.
Which would fill you up more?

Go for quality *and* quantity!

Show me the WEIGH

If you can't convince them, confuse them. When it comes to nutrition information, this seems to be the motto that some food manufacturers live by. Take the subject of cholesterol, for instance. Cholesterol, a waxy, fat-like substance that exists naturally in the body, is essential for bodily functions, including the production of cell membranes, sex hormones, and bile acids (which help digest fat). For the record, you can get your necessary supply of cholesterol from the liver (where 60-80% of it is produced) and by eating foods of animal origin: meat, fish, poultry, eggs, and dairy products. If cholesterol comes only from animal sources, why is it that some margarine and vegetable oil manufacturers tout their products (which are vegetable-based, not animal-based) as being "cholesterol-free"? They never had cholesterol to begin with! What's more, some foods labelled "cholesterol-free" such as cookies, crackers, and salad dressings may in fact be packed with saturated fat, and that spells disaster. Excess consumption of saturated fat reduces the liver's ability to clear cholesterol from the bloodstream, and that could lead to hardening of the arteries, a heart attack, or a stroke. Basically, it's the saturated fat in a food rather than its cholesterol content that has the greater impact on blood cholesterol levels. So the smart shopper is the one who pays less attention to all of the confusing hype about cholesterol, and starts minding the fats. When it comes to good health, cutting fat is where it's at.

All in the Yamily

You'd be no "meathead" for filling up on creamy-tasting, nutrient-rich gingered yams and sweet potatoes. They're loaded with potassium, beta-carotene, vitamin A, vitamin C, and calcium. "Eatith" as much as you like!

4 medium yams or sweet potatoes, peeled and sliced crosswise into 1/4-inch thick rounds
3/4 cup unsweetened apple juice
2 teaspoons grated ginger root
1 tablespoon brown sugar

Preheat oven to 425°.

Combine all ingredients in a large bowl and mix well. Spread mixture evenly in a medium casserole dish.

Bake, uncovered, for 30 minutes. Yams will be golden brown and most of the liquid will have evaporated. Serve immediately.

Makes 4 servings.

PER SERVING: 167 calories, 0.5 g fat, 39.5 g carbohydrate, 2.3 g protein, 20 mg sodium, 0 mg cholesterol
CALORIES FROM FAT: 2.5%

He's a light eater. As soon as it gets light, he starts eating.

Ex Grill Friends

Fab scent makes the heart grow fonder! These individual vegetable packets have an *ex*cellent taste and an *ex*cellent aroma. Cooked on the grill, they're tossed with a delicious blend of seasonings.

1 medium zucchini, cut into
   1/2-inch thick slices
1 small eggplant (about 1/2 pound),
   unpeeled, cut into 1-inch cubes
6 small red potatoes, unpeeled, cut into
   1/4-inch thick slices
1 medium red onion, cut into rings
1 yellow, orange, or red bell pepper,
   seeded, cut into 1-inch chunks
1 tablespoon olive oil
1/2 cup crumbled feta cheese
   (2 ounces)
3 cloves garlic, minced
1 teaspoon *each* dried rosemary
   and dried basil
1/4 teaspoon black pepper
6 12 x 15-inch pieces aluminum
   foil

BELLE, I LOVE WHAT YOU'VE DONE WITH YOUR STEM

VEGGIE REUNION

Prepare grill (medium heat setting).

Combine all ingredients in a large bowl and mix well to evenly distribute seasonings.

Spray foil sheets with non-stick spray. Place equal amounts of vegetable mixture in the center of each foil sheet. Fold up sides to create a loosely sealed pouch (you'll want the steam to be able to escape).

Place packets on grill and close lid. Cook for 30-35 minutes, until potatoes are tender. Serve immediately.

Makes 6 servings.

Hint: If you don't have a barbeque, bake veggie packets in a 400° oven for about 35 minutes.

WHAT'S IN IT FOR ME?

PER SERVING: 223 calories, 4.7 g fat,
41.7 g carbohydrate, 5.7 g protein,
120 mg sodium, 8 mg cholesterol
CALORIES FROM FAT: 18.2%

SAY IT AIN'T SO!

You've been duped! You probably thought a large Caesar salad was the healthiest thing on the lunch menu. Truth is, it weighs in at roughly 650 calories, and about 90% come from fat! Say it ain't so! You might as well have had the juicy burger and fries that you *really* wanted, because you've managed to load up on just as much fat. If you look for alternatives to the fatty dressing, salad really is a wise and healthy choice.

D. I. E. T.

is a four-letter word that really means...
DONE IN EVERY TIME

Ultimately, there isn't a diet on earth that works. Diets set people up for failure because they're impossible to sustain. They're temporary, unrealistic, and impractical. In fact, diets only benefit the manufacturers of diet food products and those preying on the desperation of millions and millions of overweight North Americans. Permanent changes in eating habits are needed to maintain a healthy weight and to promote overall health. Diets are only short term solutions, but low-fat, healthy eating is forever.

MIRROR, MIRROR ON MY OVEN LOW-FAT COOKIN' I AM LOVIN'

Show & Tell

Mother knows best—especially when it comes to extolling the virtues of broccoli. When she sternly insisted that you "eat your broccoli," she was obviously well aware that broccoli harbors a chemical called sulforophane which is thought to detoxify carcinogens. Studies have shown that broccoli and other cruciferous vegetables (those with cross-shaped flower petals, such as brussels sprouts, cabbage, kale, and cauliflower) may play a role in reducing the risk of developing certain forms of cancer. Not only does broccoli have one of the highest concentrations of calcium of any vegetable, but it's rich in vitamins A and C, potassium, iron, and B vitamins, too. Oh my gosh! This broccoli bragging makes us sound just like Mother!

Gotta MOVE It!

What ever happened to the days when kids used to frolic in the fresh air for hours on end until finally cajoled into the house for dinner? Today, it seems as though the average kid has traded in his baseball bat and hockey stick for a TV remote control and a Nintendo joystick. The result: overweight, lethargic, unhealthy children. North American children now spend, on average, more than two and a half hours each day watching television, which some suggest may promote weight gain not only because it's sedentary, but because it creates a semi-conscious state that lowers metabolism. The TV trance contributes even further to obesity when you consider the thousands of commercials for sugary, fatty foods that are bombarded upon children. It soon becomes a vicious circle: Overweight children often face the taunting and teasing of peers, and the resulting lack of self-esteem may be enough to keep him or her away from team sports and co-operative games. The child ends up sitting in front of the television more often. If that's not enough fuel to spark you, as a parent, to encourage physical activity for your kids, then consider this: A recent issue of *Life* magazine cited a 1993 study based on autopsies of 1,532 teenagers and young adults. It was discovered that all of them had fatty patches in their aortas and 50% actually had heart disease! If that doesn't break your heart, then what will?

♪ Rice 'n Easy Casserole

Traditional broccoli and rice casserole has taken an abrupt "lite" turn. Our version is so creamy and satisfying, you won't believe it's low in fat. Cauliflower lends a little excitement to this classic, uncomplicated favorite.

♪ YOU...LITE UP MY LIFE ♪

1 package (6 ounces) Uncle Ben's long grain and wild rice
2 cans (10-3/4 ounces each) reduced-fat Cream of Mushroom Soup, undiluted (Campbell's Healthy Request)
3/4 cup shredded reduced-fat sharp cheddar cheese (3 ounces)
2 teaspoons Dijon mustard
1-1/2 cups each broccoli and cauliflower florets

Prepare rice according to package directions, omitting butter. Set aside.

Preheat oven to 350°.

In a medium bowl, stir together soup, cheese, and Dijon mustard. Mix well.

Spray a medium casserole dish with non-stick spray. Layer 1/2 the soup mixture over bottom. Top with 1/2 the broccoli and cauliflower, followed by 1/2 the rice. Repeat layers. Cover and bake for 1 hour. Let cool for 5 minutes before serving.

Makes 6 servings.

PER SERVING: 166 calories, 4.5 g fat, 22.9 g carbohydrate, 8 g protein, 827 mg sodium, 14 mg cholesterol
CALORIES FROM FAT: 24.6%

WHAT'S IN IT FOR ME?

Intimate little dinners for two are damaging to the waistline—unless there's someone with you.

Cookoo Over Couscous

I'm cookoo over couscous! Crazy over the taste! Insane over the texture! Nuts about how healthy it is! And as soon as I get outta this straightjacket, I'm gonna dive into a heaping plateful!

1/2 cup chopped onions
1 clove garlic, minced
1-1/2 cups sliced mushrooms
1 cup chopped tomato
1/2 teaspoon *each* dried oregano
   and ground cumin
2 cups low-sodium, reduced-fat
   chicken broth
1/4 teaspoon crushed red pepper flakes
2 cups couscous (see page 154)
1/4 cup chopped fresh parsley

Spray a medium saucepan with non-stick spray. Add onions, garlic, and mushrooms. Cook and stir over medium heat until vegetables are tender, about 5 minutes.

Add tomatoes, oregano, and cumin. Cook for 1 more minute. Stir in broth and crushed red pepper flakes. Bring to a boil. Stir in couscous and parsley. Remove from heat. Cover and let stand for 5 minutes. Fluff with a fork before serving.

Makes 8 servings.

WHAT'S IN IT FOR ME?

PER SERVING: 191 calories, 0.5 g fat,
38.8 g carbohydrate, 7.3 g protein,
126 mg sodium, 0 mg cholesterol
CALORIES FROM FAT: 2.5%

Panting and perspiring heavily, two men on a tandem bicycle finally got to the top of a steep hill. "That was an unbelievably stiff climb," said the first man. "It certainly was," replied the second man. "And if I hadn't kept the brake on, we probably would have slid down backward!"

SAY IT AIN'T SO!

Feeling a little nutty? Well, there's nuttin' funny about the fat in cashews. One cup of salted cashews has 63 grams of fat, 787 calories, and 69% calories from fat! It's smarter to serve pretzels at your poker table. Remember, a full house beats a fat house any day.

Show me the WEIGH

"Eat, drink, and be merry" are truly words of wisdom. Food makes us feel better when times are tough and it nourishes us in ways that go well beyond carbohydrates and proteins. We eat out of emotional needs—we eat when we're happy, we eat when we're sad. Food is like an affirmation of life. Think of all the special occasions in life that are marked by happy meals with family and friends. With this in mind, it's easy to understand why dieting, which requires deprivation and starvation, doing without the many pleasures of food, means you're setting yourself up for disappointment. Dieting is downright dumb. Be smart and learn to love low-fat, nutritious foods. If you can eat when you're hungry, the chances are, you'll be much happier.

What the heck is "Cajun Spice" and where can I get it?

Cajun Spice is a pre-mixed blend of several spices including paprika, black and white pepper, cayenne pepper, garlic powder, onion powder, oregano, and thyme. It's widely available in most grocery stores. If you like, you can substitute a blend of your own favorite spices in this recipe. Just about anything goes with good ol' potatoes!

Show & Tell

Although the controversy about salt contributing to high blood pressure rages on, salt does have its virtues, too. It helps regulate the balance of bodily fluids and plays a role in muscle contractions and the transmission of electrical nerve impulses. The American Heart Association recommends that sodium intake should not exceed 2400 milligrams a day (one teaspoon of salt contains about 2000 milligrams of sodium). Remember, everything in moderation.

The Wedge of Light

At the conclusion of last week's episode, things were really heating up between Victoria and Drake as they both professed their undying love of seasoned potato wedges—baked, not fried. "These wedges are super tasty plain, with salt and vinegar, salsa, or ketchup," Victoria whispered suggestively. Stay tuned to find out if it's love at first bite!

4 large potatoes,
   unpeeled, scrubbed
1 tablespoon olive oil
1-1/2 teaspoons "Cajun Spice"
   seasoning

I ONLY HAVE EYES FOR YOU

Preheat oven to 400°.

Cut each potato lengthwise into 4 slices. Then cut each slice into 2 wedges.

Place potatoes in a large bowl. Add olive oil and Cajun spice. Toss well to coat potatoes evenly with oil and seasoning.

Transfer potatoes to a large baking sheet that has been sprayed with non-stick spray. Spread evenly in a single layer. Bake for 20 minutes. Turn wedges over and bake another 20-25 minutes, until golden brown on the outside and tender on the inside.

Makes 4 servings.

PER SERVING: 280 calories, 3.8 g fat, 57.9 g carbohydrate, 5.4 g protein, 72 mg sodium, 0 mg cholesterol
CALORIES FROM FAT: 11.8%

WHAT'S IN IT FOR ME?

GEE, IT LOOKS LIKE JOE'S REALLY COME OUT OF HIS SHELL TONIGHT

If dieticians say we are what we eat, then nuts must be one of the most popular foods.

Everybody Salsa

An all-purpose corn and black bean salsa—great by itself, spooned over chicken, fish, or baked potatoes, or stuffed in a pita pocket with tuna and chopped lettuce. Potential uses are limited only by your imagination. Tap into your creativity and go wild!

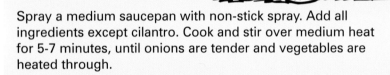

- 1 cup whole-kernel corn (thaw first if using frozen)
- 1 cup diced tomato
- 1 cup canned black beans, drained and rinsed
- 1/2 cup *each* diced onions and diced red bell pepper
- 1/4 cup grated carrots
- 1 jalapeño pepper, seeded and minced
- 1 clove garlic, minced
- 1 teaspoon ground cumin
- 1/2 teaspoon chili powder
- 1/4 teaspoon black pepper
- 1/4 cup chopped fresh cilantro

Spray a medium saucepan with non-stick spray. Add all ingredients except cilantro. Cook and stir over medium heat for 5-7 minutes, until onions are tender and vegetables are heated through.

Stir in cilantro. Serve warm or cold.

Makes about 4 cups.

WHAT'S IN IT FOR ME? ➤ PER SERVING (1/2 cup): 62 calories, 0.6 g fat, 13.4 g carbohydrate, 2.5 g protein, 152 mg sodium, 0 mg cholesterol CALORIES FROM FAT: 8.4%

Slim Pickin's

You'd have to oink out on **100 BAKED POTATOES** to consume the **10 GRAMS OF FAT** found in a measly **1 OUNCE OF POTATO CHIPS** (an average handful). Which would fill you up more?

Go for quality *and* quantity!

Show me the WEIGH

Chilies have been recognized for centuries as a cure for a number of illnesses, from indigestion to impotence. Capsaicin, the chemical agent that delivers the chili's heat, is actually used in some topical creams to relieve the agony of shingles, arthritis, and other painful conditions. Like the effect it has on our taste buds, capsaicin first stuns, then anesthetizes when used as a salve. When we eat chili peppers, our palate translates the heat as burningly tasty, causing our endorphins to kick in. This results in what some people describe to be a "runner's high." A fiery chili pepper is also a sure-fire remedy for a head cold since it irritates the mucous membranes lining your nose and throat, making the tissues "weep." In addition to these medicinal qualities, hot chili peppers are often used to repel muggers (mace) and to kill parasites. Pretty potent powers packed into one pepper!

The judge couldn't be disturbed at dinner because His Honor was at steak.

Dream Team Cream Pie

When chocolate and banana are teamed up, it's a guaranteed victory, especially with a winning formula that cuts fat from the roster. Also in the starting line-up for this creamy, dreamy pie are chocolate wafers to add some crunch power to the crust! Can't beat that!

1-1/2 cups crushed chocolate graham wafers
1 egg white
2 cups 1% milk
2 cups low-fat sour cream
2 packages (4 ounces each) instant chocolate pudding mix
1-1/2 cups sliced bananas

Preheat oven to 375°.

In a medium bowl, stir together crumbs and egg white until well mixed. Spray a 9-inch pie plate with non-stick spray. Press crumb mixture on bottom and up sides of pie plate. Bake for 8 minutes. Let cool before filling.

Pour milk into a deep bowl. Add sour cream and pudding mix. Beat with electric mixer on low speed for 2 minutes, until very thick and creamy.

Arrange 1/2 the bananas over bottom of cooled pie crust. Spread 1/2 pudding mixture over bananas. Top with remaining bananas, followed by remaining pudding mixture. Spread pudding to edges of pie. Refrigerate for 2-3 hours before serving. Garnish with light whipped topping, if desired.

Makes 8 servings.

The Way the Cookie Crumbles: To crush cookies or wafers for use in crumb crusts and toppings, first place the required number of cookies in a large plastic freezer bag and seal closed. Using a rolling pin, roll back and forth over cookies until they are reduced to fine crumbs. If you have a food processor, you can crumble the cookies quickly by using the chopping blade and pulsing on and off. If you want, you can substitute 1-1/2 cups Oreo Baking Crumbs for the crushed chocolate wafers in this recipe.

Show me the WEIGH

A quick lesson about the "Milky Weigh": 2% milk does *not* derive 2% of its calories from fat—35% of its calories actually come from fat! Homogenized milk is 49% fat, 1% milk is 23% fat, and skim milk is 4% fat. If you're still consuming homogenized milk, make the switch gradually to 2%, then to 1%, and eventually to skim. Your waistline will thank you!

Compare the fat grams:

Homogenized milk	8 grams fat/cup
2% milk	4.7 grams fat/cup
1% milk	2.6 grams fat/cup
Skim milk	0.4 grams fat/cup

WHAT'S IN IT FOR ME? ➡ PER SERVING: 289 calories, 4.9 g fat, 55.1 g carbohydrate, 8.7 g protein, 463 mg sodium, 4 mg cholesterol CALORIES FROM FAT: 14.8%

HOW DO I STAND, DOC?
I DON'T KNOW, IT'S A MIRACLE

Show & Tell

Cocoa butter is the vegetable fat of the cacao bean. The edible part of the bean (called the cocoa nib) is roasted, ground, and liquified to create chocolate liquor, and the fat content is extracted when the liquor is subject to high pressure. The brown powder remaining after most of the cocoa butter has been extracted is cocoa powder. Cocoa butter is the second most highly saturated vegetable fat, second only to coconut oil. Incidently, cocoa butter melts at 92-95°F, the temperature of the human tongue, an attractive quality that has often been milked by chocolate manufacturers.

Hot Fudge Monday

You read it right—it's not "sundae" and there's no ice cream, either. Instead, it's a heavenly fudgy cake smothered in a hot, chocolaty sauce. Incidently, serving this with a scoop of low-fat frozen yogurt makes for an incredible hot/cold melt-in-your-mouth experience!

Cake
1 cup all-purpose flour
3/4 cup unpacked brown sugar
1-1/2 tablespoons unsweetened cocoa powder
2 teaspoons baking powder
1/4 teaspoon salt
1/2 cup skim milk
2 tablespoons vegetable oil

Sauce
1 cup unpacked brown sugar
1/4 cup unsweetened cocoa powder
1-3/4 cups boiling water

I LOVE MONDAYS!

Preheat oven to 350°.

To prepare cake batter, combine flour, brown sugar, cocoa, baking powder, and salt in a medium bowl. Set aside.

In a small bowl, whisk together milk and oil. Add milk mixture to flour mixture. Using a wooden spoon, stir vigorously until well blended (you may also use an electric mixer on low speed). Pour batter over the bottom of an ungreased 8 x 8-inch baking pan. Spread evenly.

In a small bowl, mix together second amount brown sugar and second amount cocoa. Sprinkle mixture evenly over batter. Pour boiling water over top. DO NOT STIR! Bake for 40-45 minutes, until top of cake feels dry to touch. Remove from oven and let stand 5 minutes before serving. Cut into 6 pieces. Spoon sauce from bottom of pan over individual servings of cake.

Makes 6 servings.

PER SERVING: 285 calories, 5.7 g fat, 58.1 g carbohydrate, 4 g protein, 234 mg sodium, 1 mg cholesterol
CALORIES FROM FAT: 17%

WHAT'S IN IT FOR ME?

Chocolate Boy Scouts

Why should "Brownies" get all the attention? Our version of the traditional brownie is just as chewy and chocolaty, but it's also amazingly low in fat. Mmmmm!

1/3 cup unsweetened cocoa powder
1/2 cup all-purpose flour
1/4 teaspoon salt
1 cup packed brown sugar
1/2 cup baby food prunes
3 tablespoons butter, melted
2 egg whites
1 teaspoon vanilla
1/4 cup chopped walnuts

Preheat oven to 325°.

Combine cocoa, flour, and salt in a small bowl. Set aside.

Using a wooden spoon or an electric mixer on low speed, blend together brown sugar, prunes, butter, egg whites, and vanilla. Gradually add flour mixture and blend after each addition. Stir in walnuts.

Spray an 8 x 8-inch baking pan with non-stick spray. Pour batter into pan and spread evenly. Bake for 20-22 minutes, until edges feel dry to touch but center appears fudgy. Do not overbake.

Remove from oven and let cool in pan before slicing. For maximum moistness, store squares in an airtight container.

Makes 12 Boy Scouts.

WHAT'S IN IT FOR ME?

PER SERVING: 145 calories, 4.7 g fat, 25.1 g carbohydrate, 2.5 g protein, 62 mg sodium, 8 mg cholesterol
CALORIES FROM FAT: 27.8%

What the heck are "baby food prunes" and what are they doing in this recipe?

Prunes are an excellent fat substitute when used in baked goods. By using puréed prunes to replace most of the butter or oil normally found in fudge brownies, you'll save at least 25 grams of fat, without jeopardizing flavor or moistness. Look for a baby food jar that says "Strained Prunes" or make your own prune purée by processing 1-1/2 cups pitted prunes and 8 tablespoons water in a food processor until smooth. Use the amount specified in the recipe and store the rest in the refrigerator.

Slim Pickin's

If you choose to eat a measly
2 GOURMET-STYLE SEMI-SWEET CHOCOLATE CHIP COOKIES,
you'll be choosing a humungous
21 GRAMS OF FAT,
the equivalent of eating
35 CUPS OF WILD RICE.
Which would fill you up more?

Go for quality *and* quantity!

Trivial Tidbit

In the 18th and 19th centuries, chocolate was believed to have medicinal properties and was sold by pharmacists to relieve coughs, as an anti-inflammatory, as an aid to digestion, as an anti-spasmodic, and as an aid to weight gain.

TAKE TWO OF THESE CHOCOLATE BARS AND CALL ME IN THE MORNING

Show & Tell

Don't be misled by the % MF (milk fat) or % BF (butterfat) figures that appear on the labels of dairy products. This percentage refers to the *weight* of fat in the product, not to the percentage of calories from fat. For instance, cream cheese with 23% MF may still derive 83% of its calories from fat! It's best to stick with skim and 1% milk, and look for the words "low-fat" on other dairy products like sour cream, cottage cheese, and yogurt.

Gotta MOVE It!

Forget the slogan "no pain, no gain." Pain is often an early warning sign of injuries from strain and overuse. But killer workouts (working out at an intensity that's leaps and bounds above your normal fitness level) can damage more than just muscles, tendons, and ligaments. More damage is ultimately done to your attitude about exercise in general, and your desire to make it a regular part of your life. Who looks forward to voluntary torture? Who would want to stick with it? No one—that's who! It makes much more sense to exercise at a moderate, consistent level for a longer period of time than it does to get in there and act like a Ninja Turtle on a sugar high!

Did you hear about Snow White's brother? His name is Egg White. Get the yolk?

Say "Cheesecake"

No doubt you'll be grinning from ear to ear when you discover that this remarkably luscious cherry-topped cheesecake has less than 4 GRAMS OF FAT per slice! You read that correctly—only 4 grams—a far cry from traditional fat-laden cheesecake. A great guilt-free treat!

1-1/2 cups crushed low-fat
   graham wafers
1 tablespoon sugar
1 egg white
1 cup low-fat (1%) cottage cheese
2 cups low-fat sour cream
1/2 cup sugar
2 tablespoons all-purpose flour
1 egg
2 egg whites
2 teaspoons vanilla
1 can (21 ounces) cherry or
   blueberry pie filling, or fresh
   fruit to top cake

Preheat oven to 375°.

Spray an 8-inch springform pan with non-stick spray. Set aside.

In a small bowl, mix together graham crumbs and sugar. Add egg white. Stir until well blended. Press crumb mixture firmly over bottom and part way up sides of springform pan. Bake just until edges feel firm and dry, about 8 minutes. Be careful not to overbake. Set aside to cool. Reduce oven to 300°.

In blender, process cottage cheese and sour cream until smooth (about 1 minute). Add sugar, flour, egg, egg whites, and vanilla and process again until well blended.

Pour filling into pie crust and bake about 1 hour and 15 minutes, or until edges are dry to touch and center jiggles only slightly when pan is shaken. Remove from oven and cool completely. Cover and refrigerate for at least 5 hours before serving. Run a knife along inside edge of pan and remove sides. Serve with pie filling or fresh fruit on top.

Makes 8 large slices.

PER SLICE (with cherry pie filling):
281 calories, 3.6 g fat,
53.7 g carbohydrate, 11 g protein,
234 mg sodium, 31 mg cholesterol
CALORIES FROM FAT: 11.1%

WHAT'S IN IT FOR ME?

Charlie's Angel Food Cake

Our good friend Charlie gave us this recipe. It makes a delicious, light dessert or a tasty, fruity treat after a long day of thwarting criminals, roller-skating, and feathering your hair.

GOOD WORK, ANGELS. LET'S CELEBRATE WITH SOME CAKE

Topping
1 cup *each* strawberries, raspberries, and blueberries (if using frozen berries, buy the unsweetened variety and thaw before using)
1 tablespoon sugar
3/4 cup low-fat sour cream
3 tablespoons honey
1 tablespoon frozen orange juice concentrate

Cake
1 cup sifted cake and pastry flour
1-1/2 cups sugar
12 egg whites, at room temperature
1-1/2 teaspoons cream of tartar
1/2 teaspoon salt
1 teaspoon vanilla
1/2 teaspoon almond extract

To prepare topping, combine berries and sugar in a medium bowl. Cover and refrigerate until serving time. Combine sour cream, honey, and orange juice concentrate in a small bowl. Cover and refrigerate until serving time.

Preheat oven to 350°.

To prepare cake, sift together flour with 3/4 cup sugar. Sift again and set aside.

In a large non-plastic bowl, beat egg whites until foamy using an electric mixer on medium speed (about 45 seconds). Add cream of tartar and salt.

Beat again on medium speed until soft peaks form when beater is slowly raised (about 1-1/2 minutes). Gradually beat in remaining sugar, 1/4 cup at a time. Turn beater to high speed. Beat until egg whites are glossy and stiff peaks form (about 1-1/2 minutes).

Sprinkle vanilla and almond extract over egg whites. Sift flour mixture, 1/4 cup at a time, over egg whites. Gently fold in each addition of flour using a rubber spatula.

Pour batter into an ungreased 9 or 10-inch angel food tube pan. Using a knife, cut through batter to remove large air pockets. Smooth top.

Bake for 40-45 minutes, until cake is golden brown and top springs back when lightly touched.

Invert cake pan onto the neck of a bottle and let hang to cool, about 1-1/2 hours.

Run a knife along inside edge of pan and around tube to loosen cake. Invert onto a serving plate. Top each slice of cake with 2 tablespoons berries. Drizzle with 1 tablespoon orange cream sauce. Serve immediately.

Makes 12 servings.

WHAT'S IN IT FOR ME?

PER SERVING: 199 calories, 0.4 g fat, 44.2 g carbohydrate, 5.5 g protein, 146 mg sodium, 1 mg cholesterol
CALORIES FROM FAT: 2%

***D**on't dig your grave with a knife and fork.*

English Proverb

COOKING 101

Avoid that sinking feeling! You can prevent ingredients such as chocolate chips, nuts, and dried fruit from settling to the bottom of your cake by coating the chips, nuts, etc. with a light dusting of flour before mixing them into the batter. The flour absorbs some of the surface oil and water that exudes from these ingredients during baking, reducing their tendency to sink to the bottom.

SAY IT AIN'T SO!

Have you ever thought, "How can I possibly be gaining weight? All I have for breakfast every day is a muffin on the way to work!" Well think about this: A large commercially made muffin contains 400 to 500 calories, and typically 70% of them come from fat (more than a chocolate glazed donut). Huge quantities of oil and butter are to blame. So drive past the pastry shop at full speed and instead, bring some homemade low-fat muffins along for the ride. You won't get "hit in the rear" with these lower-fat choices.

Trivial Tidbit
As far as burning calories goes, 100 hearty, good laughs are considered the equivalent of 10 minutes of rowing. Looks like more giggling leads to less jiggling!

Fantasy Island Cake

Taking a bite of this luscious, moist cake is like being whisked away to a tropical paradise. Dream-come-true delicious!

1-3/4 cups all-purpose flour
1 cup granulated sugar
1/2 cup unpacked brown
   sugar
1 teaspoon baking powder
1 teaspoon baking soda
1 cup crushed pineapple
   in juice
1/3 cup mashed banana (ripe!)
1 egg
2 egg whites
3/4 teaspoon vanilla
1/2 cup mini chocolate chips
1/3 cup chopped walnuts
1 tablespoon all-purpose flour

Preheat oven to 350°.

Combine flour, sugar, brown sugar, baking powder, and baking soda in a medium bowl. Mix well and set aside.

In a large bowl, blend together crushed pineapple (and juice), banana, egg, egg whites, and vanilla using an electric mixer on low speed. Do not overbeat. Gradually add flour mixture and beat on medium-high speed until all flour has been incorporated.

In a small bowl, mix together chocolate chips, walnuts, and 1 tablespoon flour. Fold into batter.

Spray an 8 x 8-inch baking pan with non-stick spray. Pour batter into pan. Bake for 40-45 minutes, until wooden pick inserted in center comes out clean. Let cake cool completely in pan. Cut into 12 pieces and store at room temperature in an airtight container.

Makes 12 servings.

PER SERVING: 232 calories, 4.7 g fat, 44.7 g carbohydrate, 4.5 g protein, 153 mg sodium, 18 mg cholesterol
CALORIES FROM FAT: 17.7%

Peach on Earth

Good fill for men—and women, too! This scrumptious pie is just peachy and it's as light on the fork as it is on the hips! So take a ride on the Peach Train. Choo choose this recipe when you want to indulge in a dessert that won't weigh you down.

- 1 9-inch deep-dish frozen pie crust shell
- 3/4 cup sugar
- 2 tablespoons corn syrup
- 5 tablespoons cornstarch
- 1 cup boiling water
- 1/4 cup peach-flavored Jell-o powder
- 8-9 medium peaches, peeled and sliced

THIS PIE'S REAL PEACHY MAN

Bake pie crust according to package directions. Cool completely before filling.

To prepare filling, combine sugar, corn syrup, cornstarch, and boiling water in a medium saucepan. Cook and stir over medium-high heat until mixture thickens and becomes clear (it will become quite thick). Remove from heat and stir in jello powder. Let cool to room temperature. Add peaches and stir until evenly coated. Pour into prepared pie shell. Refrigerate for 3-4 hours before serving.

Makes 8 servings.

Hint: Look for a frozen pie crust shell that has less than 7 grams of fat per serving.

WHAT'S IN IT FOR ME? ➤ PER SERVING: 278 calories, 6.9 g fat, 52.4 g carbohydrate, 2.2 g protein, 150 mg sodium, 6 mg cholesterol CALORIES FROM FAT: 22.2%

Peaches are much easier to peel if you first immerse them in boiling water for 30 seconds. Use a sharp paring knife to remove the peel. When fresh peaches aren't in season, you may substitute canned peaches in their place. Just make sure you drain them well, and pat them dry before adding to the other ingredients.

Show me the WEIGH

Contrary to popular belief, margarine isn't always a healthy substitute for butter. In fact, most margarines contain significant amounts of saturated fats (the kind we want to avoid). The misconception arises because margarines are typically made with vegetable oils, and these oils are low in saturated fat. But in order to solidify the oils into a spread and to increase shelf life, margarine manufacturers convert the unsaturated fats into trans fatty acids (by adding hydrogen atoms). These trans fatty acids, absorbed by the body, act like saturated fats and upset the body's balance of HDL and LDL cholesterols. As a rule of thumb, the harder the margarine, the more trans fatty acids it contains, so soft tub margarines are preferable to stick margarines. Make sure you read the label before you buy. Choose margarines made from oils highest in polyunsaturated fats or look for non-hydrogenated margarines. Whether you choose to eat butter or margarine, the important thing is to cut back on your consumption of all types of fat.

Upper Crust: A number of persons stuck together by their dough.

SAY IT AIN'T SO!

It's better to "say cheese" than it is to overindulge on it. Cheddar cheese is almost 74% fat. Brie is more than 80% fat. To cheese us off even more, advertisers mislead us by comparing one teaspoon of cream cheese to one of butter. But who uses just one teaspoon of cream cheese? Well, maybe you should. One measly ounce has 10 grams of fat and 90% of its calories are derived from fat! But cheese does have nutritional value, so don't cut the cheese out of your diet entirely. Just moderate your intake a little and look for reduced-fat versions in your supermarket.

Gotta MOVE It!

If you want to get ahead in the health and fitness game, you've got to become a "mover and a shaker." Continuous physical movement that elevates your heart rate for at least thirty minutes is the best way to fight flab and build a leaner, healthier you. Any kind of movement will do: walking, biking, hiking, tennis, dancing, or skiing. Pick the aerobic activity that best suits your lifestyle and then "shake your wiggly things til they don't shake no more!"

Did you hear about the diet club that went fatty dipping?

♪ Puddin' on the Ritz

Traditional bread pudding gets all jazzed up with cinnamon-raisin bread in place of the ordinary stuff, and chopped apples tossed in for a pleasing texture and tasty goodness. A treat for breakfast with a light drizzle of maple syrup!

4 cups cubed cinnamon-raisin bread (slightly stale)
1 cup peeled and chopped Granny Smith apples
1/2 cup packed brown sugar
2 eggs
1 cup evaporated 2% milk
1/2 cup skim milk
1-1/2 teaspoons vanilla
1/4 teaspoon ground cinnamon
1/8 teaspoon ground nutmeg

Preheat oven to 350°.

Spray an 8 x 8-inch baking pan with non-stick spray. Set aside.

Toss bread cubes and apples together in a large bowl. In a separate bowl, whisk together brown sugar and eggs. Add evaporated milk, skim milk, vanilla, cinnamon, and nutmeg. Whisk again.

Pour egg/milk mixture over bread cubes and apples. Stir well. Let stand for 5 minutes for bread to absorb liquid.

Transfer mixture to baking pan. Make sure apples are evenly distributed throughout pan. Bake for 50 minutes, until bread is a deep golden brown and puffed up. A knife inserted in the center should come out clean.

Slice into 6 squares and serve warm.

Makes 6 servings.

PER SERVING: 231 calories, 4.3 g fat, 42 g carbohydrate, 8.1 g protein, 192 mg sodium, 81 mg cholesterol
CALORIES FROM FAT: 16%

WHAT'S IN IT FOR ME?

Rude Barb's Strawbapple Crisp

One Saturday afternoon I was in the supermarket, leaning over the fresh produce section, when my left contact lens fell onto a large stalk of rhubarb. "Hold on there!" I exclaimed, yanking the rhubarb from the hands of a strange-looking female shopper. "I've got my eye on these!" "Not a chance, Toots" she snapped. "I saw 'em first. And besides, this rhubarb makes my strawberry-apple-rhubarb crisp better than everyone else's!" What a rude barb that was!

Topping
3/4 cup quick-cooking rolled oats
1/4 cup whole wheat flour
1/4 cup packed brown sugar
1/2 teaspoon ground cinnamon
3 tablespoons reduced-fat butter or margarine, melted (not fat-free)

Fruit
3 cups peeled and sliced Granny Smith apples
1-1/2 cups sliced strawberries
1-1/2 cups sliced rhubarb
1/2 cup packed brown sugar
2 tablespoons orange juice
1-1/2 tablespoons cornstarch

Preheat oven to 375°.

Combine all topping ingredients in a medium bowl until mixture resembles coarse crumbs. Set aside.

Combine all fruit ingredients in a large bowl. Mix well. Spray a shallow 11 x 8-inch baking dish with non-stick spray. Pour in fruit and spread evenly. Sprinkle topping over fruit. Bake, uncovered, for 35-40 minutes, until fruit is tender and topping is golden brown. Best served warm or at room temperature.

Makes 6 servings.

WHAT'S IN IT FOR ME? ➡ PER SERVING: 248 calories, 4.2 g fat, 52.3 g carbohydrate, 3.1 g protein, 44 mg sodium, 6 mg cholesterol CALORIES FROM FAT: 14.5%

D. I. E. T.

is a four-letter word that really means...
DID I EAT TODAY?

"If I did, it wasn't very memorable." Dieting is synonymous with starvation. That's why diets stink—you're in a voluntary state of famine. Who could possibly stay motivated to starve, to survive on two pieces of Melba toast and half a grapefruit for lunch, followed by an "insta-meal chalkolate shake" for supper? The truth is, you need a lot more than 600 calories a day to support a healthy body. It's time to forget about pre-packaged chemical concoctions disguised as dinner and start enjoying *real* food. Forget about dieting and get on with living!

SAY IT AIN'T SO!

It's a love/hate relationship! Pizza lovers will probably hate it when they hear the truth about the fat content in a Pepperoni Lover's Pan Pizza. One slice offers 25 grams of fat, 362 calories, and 62% calories from fat! If you must get a "pizza" the action, at least try veggie toppings so you'll cut down on artery-clogging fat, the real heartbreaker.

Wake Up and Smell the Coffee Cheesecake

"I love the taste of coffee!" Joe said perkily (and it's especially good in this sumptuous, creamy cheesecake).

Crust
1-1/2 cups crushed low-fat graham wafers
1 tablespoon sugar
1 egg white

Filling
2/3 cup sugar
1/3 cup all-purpose flour
1 tablespoon cornstarch
1-1/2 cups low-fat (1%) cottage cheese
1 package (8 ounces) "light" cream cheese
1 egg
2 egg whites
1 teaspoon vanilla
1/2 cup skim milk
2 tablespoons instant coffee granules
1/3 cup low-fat sour cream
3 egg whites, at room temperature
4 tablespoons sugar

Preheat oven to 375°.

Combine graham crumbs and sugar in a small bowl. Add egg white and mix well. Press onto bottom of 9-inch springform pan that has been sprayed with non-stick spray. Bake just until edges feel firm and dry, about 8 minutes. Let cool.

Reduce oven temperature to 300°. Combine first amount sugar, flour, and cornstarch in a small bowl. Set aside.

Process cottage cheese in a blender until smooth. Transfer to a large bowl. Add cream cheese, egg, and first amount egg whites. Beat with an electric mixer on high speed until smooth, about 3 minutes.

ONLY 5 GRAMS OF FAT PER SLICE -- AND THAT'S NO JAVA!

Gradually add flour mixture and beat until well blended. Add vanilla and beat again.

Mix coffee granules with skim milk until dissolved. Add to cheese mixture along with sour cream. Beat until smooth.

In separate bowl, beat second amount egg whites with a mixer at high speed until soft peaks form. Add second amount sugar, 1 tablespoon at a time, beating at high speed until stiff peaks form. Fold egg white mixture into cheese mixture.

Pour batter into prepared crust. Bake for 1 hour and 10 minutes, or until almost set. Turn oven off. Leave cake in oven for 1 hour. Cool completely. Cover and refrigerate for 8 hours or overnight. Run knife along edges of cake before removing sides of pan.

Makes 12 servings.

PER SERVING: 203 calories, 5.4 g fat, 30.9 g carbohydrate, 9.8 g protein, 309 mg sodium, 28 mg cholesterol
CALORIES FROM FAT: 23%

WHAT'S IN IT FOR ME?

ALL YOU CAN EAT BUFFET

DOGGIE BAG

He who stuffeth, puffeth.

Viceless Riceless Pudding

Made with couscous instead of rice, this pudding is creamy and filling, just like Mom's, but it's probably better for you (sorry, Mom). Great for dessert or for breakfast.

1 cup skim milk
1/2 cup plus 1 tablespoon couscous
2-1/2 tablespoons brown sugar
1/4 cup dark raisins
1/4 teaspoon ground cinnamon
1/3 cup non-fat vanilla yogurt

Heat the milk in a small saucepan until just boiling. Stir in couscous, brown sugar, raisins, and cinnamon. Remove mixture from heat and cover with a tight-fitting lid. Allow to sit until milk is absorbed (about 10 minutes).

Stir in yogurt and serve warm. Sprinkle top lightly with more cinnamon, if desired.

Makes 4 servings.

YOU'VE EARNED YOUR WINGS

WHAT'S IN IT FOR ME? → PER SERVING: 180 calories, 0.4 g fat, 38.2 g carbohydrate, 6.7 g protein, 50 mg sodium, 2 mg cholesterol CALORIES FROM FAT: 2%

Did you hear about the new restaurant on the moon? The food's great but it just doesn't have any atmosphere.

What the heck is "couscous" and where can I get it?

Couscous is a Moroccan grain that's loaded with fiber, vitamins, and minerals. It's an excellent source of carbohydrates and is virtually fat-free. The name comes from the Arab word "Kuskus" which means "to grind small." Couscous is simply small grains of semolina, the heart of durum wheat. It can be served in any main dish, salad, or side dish as an alternative to rice or pasta. If you can boil water, you can cook couscous. You'll find it in the rice section of your grocery store.

Show me the WEIGH

Do you have Great Expectations? One of the biggest mistakes that people make when embarking on a new eating and exercise plan is having unrealistic expectations. And it's no wonder. Look at the national ideals against which men and women compare themselves. Take the average female model, for instance, who registers in at 5 feet 9 inches tall and weighs 123 pounds. What happens if you're 5 foot 4 and pear-shaped (like the majority of North American women)? Instead of setting yourself up for a huge disappointment, why not scrap the notions of being pencil thin or perfectly-chiseled? Throw those notions out the window and instead think "fit." Fitness is a lot easier to attain than thinness. Anyone, of any basic body shape, of any height, of any age, can become fit. In the long run, becoming fit will help you feel better, look better, and lead an energy-filled life. More importantly, striving for a realistic, attainable personal fitness level means that you were able to look long and hard at the reflection in the mirror and proudly accept the person who was staring back at you.

COOKING 101

Be careful not to over-bake low-fat baked goods. When a baking time range is given, always check for "doneness" at the lowest point of the range. An automatic timer with a buzzer or bell is an essential gadget. It's also a good idea to purchase an oven thermometer to check your oven for temperature accuracy.

Gotta MOVE It!

We all know that if we want to burn fat, and lots of it, we need some form of aerobic exercise—"aerobic" meaning elevating your heart rate to moderate intensity levels by moving for at least 30 minutes. This type of continuous movement feeds the body with oxygen, and fat burns in oxygen. But don't kill yourself! If you work out beyond your fitness level (to the point where you're gasping for air and you can't squeak out a word of conversation), you won't be burning fat because oxygen can't be supplied to the body fast enough to burn fat. Go slow at first if you have to. You might feel like a slug and you might be moving at the pace of a slug, too. But keep it up, keep moving for 30 minutes, 4 or 5 times a week, and eventually you'll be a lean, mean, fine-tuned machine.

She diets religiously—one day a week.

"Oops! There it is!" Chocolate Cake

The accidental dessert—that's what this is! We still don't know how or why this combination of ingredients ended up in the pan, but what a spectacular result! Super moist and chocolaty, you won't believe this cake is low in fat. Kids will love it!

1 cup all-purpose flour
1/3 cup unsweetened cocoa powder
1-1/2 teaspoons baking powder
1 teaspoon baking soda
3/4 teaspoon cinnamon
1/4 teaspoon salt
1-1/4 cups packed brown sugar
1 egg
2 egg whites
3 tablespoons canola or vegetable oil
1 teaspoon vanilla
1/4 teaspoon almond extract
1 cup low-fat sour cream
1/2 cup mini chocolate chips

Preheat oven to 350°.

In a small bowl, mix together flour, cocoa, baking powder, baking soda, cinnamon, and salt. Set aside.

In a medium bowl, blend together brown sugar, egg, egg whites, and oil with an electric mixer on medium speed. Add vanilla, almond extract, and sour cream. Beat on low speed until well blended.

Gradually add flour mixture to sour cream mixture, beating on medium speed. Fold in chocolate chips.

Spray an 8 x 8-inch pan with non-stick spray. Spread batter evenly in pan. Bake for 40-45 minutes, until wooden pick inserted in center comes out clean. Be sure to check cake after 40 minutes, as you don't want to overbake it. Remove from oven and let cool in pan for 15 minutes. Cut into 12 squares. For maximum moistness, store at room temperature in an airtight container.

Makes 12 servings.

PER SERVING: 218 calories, 6.6 g fat, 37.4 g carbohydrate, 4 g protein, 174 mg sodium, 18 mg cholesterol
CALORIES FROM FAT: 26.4%

No Pudge Chocolate Fudge

Chocoholics unite and rejoice! This "died and gone to heaven" chocolaty treat is getting rave reviews, mostly because we've taken out the pudgy ingredients but kept the really fudgy ones.

2 cups granulated sugar
6 tablespoons unsweetened cocoa powder
2/3 cup evaporated 2% milk
3 tablespoons butter, divided
2 tablespoons light corn syrup
1 teaspoon vanilla

Fill sink with 1/2 inch of cool water. Line bottom of a 9 x 5-inch loaf pan with a piece of wax paper that sticks up 2 inches at the ends of pan (so you can lift the fudge out of the pan when it's ready). Set aside.

Combine sugar, cocoa, evaporated milk, 2 tablespoons butter, and corn syrup in a medium saucepan. Place over medium-low heat. Cook slowly, stirring often, until sugar is completely dissolved and butter is melted. Mixture should be very smooth. This takes about 10 minutes.

Increase heat to medium-high. Insert candy thermometer at this point, if you're using one.

WHAT'S IN IT FOR ME? ➡ PER SERVING: 136 calories, 2.6 g fat, 28.9 g carbohydrate, 1.1 g protein, 16 mg sodium, 7 mg cholesterol CALORIES FROM FAT: 16.2%

Bring mixture to a boil. Boil until fudge reaches the "soft ball stage," stirring occasionally (see "Finicky Fudge"). This stage is usually reached anywhere between 234° and 240°. Remove immediately from heat. Place pot in sink. Make sure water only comes up 1/2 inch on side of pot (you don't want to cool it too quickly). Add remaining 1 tablespoon butter and vanilla. Do not stir yet.

Allow fudge to cool for 5 minutes in water. Lift from sink and let fudge cool at room temperature for another 20 minutes (if you're using a thermometer, let the fudge cool to 110°). When you press down lightly on the fudge it should indent a little. A "skin" will have formed on top. This is good.

Using a wooden spoon and a bit of muscle, begin to stir the fudge. Stop stirring and observe the fudge every once in a while. You're looking for it to lose its shine, lighten slightly in color, and become thicker. Repeat stirring and observing until these changes take place.

Spread fudge into prepared pan. Refrigerate until fudge is "set," about 1 hour. Run knife around edge of pan and lift out fudge by holding on to wax paper. Slice into 16 rectangular chunks. Store covered in fridge.

Makes 16 pieces.

Finicky Fudge

Making a great batch of creamy, smooth fudge is a little bit of art and a little bit of science. Testing for the "soft-ball stage" that's so critical to fudge-making really isn't that difficult if you follow these simple steps:

1. Pour about 1/2 a teaspoon of the boiling hot syrup into a custard cup or small dessert dish filled with ice cold water.

2. Watch the fudge. If it dissipates immediately, it's not ready. If it forms a round mass and the end of the pour remains elevated, it should be ready. If the syrup

becomes quite stiff and sticks up in the air, remove pot from heat immediately, as you're now pushing your luck.

3. Form syrup into a ball. The best way to do this is to empty the water from the cup, then gather up the syrup. If it won't gather or falls apart, it's not ready. If it's fairly round and holds its shape, taste it. If it's a bit chewy and offers some resistance, it's ready! If it's really chewy and you can stretch it, then you've probably made caramel.

4. At the first sign that your fudge is ready, remove it from the heat, place the pot in 1/2 an inch of cool water, and proceed according to recipe instructions.

Show & Tell

Why are oats so oat-standing? Well, first of all, they're really loaded with complex carbohydrates and fiber. Even better, oats have very little fat. They're also a source of vitamin E, iron, manganese, zinc, and folacin. And if that isn't enough to convince you of the merits of eating your oatmeal, in Germany they insist that eating a bowl of oatmeal with fried onions is a sure-fire cure for a hangover! (*Nein Danke!* *No Thanks!*)

Slim Pickin's

You'd have to oink out on
17 BANANAS
to consume the unbelievable
17 GRAMS OF FAT
found in
1 CUP OF EGGNOG.
Which would fill you up more?

Go for quality *and* quantity!

IT SAYS HERE YOU WERE THE STARTING CENTER FOR THE CHICAGO BULLS...

The closest to perfection a person ever comes is when they fill out a job application form.

Strike Three, Yer Oat Cookies

Batter up! At the plate we have oatmeal-raisin cookies that are:

1. Delicious
2. Chewy and moist
3. Low in fat

Strike three, yer oat-standing!

STRIKE THREE, YER OAT!

2 cups quick-cooking rolled oats
3/4 cup plus 2 tablespoons
   all-purpose flour
1/2 teaspoon baking soda
1/2 teaspoon salt
1 cup lightly packed brown sugar
1/3 cup reduced-fat butter or
   margarine (not fat-free)
1/4 cup buttermilk
1 teaspoon vanilla
1/2 cup dark raisins

Preheat oven to 325°.

Combine oats, flour, baking soda, and salt in a medium bowl. Mix well.

In a large bowl, combine brown sugar, butter or margarine, buttermilk, and vanilla. Beat with electric mixer on low speed for 1-2 minutes, until well blended. Add oat mixture to sugar mixture. Stir until dry ingredients are moistened. Stir in raisins.

Shape dough into 16 balls (1-1/2-inch diameter). Place 2 inches apart on a large cookie sheet that has been sprayed with non-stick spray. Flatten cookies to 1/4-inch thickness using the back of a spoon. Dip the spoon in water to prevent it from sticking to cookies. Bake for 13-14 minutes, until tops of cookies are dry to touch and bottoms are golden brown. Do not overbake! Remove from tray immediately and let cool.

Makes 16 large cookies.

PER SERVING: 134 calories, 2.8 g fat, 25.5 g carbohydrate, 2.8 g protein, 174 mg sodium, 4 mg cholesterol
CALORIES FROM FAT: 18.1%

WHAT'S IN IT FOR ME?

GUNGA GALUNGA

Recipes without a home

You're probably wondering, "What the heck is Gunga Galunga?" Truth is, we just couldn't come up with a name for this category. It's the place where we put recipes that don't really belong in any other section. So, we decided to quote some famed gibberish that was uttered by the Dalai Lama to a famous caddy during a round of golf in the classic movie "Caddyshack." What does Gunga Galunga mean? Only the Dalai Lama knows!

Tortilla Orlando at Dawn

The idea for these delectable breakfast tortillas came from the guy who lived in the apartment one floor above us. Whenever he would make them, he would tell us to "knock three times on the ceiling" if we wanted some. Well, we darn near put a hole through his floor every time!

1/2 cup diced red bell pepper
4 ounces lean cooked ham slices, chopped
1/4 cup *each* minced onions and chopped green onions
2 tablespoons diced mild green chilies (canned, drained)
3 eggs
5 egg whites
1/2 teaspoon ground cumin
1/4 teaspoon *each* salt and garlic powder
8 7-inch flour tortillas
3/4 cup shredded reduced-fat sharp cheddar cheese (3 ounces)
1-1/2 cups salsa (mild, medium, or hot)

Preheat oven to 350°.

Spray a large skillet with non-stick spray. Add red pepper, ham, onions, green onions, and chilies. Cook and stir over medium heat for 5 minutes.

Whisk together eggs, egg whites, cumin, salt, and garlic powder in a medium bowl. Add to ham and vegetables. Increase heat to medium-high. Cook until eggs are set, stirring often (about 4-5 minutes). Make sure the egg mixture is no longer runny. Remove from heat.

Reserve 1/4 cup shredded cheese. Working one at a time, spread 1/8 egg mixture in center of tortilla. Sprinkle with 1 tablespoon cheese. Roll up to enclose filling. Place seam side down in a 13 x 9-inch baking dish. Repeat with remaining egg mixture, cheese, and tortillas.

Pour salsa evenly over tortillas. Top with reserved 1/4 cup cheese. Cover with foil and bake for 25 minutes. Remove from oven. Uncover and let stand for 5 minutes before serving.

Makes 4 servings.

WHAT'S IN IT FOR ME? ➡ PER SERVING: 372 calories, 12.4 g fat, 46.9 g carbohydrate, 27 g protein, 1089 mg sodium, 184 mg cholesterol CALORIES FROM FAT: 27.3%

SAY IT AIN'T SO!

There are 34 grams of fat and 370 calories in the average avocado, with 81% of calories coming from fat. Holy Moly! What about guacamole! The guacamole that you dip your nacho chips into is made largely with avocados, so a little dip goes a long weigh!

Show me the **WEIGH**

"I feel like eating, so I must be hungry." Actually, you might not be. Thirst, stress, boredom, anxiety, and fatigue are often mistaken for hunger. And why fill the tank when it's still 3/4 full? If you're not truly hungry, try drinking a glass of water or a diet soda, going for a walk, or taking a nap before succumbing to the fridge's beckoning. If you find that you're obsessed by overpowering cravings, like the ones that some people have for "chocolate anything," indulge *a little* and then get on with healthy, low-fat eating. Or better yet, try sensible, appropriate alternatives. For instance, when it comes to satisfying your craving for chocolate covered almonds, a bag full of carrot and celery sticks just won't cut it. However, chocolate pudding made with skim milk or a low-fat Fudgsicle might do the trick.

HEY! I RESENT THAT!

If swimming is good for the physique, how do you account for ducks?

WHO NEEDS DONUTS?

COOKING 101

Cutting down on fat doesn't mean cutting down on flavor, and here's a fantastic example. These pancakes are absolutely bursting with taste and texture. A creamy, low-fat banana topping helps curb the urge to pile on the butter or margarine. Top that off with luscious maple syrup (0 grams of fat). By skipping the butter, you've saved yourself about 11 grams of unnecessary fat! That's a lot!

By the way, despite its rich-sounding name, buttermilk is low in fat. It falls between skim milk and 1% milk in percentage of calories from fat (about 20%). However, not all brands are created equal. Some are much higher in fat content than others, so make sure you read the label before buying.

VOILÀ! FILET OF SOLE!

All she knows about cooking is how to bring him to a boil.

N.Y.P.D. Blueberry Pancakes

These mouthwatering pancakes are so scrumptious and so huge, they were awarded top prize in the New York Pancake Department's *Fabulous Flapjack Flip-off.* Apparently, they're also the hands-down (or hands-up) favorite at the local police station.

3/4 cup *each* whole wheat flour and all-purpose flour
1 teaspoon *each* baking powder and baking soda
1-1/2 tablespoons sugar
2 egg whites
1-1/2 cups buttermilk
1/4 cup low-fat (1%) cottage cheese
1/2 teaspoon vanilla
1/4 cup blueberries
Banana Cream Topping (recipe follows)
3/4 cup pure maple syrup

In a large bowl, combine flours, baking powder, baking soda, and sugar. Set aside.

In a medium bowl, whisk together egg whites, buttermilk, cottage cheese, and vanilla.

Add buttermilk mixture to flour mixture. Stir just until dry ingredients are moistened. Gently stir in blueberries.

Spray a large, wide skillet or electric griddle with non-stick spray. Heat over medium heat. For each pancake, spoon about 1/2 cup batter onto skillet. Spread to make a 5 or 6-inch circle. Cook until bubbles break through the top and undersides are lightly browned. Flip and cook other side until lightly browned, 2-3 more minutes. Serve pancakes topped with 2 tablespoons Banana Cream Topping. Drizzle with maple syrup.

Makes 4 generous servings (8 large pancakes).

Banana Cream Topping
1/2 cup low-fat sour cream or yogurt
1/2 cup mashed banana (about 1 large)
2 tablespoons brown sugar
1/8 teaspoon ground cinnamon

Combine all ingredients in a small bowl. Cover and refrigerate until ready to use.

PER SERVING (with topping):
444 calories, 2.2 g fat,
94.3 g carbohydrate, 13.9 g protein,
582 mg sodium, 6 mg cholesterol
CALORIES FROM FAT: 4.4%

WHAT'S IN IT FOR ME?

Acropolis Sandwich

Finding a better-tasting Greek-style sandwich would be a Herculean task, for sure. Venus would have loved this one!

Tzatziki Sauce
1 cup non-fat plain yogurt
3/4 cup peeled, seeded, and finely chopped English cucumber
1 tablespoon chopped fresh dill
1 clove garlic, minced

4 boneless, skinless chicken breast halves, cut into strips
1-1/2 tablespoons lemon juice
1 teaspoon dried oregano
1 clove garlic, minced
4 7-inch "Greek-style" pitas
4 lettuce leaves
1 cup chopped tomato
1 medium red onion, cut into rings

In a small bowl, stir together yogurt, cucumber, dill, and garlic. Cover and refrigerate for at least 1 hour.

Combine lemon juice, oregano, and garlic in a medium bowl. Add chicken and toss until coated. Let stand 5 minutes.

Spray wok or skillet with non-stick spray. Add chicken and cook, stirring often, until no longer pink. Continue to cook until chicken is lightly browned.

Meanwhile, wrap pitas in foil and warm in 350° oven for 8 minutes.

To assemble, place lettuce leaf and 1/4 of the chicken on pita bread. Top with chopped tomatoes, onion rings, and 2 tablespoons tzatziki. Fold pita over filling and serve immediately. (Wrap bottom half of sandwich in aluminum foil to secure.)

Makes 4 servings.

WHAT'S IN IT FOR ME?

PER SERVING: 471 calories, 7.7 g fat, 55 g carbohydrate, 42.5 g protein, 450 mg sodium, 84 mg cholesterol
CALORIES FROM FAT: 15.1%

What the heck is a "Greek-style" pita and where am I supposed to find it?

"Greek-style" pitas are similar to Italian flatbread, only they're slightly thinner and a bit softer. When warmed, you can easily fold them over without breaking them in half (ideal for sandwiches). A distinguishing feature of "Greek-style" pitas that differentiates them from regular pitas is the absence of a hollow "pocket" inside. Also called "East Indian-style pitas," they're sold in most well-stocked supermarkets and specialty bakeries. These pocketless pitas make fantastic low-fat pizza crusts!

D. I. E. T.

is a four-letter word that really means...
DENY INGESTING EVERYTHING TASTY

Diets don't work. One of the problems is that they forbid you to eat the foods you enjoy. Instead, you're forced to eat packaged dinners that taste like cardboard, to drink shakes with the taste and texture of chalk, and to pacify a growling stomach with lettuce and grapefruit. With so many restrictions on what can and can't be eaten, it's no wonder that 95% of dieters end up regaining any lost weight.

There are just two things you can't eat for dinner—breakfast and lunch.

Burger Alarm

Someone call the cops! There's a cooking misdemeanor in progress! It's gotta be a crime for burgers to taste this good! And low in fat, too? You're definitely busted! The fuzz will be *grilling* you for an explanation, but you can just shrug your barbeque tongs and say, "No condiment."

1/2 pound extra-lean ground beef
1/2 pound lean ground turkey (skinless)
2 tablespoons minced onions
2 cloves garlic, minced
1 egg white
1 tablespoon ketchup
1 teaspoon "lite" Worcestershire sauce
1/2 teaspoon *each* chili powder and celery seeds
1/4 teaspoon *each* ground cumin, salt, and
 black pepper
4 hamburger rolls
Show Stopper Burger Topper (see recipe)
 plus your favorite low-fat toppings

Combine all burger ingredients (beef through black pepper) in a large bowl. Mix well (using your hands works best). Divide into 4 equal portions. Shape each portion into a 1/2-inch thick patty. Separate patties using wax paper. This also makes it easier to transfer them to the grill.

Prepare grill. Cook burgers 4-5 minutes on each side, or until desired "doneness" is reached. Baste with your favorite barbeque sauce.

Serve on hamburger rolls with your favorite toppings.

Makes 4 servings.

Show Stopper Burger Topper

This salsa is a snap to make and tastes fabulous on grilled burgers or grilled chicken sandwiches.

2 cups seeded and diced tomatoes
3/4 cup diced onions
1 jalapeño pepper, seeded and minced
2 tablespoons chopped fresh cilantro
2 teaspoons lime juice
1/2 teaspoon sugar
Salt and pepper to taste

Combine all ingredients in a small bowl. Mix well. Allow to stand for 30 minutes for flavors to develop.

Spoon salsa over hot burgers.

Makes about 2 cups.

Hint: Top your burger with non-fat or low-fat cheese slices instead of the regular kind and save about 7 grams of fat per burger!

Burger
PER SERVING:
307 calories, 9.5 g fat,
23 g carbohydrate, 30.8 g protein,
506 mg sodium, 70 mg cholesterol
CALORIES FROM FAT: 28.5%

Salsa
PER SERVING (2 tablespoons):
9 calories, 0.1 g fat,
2 g carbohydrate, 0.2 g protein,
18 mg sodium, 0 mg cholesterol
CALORIES FROM FAT: 9.4%

WHAT'S IN IT FOR ME?

—JUST THE WAY I LIKE IT—PINK ON THE INSIDE, CHARRED ON THE OUTSIDE. THE BAD NEWS IS, IT'S MY THUMB

Tuna Topped Taters

A tantalizing treat for those of you who just can't get enough potatoes! Smothered in an absolutely delicious tuna/veggie topping, these baked potatoes make a filling, hearty meal on their own, or you can serve them as a memorable side dish.

1 cup broccoli florets
1/2 cup *each* chopped onions, diced celery, and diced red bell pepper
1 can (10-3/4 ounces) reduced-fat Cream of Mushroom Soup (Campbell's Healthy Request), undiluted
1/2 cup shredded reduced-fat sharp cheddar cheese (2 ounces)
1/2 teaspoon *each* dry mustard and celery seeds
1/4 teaspoon *each* salt and black pepper
1 can (6 ounces) water-packed tuna, drained
2 tablespoons chopped fresh parsley
4 large baked potatoes (hot)

Place broccoli in a microwave-safe dish with 1/4 cup water. Cook on high power for 3-4 minutes, until broccoli is tender-crisp. Drain and set aside.

Spray a medium saucepan with non-stick spray. Add onions, celery, and red peppers. Cook over medium heat for 5 minutes, stirring often, until vegetables are softened.

Add undiluted mushroom soup and stir well. Cook until mixture is bubbly. Add shredded cheese, dry mustard, celery seeds, salt, and pepper. Cook and stir until cheese is melted.

Add tuna, cooked broccoli, and parsley to sauce. Stir well. Cook for 2-3 more minutes, until heated through.

Split open hot baked potatoes and pour tuna mixture over top. Serve immediately.

Makes 4 servings.

WHAT'S IN IT FOR ME?

PER SERVING: 380 calories, 4.4 g fat, 61.6 g carbohydrate, 24.7 g protein, 604 mg sodium, 21 mg cholesterol
CALORIES FROM FAT: 10.4%

SAY IT AIN'T SO!

What's so "smart" about the popular white cheese-flavored popcorn? Not much, when you take a real look at the fat content of this deceptively healthy-sounding snack. A 1-ounce serving packs in 160 calories and 10 grams of fat (56% of calories from fat)! Sounds more like a dumb food choice, doesn't it?

Gotta MOVE It!

People who are already thin don't need to exercise. No weigh! Everyone needs exercise—every weight, every age, everyone! Exercise does more than just burn calories, it strengthens the heart and lungs, lowers the risk of disease, increases immune system functioning, helps us sleep well, and relieves depression and stress. You don't need to exercise if you don't care about being healthy, physically fit, having energy, or looking and feeling good. And if you don't care about these things, then what exactly do you care about?

Attitude is a little thing that makes a BIG difference.

COOKING 101

Don't attempt to make this omelette without a non-stick skillet, unless you're fully prepared to add 1 tablespoon butter (and 11 grams of fat) to the recipe to prevent your eggs from sticking! When cooking or sautéing without butter or oil, try using a lower heat setting than you would normally use. This will prevent the food from sticking or burning. It may take slightly longer to cook your food this way, but you can use the extra time to calculate all the fat calories you'll be saving.

Slim Pickin's

You'd have to oink out on
31 CUPS OF FRESH STRAWBERRIES
to consume the
19 GRAMS OF FAT
found in
1 PLAIN CROISSANT.
Which would fill you up more?

Go for quality *and* quantity!

"I DO" "PEE YEW!"

Trivial Tidbit

Attention all bridegrooms! An ancient Palestinian superstition says that a clove of garlic worn in a groom's buttonhole will ensure a successful wedding night. Why buy cologne when you can use Bold Spice?

Omelettel Bit Country

He's a little bit rock and roll. This country-style omelette is really "Osmond"—Uh... er... we mean "awesome!"

GOT A LITTLE BIT OF MOTOWN IN MY SOUL

1/4 cup chopped onions
1 clove garlic, minced
1 cup sliced mushrooms
1/2 cup thinly sliced zucchini
1/4 cup diced red bell pepper
1/4 teaspoon dried basil
2 ounces lean cooked ham slices, chopped
1 egg
3 egg whites
1 tablespoon water
1/2 teaspoon *each* salt and black pepper
2 low-fat cheese slices (cheddar, mozzarella, or Swiss)

Spray a 10-inch non-stick skillet with non-stick spray. Add onions and garlic. Cook over medium heat for 2 minutes. Add mushrooms, zucchini, red pepper, and basil. Cook for 5 minutes, stirring often, until vegetables are tender. Stir in chopped ham. Transfer vegetable mixture to a small bowl and set aside.

Re-coat skillet with non-stick spray. Whisk together egg, egg whites, water, salt, and pepper. Add to skillet. Cook over medium heat. As eggs set, run a spatula around edge of skillet, lifting eggs and letting uncooked portion flow underneath.

When eggs are set, spread vegetable mixture over one half of omelette. Top with cheese slices. Fold opposite side over to cover vegetables. Cook 1 more minute. Slide omelette onto a plate. Cut into 2 pieces and serve immediately.

Makes 1 large omelette, 2 servings.

Hint: Look for low-fat cheese slices where you buy regular cheese slices at the grocery store.

PER SERVING: 110 calories, 3.3 g fat, 5.7 g carbohydrate, 14.3 g protein, 417 mg sodium, 119 mg cholesterol
CALORIES FROM FAT: 27.1%

WHAT'S IN IT FOR ME?

I Dream of Wienies

We were just lounging around one day, when all of a sudden, a mysterious bottle washed up from the unexplored depths of our swimming pool! Inside, we found this recipe that completely transforms humdrum beans and wieners into a magical treat! If wieners just aren't your thing, then leave them out. You'll have "I Dream of Beanies"! A great one for the kids!

I WISH FOR MAGICALLY DELICIOUS BEANS AND WIENERS !

1 cup diced carrots
1/2 cup chopped onions
1 can (28 ounces) baked beans
in tomato sauce
1 cup unsweetened crushed pineapple,
undrained
4 veggie wieners, cut into 1/2-inch
thick slices
1 tablespoon *each* molasses and
ketchup
1 teaspoon prepared mustard
1/4 teaspoon *each* salt and black pepper

Place carrots in a small microwave-safe dish with 1/4 cup water. Microwave on high power for 4-5 minutes, until tender. Drain and set aside.

Spray a medium saucepan with non-stick spray. Add onions. Cook and stir over medium heat until onions are tender, about 5 minutes. Add cooked carrots and all remaining ingredients. Reduce heat to low. Cover and simmer for 10 minutes, until wieners are heated through. Stir gently, otherwise beans will be mushy.

Makes 4 servings.

Hint: The high sodium content of this recipe comes from the canned beans. Try to find a reduced-sodium variety if you're watching your sodium intake.

WHAT'S IN IT FOR ME?

PER SERVING: 338 calories, 3.2 g fat, 59.3 g carbohydrate, 19 g protein, 1404 mg sodium, 15 mg cholesterol
CALORIES FROM FAT: 8.5%

Show & Tell

Regular hot dog wieners are loaded with fat. Fortunately, we can now buy "veggie" wieners that have just as much flavor as all-beef or all-pork wieners, but that contain only a smidgen of the fat. Be careful, though! Different brands of veggie wieners have different fat contents! Some products use deceptive phrases like "healthy," "all-natural," "lite," or "contains absolutely no meat" to entice health-conscious shoppers, yet they contain as much as 70% fat! So let's be frank. Your best bet is to read the label before you buy.

Show me the WEIGH

When it comes to fat, you can take it or leave it. If you're keeping an eye on your health and your waist size, the best advice is to leave it, or learn to leave it off your food once and for all. Butter, margarine, oil, and salad dressing are all adipose outlaws, and so are cream, sour cream, and mayonnaise. Small amounts add up quickly. A gram here, a gram there, you haven't eaten much, but the flab is everywhere! There are many other ways to add zip to foods without wreaking havoc on your health: herbs, spices, vinegar, mustard, salsa, and lemon juice to name a few. So do yourself a flavor, and keep fat in its place.

An elegant frankfurter is a haute dog.

LEANing Tower of Pizza

A sight to behold! This pizza's stacked so high to the sky with tasty toppings, it's hard to believe that it's not towering with fat! We're a little mixed up with our geography, though. This leaning tower has *Greek*-style toppings, not Italian. Oh well.

Pizza Dough
1 package (1/4 ounce) active dry yeast
2 teaspoons sugar
2/3 cup warm water
2 cups all-purpose flour
1 tablespoon cornmeal
1/2 teaspoon salt
1 tablespoon olive oil

Toppings
1 cup thinly sliced zucchini
1/2 cup pizza sauce
1 cup chopped cooked chicken breast
5 sun-dried tomatoes, softened and chopped (see page 85)
3 extra-large pitted black olives, thinly sliced
1 small red onion, cut into thin rings
2 plum tomatoes (Roma), thinly sliced
1/4 cup crumbled feta cheese (1 ounce)
1/2 cup shredded reduced-fat mozzarella cheese (2 ounces)

To prepare dough, combine yeast, 1 teaspoon sugar, and warm water in a large bowl. Let sit for 10 minutes, until frothy.

Combine flour, cornmeal, remaining 1 teaspoon sugar, and salt in a small bowl. Set aside.

Stir olive oil into yeast mixture. Add 1-3/4 cups of the flour mixture and stir until a soft ball forms. Turn dough out onto a lightly floured surface and knead for 3-4 minutes. If necessary, add some of the remaining flour mixture to prevent dough from sticking to hands.

Spray a large bowl with non-stick spray and place dough inside. Cover with a tea towel and let rise in a warm place for 1 hour, until double in size. Punch down dough, form a ball, and place on lightly floured surface. Using a rolling pin, roll out into a 12-inch circle. Place dough on 12-inch round pizza pan sprayed with non-stick spray.

Place zucchini in a small microwave-safe dish with 1/4 cup water. Cook on high power for 5 minutes. Drain.

Layer toppings on pizza dough in the following order: sauce, chicken, sun-dried tomatoes, olives, onions, zucchini, tomato slices, feta, then mozzarella. Bake at 425° for 15 minutes, or until cheese is melted and crust is golden brown.

Makes one 12-inch pizza, 8 slices.

PER SLICE: 201 calories, 5 g fat, 26.2 g carbohydrate, 11.8 g protein, 316 mg sodium, 21 mg cholesterol
CALORIES FROM FAT: 21.9%

WHAT'S IN IT FOR ME?

Nothing beats a homemade pizza crust, but when time is a factor, simply pile the toppings on a 12-inch pre-cooked Italian-style flatbread and shorten cooking time by about 2 minutes. Quick *and* delicious!

Ross Perogies

If you're searching for an adventurous, crowd-pleasing dish to serve for dinner, this one's an ideal candidate. Cast your vote for spectacular potato and cheese-stuffed perogies topped with a taste of Texas!

4 medium baking potatoes
1 tablespoon reduced-fat butter or margarine
  (not fat-free)
1/2 cup chopped onions
1/2 cup shredded reduced-fat sharp cheddar
  cheese (2 ounces)
20 jumbo pasta shells, uncooked

Sauce
1 pound lean ground chicken or turkey (skinless)
1 cup *each* chopped onions and chopped green
  bell pepper
2 cloves garlic, minced
1 can (28 ounces) tomatoes, undrained, cut up
1 can (6 ounces) tomato paste
1-1/2 teaspoons *each* dried oregano and
  ground cumin
1/2 teaspoon *each* chili powder and crushed
  red pepper flakes
1/4 teaspoon black pepper
2 tablespoons chopped fresh cilantro
Low-fat sour cream (optional)

Wash the potatoes and prick them in several places with a fork. Microwave on high power for 12-15 minutes, rotating potatoes halfway through cooking time. When potatoes are cool, peel off and discard skin, then mash. Set aside.

Melt butter in a small skillet or saucepan. Add onions and cook over medium heat until tender, about 5 minutes. Add onions to potatoes, along with shredded cheese. Mix well. Cover and refrigerate until ready to use.

Prepare shells according to package directions. Drain. Rinse with cold water and drain again. Set aside.

To prepare sauce, spray a large saucepan or skillet with non-stick spray. Add ground chicken, onions, green pepper, and garlic. Cook over medium-high heat until chicken is no longer pink and vegetables are tender, about 7-8 minutes. Drain off any fat. Add remaining ingredients, except cilantro and sour cream (if using). Stir well. Bring mixture to a boil. Reduce heat to medium-low. Simmer, uncovered, for 5 minutes. Remove from heat and stir in cilantro.

Spoon potato/cheese mixture into each pasta shell. Pinch closed to hold in filling. Arrange filled shells in a single layer in a 13 x 9-inch casserole dish. Pour sauce over top. Bake at 375°, uncovered, for 20 minutes. Serve with a dollop of low-fat sour cream, if desired.

Makes 4 servings.

WHAT'S IN IT FOR ME?

PER SERVING: 612 calories, 5.3 g fat, 98.3 g carbohydrate, 45 g protein, 636 mg sodium, 65 mg cholesterol
CALORIES FROM FAT: 7.6%

Use these hints to make the job of stuffing pasta shells a cinch: 1) Slightly undercook the shells so they're easier to handle and less likely to tear; 2) After draining the shells, place them in a bowl of cold water to keep them separate. Remove them one at a time for stuffing; 3) Use a teaspoon (the non-measuring kind) to stuff the shells.

COOKING 101

We've Got the Shakes!

GULPABILITY JUDGING

And we can barely contain our excitement over these absolutely delectable, ever-so-tasty milkshakes that are also guilt-free! Rated extremely high on the Gulpability Scale!

These shakes are simple to make, so you won't need to blend over backwards. The directions are the same for each of the recipes: Simply throw everything in a blender and whirl away until smooth. Each recipe makes enough for 2 people.

Bikini Breezer

3/4 cup non-fat strawberry yogurt
1/2 cup skim milk
1/2 cup orange juice
1 medium banana (ripe)
1 teaspoon honey
Handful of crushed ice

Martian Meltdown

1 cup non-fat plain yogurt
1 cup skim milk
1/4 cup pistachio-flavored instant
    pudding mix
1 medium banana (ripe)
Handful of crushed ice

Tropical Twister

1 can (15-1/2 ounces) Dole Tropical
    Fruit Salad
1 cup low-fat vanilla frozen yogurt or
    ice milk
1/2 medium banana (ripe)
1/2 cup skim milk
1/3 cup reserved syrup from fruit salad

Drain fruit salad, reserving 1/3 cup syrup.
Add reserved syrup and remaining
ingredients to blender. Whirl until smooth.

Peach Therapy

3/4 cup non-fat peach yogurt
1 can (15-1/2 ounces) sliced peaches,
    drained
1/2 cup skim milk
1 teaspoon vanilla
Handful of crushed ice

Martian Meltdown
PER SERVING:
249 calories, 1.5 g fat,
50 g carbohydrate, 11.4 g protein,
391 mg sodium, 6 mg cholesterol
CALORIES FROM FAT: 5.1%

Bikini Breezer
PER SERVING:
216 calories, 1.6 g fat,
45.8 g carbohydrate, 7.1 g protein,
102 mg sodium, 2 mg cholesterol
CALORIES FROM FAT: 6.2%

Peach Therapy
PER SERVING:
171 calories, 1.2 g fat,
34.7 g carbohydrate, 7.1 g protein,
106 mg sodium, 2 mg cholesterol
CALORIES FROM FAT: 6.1%

Tropical Twister
PER SERVING:
254 calories, 2.4 g fat,
51.7 g carbohydrate, 6.4 g protein,
102 mg sodium, 7 mg cholesterol
CALORIES FROM FAT: 8.4%

WHAT'S IN IT FOR ME?

Tidy Joes

Meet Sloppy Joe's wholesome and healthy cousin, Tidy, from down south. Masked underneath a shipshape exterior lurks a wilder, spicier alter ego. Smmmmokin'!!

1 pound lean ground chicken or
  turkey (skinless)
1/2 cup chopped onions
2 cloves garlic, minced
1/2 cup chopped celery
1/4 cup grated carrot
1 cup cooked pinto beans,
  mashed
1 cup cooked brown or white rice
1 cup diced tomato
2/3 cup ketchup
1/2 cup chopped green onions
2 jalapeño peppers, seeded
  and minced
2 tablespoons white vinegar
1 tablespoon *each* "lite"
  Worcestershire sauce and
  brown sugar
1-1/2 teaspoons chili powder
1 teaspoon *each* ground cumin and prepared mustard
1/2 teaspoon crushed red pepper flakes
1/4 teaspoon black pepper
8 hamburger rolls or soft Kaisers

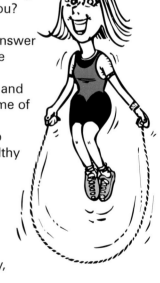

Spray a large saucepan with non-stick spray. Add ground chicken, onions, garlic, celery, and carrot. Cook over medium-high heat until chicken is browned, about 8 minutes. Stir often. Break up any large chunks of chicken with a fork. Drain off any fat.

Stir in remaining ingredients. Reduce heat to medium-low. Cover and simmer for 10 minutes, stirring occasionally. Spoon chicken mixture over bottom half of hamburger or Kaiser bun, cover with top half, and enjoy!

Makes 8 Tidy Joes.

WHAT'S IN IT FOR ME? ➡ PER SERVING: 276 calories, 3.9 g fat, 41.6 g carbohydrate, 20.2 g protein, 715 mg sodium, 32 mg cholesterol CALORIES FROM FAT: 12.5%

COOKING 101

Since jalapeño peppers contain capsaicin, the source of their fiery flavor, they should be handled with care. (Let's just say it doesn't tickle if this compound gets in your eye!) After chopping a hot pepper, make sure you immediately wash your hands as well as all surfaces that came in contact with the pepper. If you're not a lover of spicier fare, you can eliminate the jalapeños altogether from this recipe.

Gotta MOVE It!

When planning their daily activities, people often don't make time for exercise because they place it in the play/recreation category, making it seem unimportant. Now, let's really think about this for a moment. Is it important to be healthy and energetic? Is it important to feel good and to look good? Is having self-esteem and self-confidence something that matters to you? Is sleeping well important? The answer to all of the above questions is a resounding YES, and these are just some of the reasons why people should do some sort of healthy physical activity every single day. Putting exercise higher on the priority list is a good first step towards a healthy, energy-filled life.

It's a common fallacy that eating oysters increases your mussel tone.

Appendix

Calculating Your Daily Fat Consumption Target

For a healthy diet, experts recommend that we get no more than 30% of our daily calories from fat. Some people believe that this figure is too high, and suggest a diet that is 20-25% fat. The choice is yours. We've found that most people can maintain their ideal weight at 30%, but in order to lose weight, it might be necessary to cut fat intake to 20-25% of total calories. You may want to start out at the 30% target, then gradually drop to 25%, depending on your goals. Remember, you're not likely to stick with drastic measures, so start out slowly, making gradual changes in your eating habits. Choose a target you can stick to and live with!

If you consume 2000 calories per day, and want to derive no more than 30% of those calories from fat, your daily fat consumption target would be calculated as follows:

1. **Multiply your total daily calories by the desired percentage from fat**
   example: 2000 x 30% = 600 fat calories

2. **Divide the number of fat calories by 9 (the number of calories in 1 gram of fat) to determine your daily fat consumption target**
   example: 600÷9 = 67 grams of fat

In this example, your daily fat consumption would be limited to 67 grams. You can use the chart at the bottom of the page to determine a daily fat consumption target that's right for you.

For the first few weeks, try to keep a running total each day. You won't need to do this forever (phew!). We're not encouraging you to become obsessed with numbers. But keeping track at first will help you develop the habit of reading food labels, and you'll become an expert at knowing which foods are low in fat, and which foods are loaded with it. Think of it as an educational process. After about 3 weeks, making low-fat food choices will become second nature. You'll just "know" whether you've consumed too much fat in one day.

Understanding Label Lingo

In order to make healthier food choices at the grocery store, you'll have to do some homework to understand the language of food labels. If you're a health-conscious shopper, you've probably found yourself wondering what the terms "low-fat," "light," and "low cholesterol" really mean. Some labeling terms are pretty straightforward, while others can mean several different things, depending on the context.

Manufacturers in the U.S. are required by law *(Nutrition Labeling and Education Act of 1990)* to provide accurate, easy-to-understand nutrition labels on their products, with a few exceptions (freshly baked goods, single foil-wrapped chocolates, deli-counters, take-out and fast food restaurants are exempt). The label on the following page depicts the standard "Nutrition Facts" label that is now mandatory in the United States. Canadian consumers

Daily Fat Consumption Targets			
If you consume...	**Your daily fat consumption target is...**		
	20%	**25%**	**30%**
1500 calories	33 grams	42 grams	50 grams
1800 calories	40 grams	50 grams	60 grams
2000 calories	44 grams	56 grams	67 grams
2500 calories	56 grams	69 grams	83 grams
3000 calories	67 grams	83 grams	100 grams

should try to recognize and understand this label as well, because many products in Canadian grocery stores originate in the U.S., and if you take a good look around the next time you're food shopping, you'll see it on a variety of products (especially snack foods).

You'll notice that the label is quite comprehensive, including all of the information a consumer needs to make smart food choices. The only important figure that's missing is the percentage of calories that come from fat. Luckily, this isn't very difficult to calculate. Find the value for "Calories from Fat." In this case it's 120 calories. Divide the "Calories from Fat" by the "Calories" (260), then multiply by 100. This will give you the percentage of calories that come from fat. According to the sample label, this product gets 46% of its calories from fat—that's a lot. Remember, experts recommend a diet that derives no more than 30% calories from fat, so a food that contains 46% fat should be consumed in moderation.

On the U.S. label you'll also find reference values that help teach consumers good diet basics, and that show how the particular food fits in to the overall daily diet. For example, you can see that the product contains 13 grams of fat, or 20% of the reference daily intake of this nutrient (65 grams/day based on a 2000 calorie diet).

In Canada, nutrition labeling is voluntary, unless a specific claim is made about the product. For example, a product stating that it's "25% lower in fat than our regular fudge cookies" will need to show the nutritional information to support this claim. We've found that most Canadian manufacturers are responding to the demand for accurate, complete nutritional information by labeling their products even though it's not mandatory. The labels aren't as comprehensive as those appearing in the U.S., but they almost always cover the basic nutrients: fat, saturated fat, cholesterol, carbohydrate, protein, and sodium. With Canadian labels you'll need to add one more step to the math equation when calculating the percentage of calories from fat. First, find the number of fat grams per serving. Multiply this number by 9 (the number of calories in one gram of fat). This gives you the "Calories from Fat" figure that appears on American labels. As in the example above, divide the "Calories from Fat" by the total calories per serving, then multiply by 100.

Now, what about all those claims? When can a product be labeled "fat-free" or "low-fat"? Well, the laws and guidelines are different in Canada than in the U.S. for most products, but here's a run-down of what the rulebook says regarding labeling terms:

Nutrition Facts

Serving Size 1 cup (228g)
Servings Per Container 2

Amount Per Serving	
Calories 260 Calories From Fat 120	
	% Daily Value*
Total Fat 13g	20%
Saturated Fat 5g	25%
Cholesterol 30mg	10%
Sodium 660mg	28%
Total Carbohydrate 31g	28%
Dietary Fiber 0g	0%
Sugars 5g	
Protein 5g	

Vitamin A 4%	●	Vitamin C 2%	
Calcium 15%	●	Iron 4%	

*Percent Daily Values are based on a 2,000 calorie diet. Your daily values may be higher or lower depending on your calorie needs:

		Calories:	2,000	2,500
Total Fat	Less than		65g	80g
Sat Fat	Less than		20g	25g
Cholesterol	Less than		300mg	300mg
Sodium	Less than		2,400mg	2,400mg
Total Carbohydrate			300g	375g
Dietary Fiber			25g	30g

Calories per gram:
Fat 9 ● Carbohydrate 4 ● Protein 4

Source: Food Labeling Education Information Center, FDA/USDA

Fat-Free:

U.S.—the product contains less than 0.5 g fat per serving
Canada—the product contains less than 0.5 g fat per serving

Low-Fat:

U.S.—the product contains no more than 3 g fat per serving
Canada—the product contains no more than 3 g fat per serving

Reduced-Calorie:

U.S.—the product contains 25% less calories than a comparable food
Canada—the product must have at least 50% less calories compared to the same food not calorie-reduced

Low-Calorie:

U.S.—the product contains 40 calories or less per serving
Canada—a calorie-reduced food that provides no more than 15 calories per average serving and not more than 30 calories in a reasonable daily intake of that food

Low-Cholesterol:

U.S.—the product contains no more than 20 mg of cholesterol and 2 g of saturated fat per serving
Canada—the product contains no more than 20 mg of cholesterol per 100 g and per serving; the food contains no more than 2 g saturated fat per serving and must not derive more than 15% of calories from saturated fat

Light/Lite:

A confusing term in both the U.S. and Canada, "light" can mean light in calories, light in fat, light in cholesterol, light in sodium, light in color, or light in flavor, so it's best to read the nutrition label to check the content of the specific nutrient you're interested in. For example, "light" olive oil is light in color and light-tasting, but not light in fat or calories. It has just as many calories and just as much fat as regular olive oil.

Lean:

U.S.—used to describe meat, poultry, fish, and shellfish products which contain less than 10 g fat, 4.5 g or less saturated fat, and less than 95 mg of cholesterol per serving and per 100 g
Canada—used to describe meat, poultry, fish, and shellfish products which contain no more than 10% fat (*by weight*), except for ground beef and ground pork, which may contain up to 17% fat (*by weight*) and still be described as "lean"

Labels on meat products are a source of confusion for most shoppers. People often interpret a label that states "less than 15% fat" as meaning less than 15% of calories from fat. It's a common misconception—what else could the manufacturer mean by "less than 15% fat"? Why would they deliberately mislead us? Hopefully the following true example of a misleading meat label will incite you to read nutrition panels *in addition* to the claims on the front of the package.

Some friends of ours recently decided to make a commitment to healthier eating by lowering the amount of fat in their diet. Lovers of greasy, fried bacon, they quickly made the switch to turkey bacon, since the label screamed in big, bold letters that Brand XYZ Turkey Bacon was "Less than 15% fat!" They gobbled up this bacon freely and frequently, bragging about the amount of fat they were cutting from their diet. When shown how to calculate the actual percentage of calories from fat that this "wonder" product contained, our friends were horrified to discover that the turkey bacon derived *70%* of its calories from fat! The claim "Less than 15% fat!" referred to the amount of fat *by weight* of the product, not the percentage of calories from fat. And remember, according to North American labeling guidelines, it would be perfectly acceptable to call this "70% fat" turkey bacon "lean." It seems unbelievable, but it's true. Our best defense against misleading claims is education—learn to understand the nutrition label.

Another source of information on packaged goods is the ingredient list. In general, ingredients must be listed in descending order of their proportion or percentage by weight, with the exception of food additives, which may be shown, grouped together, at the end of the list. The list of ingredients can tell you a lot about the nutritional content of the product. Sugars are often disguised by their scientific-sounding real names—names that aren't familiar to the average consumer. Whenever you see an ingredient that ends in "ose," you can be sure it's a form of sugar. Fructose, dextrose, and sucrose are a few examples. And don't forget about honey, molasses, and corn syrup—all sugars. If you see these names at the beginning of the list, the product is likely high in sugar content.

Similarly, there are many ways of listing fats. Vegetable oil, hydrogenated vegetable oil, soybean oil, cocoa butter, butter, and coconut oil are all fats. Some vegetable oils, like olive oil and canola oil, are high in monounsaturated fats (the good type of fat). Other plant fats are highly saturated and should be avoided. These are palm oil, cocoa butter, coconut oil, and any oil that starts with the word "hydrogenated." If the fat or oil appears at the beginning of the ingredient list, you're looking at a high-fat product. Keep in mind that all oils, whether saturated or unsaturated, contain the same amount of fat and calories.

Understanding food labels is an important first step in adopting a healthier lifestyle. And while all of this label lingo might seem a bit overwhelming at first, with a little effort and practice, you'll soon become a highly skilled grocery store detective.

Less Stress and Mess in the Kitchen

Now that you've made a commitment to a healthier, low-fat lifestyle, you need to get your act together in the kitchen. Getting organized is crucial if you want your cooking experiences to be relaxed and enjoyable instead of a chaotic mess. If you're not a big fan of cooking, or you just don't have much experience at it, try to incorporate some or all of the following tips to make meal preparation as painless as possible, and much easier to manage:

■ Before you attempt to make any new recipe, read all of the instructions carefully. An hour before your guests arrive is *not* the time to find out that the pork chops need to be marinated overnight.

■ Gather all of the ingredients and cooking tools you'll need and put them on the kitchen counter. You'll know before you begin if you're missing an essential ingredient and won't need to hunt for items later on when you should be paying attention to what's happening in your pot.

■ Prepare the ingredients as the recipe specifies *before you begin to cook*. Chop all of the vegetables and cube the meat. You don't want to be peeling onions while the rest of your stir-fry burns.

■ Tidy up as you go along. If you have a dishwasher, load mixing bowls and measuring cups when you're finished with them instead of stacking up the dirty cookware. Dinner will be much more enjoyable if you don't have a disaster zone of dishes to face when the meal is over.

■ Invest in a good sharp knife. You'll be able to prepare food faster and easier. And believe it or not, you're more likely to cut yourself with a dull knife, which slips easily, than with a sharp knife.

■ Keep the garbage can nearby. This way you can keep your work space tidy and avoid dropping potato peels all over the kitchen floor en route to the trash.

■ Although it may not always be possible, try to plan weekly menus on the weekend and shop for the ingredients you'll need. This will make weekday mealtimes a lot less hectic. Even better, cook 2 or 3 one-dish meals on Sunday that can be refrigerated and reheated for lunch or dinner on Monday and Tuesday.

■ Try not to worry so much if a dish doesn't taste "how it's supposed to taste." If you and your family think it tastes good, then it *is* good.

Tip the Scale in Your Favor

20 Helpful Tips for Healthful Cooking

■ Plan your menus in advance. When you know what you're going to eat ahead of time, you avoid impulsive high-fat, high-calorie food selections. Menu planning saves you money, allows you to eat better, and helps you lose weight more effectively.

■ Learn to read and understand food labels so you can make better choices at the grocery store (see page 171).

■ In baking, when a recipe calls for whole eggs, experiment by replacing some of the yolks with additional egg whites. For example, instead of using 2 whole eggs, try 1 whole egg plus 2 egg whites for a savings of 5 grams of fat and 213 milligrams of cholesterol.

■ Jams, jellies, and preserves have zero fat and about 45 calories per tablespoon. They're a perfect spread for toasted English muffins, bagels, and bread. (But don't defeat the purpose by slathering your toast with butter first!)

■ Herbs and spices are naturally low in fat and should be used lavishly to add zip to cooking when little fat is used. Some herbs and spices are perfectly fine in dried form, but the following are *so* much better fresh, it's really worth keeping them around, especially since they're inexpensive and readily available: garlic, ginger root, parsley (dried parsley tastes like vacuum cleaner dust—don't use it), fresh peppercorns for your pepper mill, cilantro/coriander (ground coriander is really tasty, but has a completely different flavor than fresh coriander leaves—don't interchange them), and basil (most of our recipes use dried basil, however, because that seems to be what most people have handy).

■ Choose skinless turkey, chicken, and fish over red meat whenever possible. If you do eat red meat, trim off all visible fat and avoid pan frying.

■ Limit the amount of meat you use on sandwiches. Think of meat almost as a condiment and use vegetables as the main event.

■ Make a real effort to cook with and eat more fruits, vegetables, and grains. They're naturally low in fat, loaded with carbohydrates, and will fill you up.

■ If you have the time, refrigerate soups and broths before using them. Any fat will rise to the top and solidify, making it easy to remove.

■ Ve have vays of making you wok: A large sturdy wok with a non-stick coating is a great investment, and makes cooking with little or no fat much easier. Instead of using oil, sauté vegetables in chicken or vegetable broth, wine, fruit juice, or a little water. Try freezing broth in ice-cube trays. When frozen, pop the cubes out and store them in a plastic bag. Two cubes could be used instead of oil to add flavor and to prevent food from sticking (each cube equals two tablespoons broth).

■ Non-stick vegetable cooking spray is a great addition to your pantry. Use it instead of oil to coat your wok or skillet when making a stir-fry or omelette, and to prevent baked goods from sticking to the pan.

■ Durable non-stick cookware is a must when you're cooking with less fat. You want your dinner to stick to your ribs, not to your pots.

■ Choose cooking methods that don't add fat to your foods: baking, broiling, grilling, roasting, poaching, and steaming. When you do use oil, choose from those that are high in monounsaturated and polyunsaturated fats, and low in saturated fats. Two of the best choices are canola and olive oil.

■ Manufacturers are responding to consumer requests for reduced-sodium products. Try to use reduced-sodium versions of soy sauce, Worcestershire sauce, and chicken broth. If you're on a sodium-restricted diet, you may want to omit the salt in our recipes or use one of the many salt alternatives on the market. Recipes using canned products, like canned tomatoes, tend to be high in sodium, but you can always substitute no-salt-added

products in their place. Generally speaking, the more processed the food, the higher it is in sodium content.

■ Forget the butter when making mashed potatoes. Add a little low-fat sour cream or low-fat buttermilk to get that creamy taste and texture you're after.

■ For creamy dips and dressings, substitute low-fat versions of sour cream, mayonnaise, yogurt, or cottage cheese (smoothed in a blender) as a base.

■ Most men and especially children are quick to form negative opinions about food that is labeled "low-fat," "healthy," or "diet." Never tell family or friends that their dinner is low-fat before they've had a chance to taste it.

The Fine Art of Conscientious Dining or...
How to Dine and Slash (the Fat!)

You've been a nutritional saint for a while now, eating sensible, low-fat foods and exercising four or five times a week. You feel great and you look great. Now the big challenge: You're faced with your first real test of character, your first confrontation with a high-fat, high-cal, rip-roarin', gut-bustin' pig-out situation—eating at a restaurant!

Your friend orders the Godzilla burger with fries and gravy. The other orders the prime rib special. You salivate, thinking "Ah, what the heck! What's a few extra calories, anyway?" Just remember that one "Ah, what the heck" restaurant meal can amount to over 1500 calories that'll wind up around your middle. And after throwing caution to the wind even once, it's easy to talk yourself into doing it again and again.

Let's be realistic. All of us want to be able to enjoy an evening out at a nice restaurant every once in a while, and there's no need for this occasion to be fraught with guilt. What's needed is a strategy, a simple plan of attack. By learning the ABC's of low-fat dining, you'll be able to avoid eating with abandon and regretting it later.

Some Things To Think About Before You Go:

■ Avoid "All You Can Eat." Usually, you end up eating all you can *and then some.*

■ Vegetarian does not necessarily mean low-fat. A lot of vegetarian restaurants serve dishes that are soaking in oil. They may boast that they use olive oil exclusively, but remember, ALL culinary oils contain 14 grams of fat per tablespoon!

■ Sticking with a few favorite restaurants is a good way to get to know the chef, the servers, and the way the food is prepared. It's also a good way for them to familiarize themselves with your special requests (and don't be shy about asking for special orders— remember, you're the one who's paying).

■ Don't starve yourself in anticipation of a restaurant visit. It's much easier to stay in control if you've been eating sensibly throughout the day.

More Strategic "Stay Slim" Maneuvers:

■ Try to order first, so you won't be tempted or swayed by what everyone else is having.

■ Always ask how dishes are prepared. Are they baked? Are they broiled? Are they prepared with butter or oil? Ask what's in the sauce; ask what's in the soup; ask what's in the dressing. Servers are becoming accustomed to fielding these types of questions, so don't worry about pestering them.

■ Always ask for butter, gravy, sauces, and salad dressings on the side. This permits you to control how much fat you eat.

■ If it makes you feel better, lie to the server and say you're allergic or that your doctor put you on a low-fat, low-cholesterol diet. A little white lie is better than a BIG FAT one.

■ Fill up on rolls and salad, but always skip the butter. Freshly baked dinner rolls are great on their own and even better for dunking in soups and sauces.

■ Learn to ask for milk instead of cream. A measly 1 ounce of half and half cream has approximately 4 grams of fat. How many cups of coffee do you have per day? A simple switch from cream to 1% or skim milk could mean substantial fat savings.

■ Ask for salsa with a baked potato instead of sour cream and butter.

■ Order clear soups, broths, or tomato-based soups instead of chowders or creamy soups (they most likely contain cream).

■ If none of the entrées seem appropriate, consider ordering two appetizers. Steer clear of anything breaded or fried.

■ A doggy bag is your waistline's best friend and an effective way to sidestep the ol' "paying for it anyway so I'd better eat it" booby trap. Don't be shy about asking for one when you're served a plate of food that rivals the Matterhorn in height.

■ If you absolutely can't resist Double Fudge Kahlua Cheesecake, at least split the dessert with your dinner pal and let him/her eat the lion's share. People usually order dessert out of habit, but often a few bites are enough to satisfy even the sweetest sweet tooth. Besides, you wouldn't want to wear Decadent Donut Delight long after the flavor has worn away. (Cappucino with sweetener is a pretty rich-tasting alternative for dessert.)

Metric Conversion

If you are converting the recipes in this book to metric measurements, use the following charts as a guide.

Volume		
Conventional Measure	Exact Metric Conversion (mL)	Standard Metric Conversion (mL)
1/4 teaspoon	1.2 mL	1 mL
1/2 teaspoon	2.4 mL	2 mL
1 teaspoon	4.7 mL	5 mL
2 teaspoons	9.4 mL	10 mL
1 tablespoon	14.2 mL	15 mL
2 tablespoons	28.4 mL	30 mL
3 tablespoons	42.6 mL	45 mL
1/4 cup (4 tablespoons)	56.8 mL	50 mL
1/3 cup (5-1/3 tablespoons)	75.6 mL	75 mL
1/2 cup (8 tablespoons)	113.7 mL	125 mL
2/3 cup (10-2/3 tablespoons)	151.2 mL	150 mL
3/4 cup (12 tablespoons)	170.5 mL	175 mL
1 cup (16 tablespoons)	227.3 mL	250 mL
4-1/2 cups	1022.9 mL	1000 mL (1 L)

Weight		
Ounces (oz.)	Exact Metric Conversion (g)	Standard Metric Conversion (g)
1 oz.	28.3 g	30 g
2 oz.	56.7 g	55 g
3 oz.	85.0 g	85 g
4 oz.	113.4 g	125 g
5 oz.	141.7 g	140 g
6 oz.	170.1 g	170 g
7 oz.	198.4 g	200 g
8 oz.	226.8 g	250 g
16 oz.	453.6 g	500 g
32 oz.	907.2 g	1000 g (1 kg)

Oven Temperatures	
Fahrenheit (°F)	Celsius (°C)
175°	80°
200°	95°
225°	110°
250°	120°
275°	140°
300°	150°
325°	160°
350°	175°
375°	190°
400°	205°
425°	220°
450°	230°
475°	240°
500°	260°

Index

Y

Z

Where We Learned the Stuff We Didn't Know

American Medical Association, **Diet and Nutrition.** The Reader's Digest Association, 1991.

Bader, Dr. Myles H. **4001 Food Facts and Chef's Secrets.** Mylin Enterprises, 1993.

Brody, Jane. **Jane Brody's Nutrition Book.** Bantam Books, 1987.
Jane Brody's Good Food Book. Bantam Books, 1985.

Chalmers, Irena. **The Great Food Almanac.** Collins Publishers, 1994.

Chisholm, Patricia. *The War on Fat,* in **Macleans Magazine,** January 16, 1995, pp. 46-52.

Elmer-Dewitt, Phillip. *Fat Times,* in **Time Magazine,** January 16, 1995, pp. 38-45.

Gebhardt, Susan E. and Ruth H. Mathews. **Nutritive Value of Foods**. USDA, 1991.

The Good Health Fact Book. The Reader's Digest Association, 1992.

Grunwald, Lisa. *Do I Look Fat to You? 28 Questions and all the Answers About Our National Obsession,* in **Life Magazine,** February 1995, pp. 58-74.

Herbst, Sharon Tyler. **Food Lover's Companion**. Barron's Educational Series, Inc., 1995.
The Food Lover's Tiptionary. Hearst Books, 1994.

Hillman, Howard. **Kitchen Science**. Houghton Mifflin Company, 1989.

Lambert-Ortiz, Elizabeth. **The Encyclopedia of Herbs, Spices and Flavorings**. The Reader's Digest Association, 1992.

Lang, Jennifer Harvey (ed.). **Larousse Gastronomique**. Crown Publishers Inc., 1988.

Leith, Prue. **The Cook's Handbook**. Stewart House, 1989.

Nutribase Personal Nutrition Manager (software). Cybersoft Inc., 1995.

Rinzler, Carol Ann. **The Complete Book of Food: A Nutritional, Medical and Culinary Guide.** World Almanac, 1987.

Ulene, Dr. Art. **Nutrition Facts Desk Reference**. Avery Publishing Group, 1995.

University of California, Berkely Wellness Letter, Editors. **The Wellness Encyclopedia**. Houghton Mifflin Company, 1991.

Couldn't Have Done It Without Ya

Peter McMenemy and Brad McCaw share the Most Valuable Player honors on the *Looneyspoons* team. Without a doubt, we couldn't have started or finished the book without their unfailing support and unbelievable patience.

Generous with his time and expertise, intelligent, witty, and wise to the ways of publishing, **Dave Chilton** propelled the *Looneyspoons* engine full steam ahead with his enthusiastic thumbs-up.

Gary Robb believed in our project when it was only a concept and gave us the support we needed to make this book a reality.

Ted Martin, otherwise known as "The Bionic Cartoonist," managed to pump out 300 amazingly perfect cartoons in record-breaking time.

Kathy and Eric Johnson (along with Matthew, Mandi, Emily, and David) were enthusiastic taste-test guinea pigs and our 24-hour technical support department.

Wendy Knight-Agard was a super morale-booster when times were tough and a very willing cheesecake tester.

Jill and Jeff Doan, our official cheerleading squad, even managed to give birth to their first child in between generating *Looneyspoons* publicity and taking orders for our book.

Our sincere thanks to the following people who lent us their support, their time, their expert opinions, and in some cases, their money:

Heather Armstrong	Angel Guerra	Alfreda Podleski
Sharon Chang Fong	Linda Kenyon	Jim Phillips
Bob Chilton	Diane Latraverse	Pat Reid
Marge Chilton	Rhonda Logie	Margaret Robb
Helen Clark	John Lugsdin	Cindy Scott
Kerry Clark	Ian Maclean	Wendy Smith
Kim Dixon	Dawn Martin	Chuck Temple
Keith Donally	George McMenemy	Denis Trottier
Theresa Eveleigh	Kevin McNeil	Carolyn Trudel-Maclean
Pat Giesbrecht	Paul Moore	Greg Wiens
Donna Grabowski	Fred Pantalone	

How It All Happened

Born only one year apart, my sister Greta and I grew up in St. Thomas, Ontario, a charming railway city two hours west of Toronto. To the rest of the world, St. Thomas is best known as the site of the tragic 1885 train accident that claimed the life of Jumbo the Elephant, then the largest elephant in captivity. To local folk, St. Thomas is a tightly-woven, friendly community where you can expect to see a familiar face at every turn. Yes, it's a place where everyone knows your name—and the names of everyone that you've dated (or at least held hands with) since the eighth grade.

It was in this environment that our imaginations grew and our creativity thrived. We learned to make our own fun. We created our own adventures. There was the time when Greta and I tied our bicycles together with rope, creating a mini-caravan that would later compete with motorists on the city highway. Rather than frolic in a school playground like other normal kids, my sister and I preferred to stage our own episodes of Spiderman, scaling the school's rooftop in pursuit of the evil criminals who would certainly take over the world unless we intervened. Our rooftop escapades came to an abrupt end the day I (accidently) threw a full can of Coke at Greta's head, landing her in the emergency ward with four stitches. I was sent to my room with orders not to come out until I stopped insisting, "But Mom, my spider sense was tingling!"

As our vivid imaginations began to develop, so did the individual talents that would eventually drive the creation of *Looneyspoons*. As far back as I can remember, my sister was a cooking prodigy. In fact, she was born clutching a rolling pin and a chopping block, which made her delivery quite difficult for our mother. There she was at age seven, pushing her chair up to the kitchen counter to observe our mother's culinary wizardry (mostly Polish delicacies, largely unpronounceable). Before long, she was single-handedly preparing meals for the entire Podleski clan. Considering Greta is the youngest of six girls, this was a whole lot of food and a whole lot of pressure.

Setting her sights on one day becoming the host of a trendy and popular cooking show, Greta familiarized herself with terms like "folding" and "kneading." I was another story. Put me anywhere close to a kitchen and terms like "scalding" and "bleeding" come to mind. Our mother would have to face the fact that one of her daughters was domestically challenged. So she nudged me out of the kitchen and into the great outdoors, where I spent countless hours juggling a soccer ball, practising my tennis backhand, and dreaming of being the first female player in the NBA (the *real* "Dr. J").

Not that Greta wasn't an athlete, too. She was a fine gymnast, and tough as nails. The local gymnastics squad to which she belonged bore a striking similarity to a military boot camp, the drill sergeant/gymnastics coach strictly adhering to a "no pain, no gain" theory and insisting that sit-ups were only effective if you did enough repetitions to cause a steady stream of tears.

My sister and I have always shared a love of super-corny humor—real knee-slappers, true groaners, and clever puns. As a result, we've sprinkled these types of jokes and cartoons liberally throughout *Looneyspoons.* Some people theorize that we watched far too much T.V. in the '70s, that this is what shaped our irregular thought patterns and warped our sense of what's important. (Bet you didn't know that on *Gilligan's Island* the Skipper's real name was Jonus Grumby.) In fact, besides our mother, Greta's first real cooking influence was Alice Nelson, the jovial, totally-together housekeeper on *The Brady Bunch*.

That was then. This is now. (Well, not exactly now, but we're getting closer.) I moved to Ottawa in 1984. During this time apart, Greta continued to perfect her cooking skills, acquiring a love of healthy cooking and developing her sense of culinary adventure. It became a challenge for my sister to take everybody's favorite high-fat recipes and revamp them to low-fat.

Because I had spent the last twenty years of my life in soccer cleats and tennis gear, I didn't pay much attention to my diet. In fact, my idea of health food was anything eaten before the expiration date.

Here we are at ages 29 and 30, right after finishing our book. See what low-fat food and healthy living can do?

I reasoned that two hours of intense physical activity a day was enough to burn off the fastest of fast foods. But after my sixth knee operation in ten years, things changed. My creaking joints just wouldn't allow me to compete with the same intensity that I had been accustomed to and I had to give up many of the sports I was passionate about.

In walked fate. Actually, in walked Greta. As it turned out, she ended up moving to Ottawa, and in 1994, insisted on moving in with my husband and me. Newly wed, we were a bit hesitant to have a "roommate" at this stage in our relationship. It quickly dawned on us, however, that my sister's presence meant going from noodles and spaghetti sauce, day in and day out, to three hearty, impeccably prepared meals a day. It wasn't too long before we had her catering our dinner parties. (She hid in the basement while I took full credit for creating the mouthwatering meals.)

Needless to say, Greta was disgusted with my eating habits. "One cannot live on macaroni and barbequed steak alone," she would lecture.

"But I don't want to start eating that bland 'diet' stuff that *you* eat!" I retorted.

"Who said anything about 'diet'? Who said anything about 'bland'?" she answered. Then and there, she placed in front of me the most colossal, awe-inspiring piece of lasagna that I had ever laid my eyes on. "I call it *Lasagna with Mex Appeal*," she said, "and it has only 5-1/2 grams of fat. Can you believe something so delicious can also be good for you?"

"No, I can't believe it," I snorted, shovelling down this incredible feast like it was the last supper. "This tastes amazing!"

"You see," Greta said wisely, "just like you, people seem to have a negative perception of healthy eating. As soon as they hear the words 'low-fat' or 'good-for-you' they're turned off—they think 'flavorless.' Most people believe that healthy eating is something you do only when you're forced to, like when your doctor tells you something's physically wrong. What I'm trying to say is 'no weigh!' Healthy food can be unbelievably scrumptious and super-satisfying. Healthy eating can include all the foods that you love and it's not just for people who want to lose weight—it's for everyone!"

"You mean I don't have to survive on bean sprouts and tofu?" I asked.

"Nope."

"Are you telling me I can eat the hearty, filling foods I love—foods like pizza, burgers, and cheesecake?"

"Yup. And they'll taste so incredible, you'd never know they were low-fat unless I told you."

"You mean I don't have to be on a diet?"

"You got it, sister! Diets are temporary, anyway. Most people gain back any weight that was lost as soon as they 'stop' their diet and go back to their regular eating habits. Changing your attitude about food means a permanent change. Low-fat eating is forever. And it's not hard to do—really!"

Older is wiser, so they say. Funny how my little sister seemed like the smartest person in the world right then. As we sat there, hoovering down another piece of her lasagna, laughing about the time that I once called her (long distance) to ask her the recipe for a tuna sandwich, we realized that our entire lives had been preparing us for this moment. The desire to have fun with everything we do, the corny senses of humor, Greta's penchant for creating low-fat masterpieces, my experience with competitive sports and interest in writing—everything was pointing in one direction. Our destiny was obvious: We were to combine our talents and our experiences to create a book—a book that would change people's opinions about healthy eating and healthy living, a book that would make people *want* to eat and live this way not only because it produces great results as far as overall health and self-esteem, but because it's downright addictive and fun. Our goal was simple: to take the intimidation out of healthy eating and put the fun in.

We sincerely hope that *Looneyspoons* made you look at low-fat food in a different "light."

If you can't find **LOONEYSPOONS** where you shop, ask your retailer to give us a call. Meanwhile, we offer a mail order service for your convenience. Just fill out the coupon below and send it, along with your payment, to **Granet Publishing Inc., 51 1/2 West Adams, Fairfield, IA 52556**, or fax it to us at **(613) 247-9162**. Credit card orders can also be placed through our web site at **www.looneyspoons.com** or by calling **1-800-470-0738**.

For orders of 5 to 10 books, we'll pay the shipping costs to one address and throw in a free copy of **LOONEYSPOONS**! We offer an aggressive discount schedule for orders of more than 10 books. Please call us to find out the details.

Mail Order Coupon

Please send me _____ copies of **LOONEYSPOONS** @ $19.95 each   _____

Postage and handling: $2.00 for 1 book, $1.00 for each additional book (not applicable for orders of 5 to 10 books)   _____

TOTAL AMOUNT ENCLOSED   _____

Enclosed is my   ☐ check   ☐ money order

Please charge my   ☐ Visa   ☐ Mastercard

Card # _____   Expiration date _____

Signature as on card _____

Name _____

Address _____

City _____   State _____

Zip Code _____   Phone _____

Make all checks or money orders payable to Granet Publishing Inc.

Surprise a friend with a gift of food and fun!

LOONEYSPOONS makes a great gift for birthdays, wedding showers, Mother's Day, Father's Day, graduation, or holidays. We'll ship the books directly to the recipients of your choice if you give us their names and addresses. Attach a personal note or card with your order form and we'll be happy to include it in their package.